COMPOSING RESEARCH

COMPOSING RESEARCH
A Contextualist Paradigm for
Rhetoric and Composition

CINDY JOHANEK

UTAH STATE
UNIVERSITY PRESS
Logan, Utah

Utah State University Press
Logan, Utah 84322-7800

"The Writing Quality of Seventh, Ninth, and Eleventh Graders, and College Freshmen"
copyright © 1995, National Council of Teachers of English. Reprinted by permission

Manufactured in the United States of America.

Typography by WolfPack
Cover design by Barbara Yale-Read

04   03   02   01   00   5   4   3   2   1

Library of Congress Cataloging-in-Publication Data

Johanek, Cindy, 1964-
    Composing research / Cindy Johanek.
       p. cm.
    Includes bibliographical references (p.) and index.
       ISBN 0-87421-292-8 (alk. paper)
       1. English language—Rhetoric—Study and teaching—Research.
       2.English language—Composition and exercises—Research. I. Title.
       PE1404 .J58 2000
    808'.042'071--dc21
                                         00-008142
                                         CIP

To my mother,
Jeanne Marie Hokkanen Johanek
(September 11, 1942 - April 25, 1999),
who read this as far as she could.

CONTENTS

ACKNOWLEDGMENTS

Composing Research began, in truth, when I was a curious undergraduate guided and mentored by Dr. Judith Kilborn in the Write Place at St. Cloud State University. Eventually, the mixture of inquiry and text along the way resulted in a dissertation, inspired in part by Dr. James Treloar, (a former English teacher and) current statistics professor at Ball State University, though the notion would surprise him, I'm sure. That dissertation—critically read by readers like Linda Hanson and Patti White and carefully guided, hammered, discussed, debated, chewed, and ultimately, I hope, enjoyed by my advisor and dissertation director Paul Ranieri—is now in book form. To all of these inspiring teachers and colleagues, I express gratitude and a wish to be "half as good" as they are, half as inspiring. . . .

A special thanks to Eileen Oliver and Greg Siering for their participation in the studies presented in Chapters 5 and 6. Without their willing cooperation, much of the demonstration needed in this work would have been impossible.

Thanks also to a special colleague and friend, Carmen Siering, for her support in all things, and to my family for their constant love and encouragement.

INTRODUCTION

The history of composition studies is one of conflict and struggle. As a field relatively new to the academy, we have struggled to be valued, debated our very roots, and created tension among ourselves as researchers and teachers. The current debate between quantitative and qualitative researchers in composition has been discussed before. In that respect, this work is not new because it emerges from the firmly-established rift between humanists and scientists, between ethnographers and experimentalists.

But *how* we have debated about research methods is of greater concern here than *that* we have debated: in other words, the rhetoric of our own scholarship forms the foundation for this work. This foundation allows for more than merely another review of tensions among the field's researchers and allows us to address instead the false distinctions among competing epistemologies as composition scholars have defined them, reasons other than the epistemological for our new attention to personal narrative, the narrative potential of numerical evidence, and the notion of context as it is understood (and misunderstood) by our researchers.

At risk in any work that attempts to dissolve dichotomies is the tendency to create new dichotomies instead. For that reason, *context* is a pivotal, fluid term on which this work hinges: In what contexts do we construct arguments about our research? In what contexts do we conduct research in the first place? Which contexts demand certain research methods more than other methods? In what ways does the current research debate in composition decontextualize the problems we debate?

Throughout my work on this project, I engaged in conversations about it in various contexts, and I was often confused by reactions to this work-in-progress. Too often, my defense of the quantitative and my argument for better training in research design and statistics in composition programs were misunderstood, and my attempt to provide a contextualist view that collapses the qualitative/quantitative dichotomy in our research was sometimes plainly ignored or resulted in a certain defensiveness from some listeners.

For example, in one job interview in 1998, two search committee members asked me questions following the discussion of my work that clearly indicated they weren't willing to let go of the dichotomy we currently have. One asked, "Yeah, but, really: What's the *best* method most suited for writing centers?" and the other asked, "If you're so into the quantitative, why don't you answer any questions with quantitative responses?"

In addition, we can easily find examples of scholars using a defensive tone on "both sides of the fence," indicating the intense passion accompanying debates about research in our field. While I try to avoid such a tone myself, the passion that drives our language and voices in any debate makes our field incredibly rich and beautifully imperfect, especially in tone.

My own passion to contribute to this dialogue and the passion of my listeners and readers along the way resulted, of course, in several misunderstandings. Often, I wrestled with what I found to be puzzling misperceptions of something I *thought* I was making clear. So I'll try to make a few points clear from the start here:

1. A contextualist approach to research does not (cannot, should not) value one set of research methods over another. In no manner will I argue that "quantitative" or "qualitative" methods are always "better." Instead, this work calls our attention to the contexts from which our research questions come (and to the questions themselves)—contexts and questions that should guide our methodological decisions, whatever they might be. In some contexts, one method might be more appropriate and illuminating. In other contexts, another method might be better suited to our needs. In still other contexts, a blend might be necessary to fully answer our questions. But in *no* context should we choose our method first, allowing *it* to

narrow what kinds of questions we can ask, for to do so is to ignore context itself.

2. In this work, I adopt a fluid definition of the term "context." Here, context means more than merely "place" or location, such as "in a writing center" or "in my classroom," as we so often see the term defined. Indeed, location alone as a defining feature of research contexts or methods can cause confusion if we're not careful. MacNealy (1999), for instance, also attempted to avoid the qualitative/quantitative dichotomy by using instead the distinction between "library-based" and "empirical" research; however, MacNealy acknowledged that such a distinction "could also create some confusion because empirical research can be done in a library. . . . [And] in the most rigorous of scientific disciplines, considerable library research must be done" (7). Location becomes, then, a troublesome and narrow feature of research methods and contexts.

Instead, context is not so rigidly defined here, but is "released" as a flexible construct defined by its own power and its own variability— both stemming from the moment a researcher wants to know something. For instance, two researchers in the same writing center could pursue two very different questions, creating two different contexts in the same location. One researcher might ask, "Does the pattern of student attendance and student concerns differ between portfolio-based classrooms and non-portfolio classrooms?" Here, this researcher might design an instrument to keep track of student attendance and concerns, seeking numerical evidence found in attendance records and textual evidence found in tutors' records of each session. The second researcher might ask, "What tutorial strategies are being used with hearing-impaired students who attend our writing center?" This researcher would most likely observe and record tutorials, hoping to observe patterns in tutoring strategies, possibly interviewing the tutors and students observed in action. Both researchers, while working in the same location, will choose research methods based on their questions within their location, not on the location only. While place might determine what research methods are *possible*, the research question determines what research methods are *necessary*.

3. I have no personal preference for any one kind of research method. Though some friends, colleagues, and acquaintances sometimes preface their remarks with "Nothing against your interest in numbers, but" or "Given your preference for the quantitative," or while some might expect me to use such methods *all* the time, I am merely curious about everything—as I imagine you to be, too. Narrowed, personal attachment to methodological choices cloud our vision of what those choices are in the first place. Instead, my passion stems from a fascination with the myriad of possibilities we encounter when seeking information and insight. Rhetoric and composition is exciting because we have *all* research tools available to us, useful at any moment of curiosity.

4. Finally, the presence of the highly risky term "paradigm," as I construct it in this work, invokes, of course, a Kuhnian image—one on which our field does not entirely agree. When I began this work, I agreed with Connors (1983) that composition might be incapable of constructing the kind of paradigm that Kuhn (1970) outlined in *The Structure of Scientific Revolutions*. But Connors also speculated that perhaps such a paradigm might still emerge one day in the future.

To help him articulate what a paradigm is, Kuhn pointed to three kinds of work in which a field would engage if truly driven by a successful paradigm. First, a field tries to capture and describe a class of information that it feels will reveal the nature of things, and attempt to refine that information as the field moves forward. This first class of information defines the content of a field and the scope of what *kinds* of nature we hope to reveal. For us, we hope to identify, reveal, and describe the nature of *rhetoric*, the nature of *composition*.

Second, a field actively tries to make comparisons, observations, applications, and predictions relating to the information available within our content, attempting to produce the highest amount of agreement within the field, and refining our information/beliefs via new or revised theories and instruments. In other words, a field that is driven by a successful paradigm will construct a coherent, working body of *research* for its membership to consider.

Third, a field driven by a successful paradigm will turn its attention to the ambiguities in the first two kinds of work. Knowing that 1) the information describing our content and 2) our predictions or applications of that information may not always be so certain in all situations, a paradigm-driven field will continue to turn its attention to its very paradigm in order to fully articulate its underlying theory, given the changes in information from the other two kinds of work. Our underlying theory—as readers will see in chapter four—is a *Contextualist Theory of Epistemic Justification*, one that turns our attention again to our very content: the nature of rhetoric, moving us in a paradigm-driven *cycle of inquiry* —a Contextualist Research Paradigm for Rhetoric and Composition—that will, when successful, turn our attention beyond the kinds of research we *like*, to explore, more importantly, the kinds of research we and our students *need*.

But, for Kuhn, the adoption of a new, successful paradigm produces remarkable changes in a field:

> When . . . an individual or group first produces a synthesis able to attract most of the next generation's practitioners, the older schools gradually disappear. . . . But there are always some . . . who cling to one or another of the older views, and they are simply read out of the profession, which thereafter ignores their work. The new paradigm implies a new and more rigid definition of the field. Those unwilling or unable to accommodate their work to it must proceed in isolation or attach themselves to some other group. (18-19)

Embracing a Contextualist Research Paradigm for Rhetoric and Composition, which I hope has room for all members of our field, holds exciting possibilities for the future of our work.

To begin, this book's first chapter will focus on the context from which the remainder of *this* work emerges, with particular attention to current trends in publications and professional conferences in composition—especially those works and events that attempt to define our field. Of interest here also is the basic question of how a field defines itself in the first place, which must include a discussion of paradigms, paradigm shifts, and debates centered on what constitutes research and scholarship—and the language used either to organize or dismantle the boundaries of that same field.

Chapter two will continue to outline the historical and current issues in composition research, including a review of our field's earlier rejection of current-traditional rhetoric (to which we often draw parallels when discussing current research trends), a discussion of texts designed to help the composition researcher, a review of George Campbell's description of evidence, and a presentation of a simple mock study designed to teach some research concepts.

In chapter three, I will examine three other issues that we must address in the qualitative/quantitative debate: math avoidance and anxiety, feminist contributions to composition and arguments against traditional research, and a preference for storytelling as a genre more literary than the traditional research report. The mock study begun in chapter two will continue, in order to illustrate basic descriptive statistics.

Chapter four will examine seemingly incompatible research paradigms at an epistemological level and will examine the nature of "context." Of interest here is the artificial distinction composition scholars have made among three ways of knowing: expressivist, objectivist, and social-constructivist. To help dissolve the (false) boundaries among these theories of knowledge, I will present a Contextualist Theory of Epistemic Justification as a new template with which to view such theories and our research. This template, to those in rhetoric, will not be entirely new: it captures the essence of Aristotelian rhetoric, a tradition of rhetoric sensitive to context and to dialectic. This sensitivity to context, together with a new lens through which to see research contexts, will allow us to construct a Contextualist Research Paradigm for Rhetoric and Composition. The mock study will conclude with a demonstration of some concepts of inferential statistics.

In chapter five I will present a reprint of Eileen Oliver's (1995) study published in *RTE*, "The Writing Quality of Seventh, Ninth, and Eleventh Graders, and College Freshmen: Does Rhetorical Specification in Writing Prompts Make a Difference?" Dovetailing with her study, I will insert an interview with Eileen Oliver in which she comments on her work, describes the research process, and explains her decisions. Such a presentation will reveal to readers that narratives exist just below the surface of traditional quantitative research and are not separate from it. This presentation will also demonstrate the Contextualist Research Paradigm at work.

Chapter six presents a second study, a pilot of my own, in which I examine the lore surrounding red ink in teaching composition. The purpose of the study in this chapter is to demonstrate quantitative comparisons between groups and statistical analysis. This study also serves as a test of much-accepted anecdotal evidence. The form in which it is presented (as a traditional research report *combined with* anecdotal evidence) suggests the possibility of lifting the underlying narrative of such research into the text in a new, less traditional form that composition might embrace as neither "quantitative" nor "qualitative," but as a multi-modal design that is simply necessary in the context of a particular research question, one explored with the Contextualist Research Paradigm in mind.

With chapters seven and eight I will conclude by speculating on the future of composition research and examining the need for a Contextualist Research Paradigm. I will suggest new goals for the field's researchers, and ask several questions about the future and politics of our research, the voices of our researchers, and our training in research design and statistics. I will propose that we teach the results of our research in our classrooms when we teach students how to write and that we construct a more accessible way to teach research design and statistics to our scholars of the future.

A Contextualist Research Paradigm for Rhetoric and Composition invites us to shift our focus—to the contexts in which we and our students need to explore fully the nature of composing, learning, and teaching. This focus will call us to attend to the contexts in which rhetorical issues and research issues converge, producing varied forms, many voices, and new knowledge, indeed reconstructing a discipline that will be simultaneously focused on its tasks, its knowledge-makers, and its students. Such a paradigm calls us to emerge from the trap of dichotomous thought and passionate debate that keeps us locked in the past and divided against ourselves—a calling through which we may embrace the freedom necessary to conduct the research our discipline so greatly needs.

1 COMPOSITION RESEARCH
Issues in Context

> [C]omposition studies is a field in a preparadigmatic state, a
> proto-science of a sort waiting for its first genuine
> exemplars. It is difficult to argue with this assertion; since
> we cannot predict the future, and for all we know a
> complete composition-studies paradigm may emerge
> tomorrow from completely unsuspected sources.
>
> *Robert J. Connors, 1983*

The call for proposals for the 1998 NCTE Convention in Nashville, Tennessee, began with composition's newest and most popular tool: the anecdote. The call for proposals was focused on the local, the personal, and the emotional. In sharp contrast to previous calls that often placed a particular annual convention (and its theme) in a larger context—the overall field of teaching English, broad issues facing educators, or current social and political trends educators need to address—NCTE President-Elect Steiner instead told a story about "Maria":

> The semester had gone well, and I was giving the final exam to my
> senior American Literature class . . . . During the exam, Maria raised her
> hand. I walked over to her desk. She looked at me and asked, "Why do you
> teach us how to read around the word, but then test us on the word?" (1)

Investigating what she had learned from Maria's question, Steiner invited other professionals in our field to engage in similar inquiry, and while the Call for Proposals did not directly favor or debate the value of one kind of research over another, the call for teacher research through participant observation was clear as Steiner continued her reflection on Maria's story:

> A teacher's role is unique. At times, as James Britton has taught us,
> teachers are in the role of participant, actively involved in the classroom

with students. At other times, teachers are in the role of spectator. . . . The 1998 Convention is a time for us to reflect upon classroom practices and upon our relationships as learners with our students. . . . Maria is not the only student who has taught me. (1)

Such attention to participant-observation and to reflection on our experiences drew, I'm sure, numerous insightful anecdotes and observations from our teaching at the November 1998 convention. Reflection and anecdotes are important to our understanding of what we do, but the NCTE announcement suggested what was not invited: quantitative studies, experimental research, or anything else that doesn't seem to fit a conference theme that highlights participant-observation and the personal anecdote:

> Through the shifting roles of participant and spectator, teachers learn about their students and the dynamics of the classroom. Teachers also learn about themselves as professionals. . . . I invite you to share your moments of learning from or with your students at NCTE's 1998 National Convention. Please join us in Nashville, Tennessee, and place our mutual learning with students at the center of our time together. Join us in celebrating the continual learning and growing we enjoy as classroom teachers. (1)

A national announcement such as Steiner's (especially when added to the 1998 CCCC convention theme in Chicago, "Ideas, Historias, y Cuentos") indicates the degree to which our field has accepted certain forms of research—or forms we want to call research–and dialogue as a means of defining who we are professionally.

The simple dichotomy that divides what we commonly call "qualitative vs. quantitative" research has now been divided even further, it seems. Perhaps through our quest for more research, not only is "qualitative" disparaged, but systematic rigorous "qualitative" research seems to be less available, too, as we opt instead for the personalized anecdotal evidence we gain through experience. Rigorous ethnographies and case studies, though qualitative in nature, seem to be losing ground along with the quantitative–losing ground to the simpler, more diverse, more personal story or anecdote. Such reliance on the personal anecdote has contributed more to "lore" than to "research," two components of our knowledge-making that have always had an unfortunately strained relationship.

While I, too, will share several anecdotes in this work, in the hope and the belief that such anecdotes can help explain or contest larger concepts and can illuminate some of our work, "research" that shares *only* anecdotal evidence seems to have found a prominent place in our recent scholarship–and unfortunately so.

Recent collections of essays in composition studies reveal how strongly our field has embraced the anecdote, the story, as a means of and a form for our research. Several texts have been advertised primarily for their reflective approach and for their accessibility to readers; the following incomplete list offers just a few examples: *Pedagogy in the Age of Politics* (Sullivan & Qualley, 1994), *The Need for Story: Cultural Diversity in Classroom and Community* (Dyson & Genishi, 1994), *Learning in Small Moments: Life in an Urban Classroom* (Meier, 1997), *Stories from the Heart: Teachers and Students Researching their Literacy Lives* (Meyer, 1996), *Beginning in Retrospect: Writing and Reading a Teacher's Life* (Schmidt, 1996), *Narration as Knowledge: Tales of the Teaching Life* (Trimmer, 1997).

Potential problems of such collections, however, are noted by Jacobs (1997) in a review of Sullivan and Qualley's *Pedagogy in the Age of Politics* (1994). Jacobs argues that the focus on anecdotes and narratives from the individual voices of authors results in "diffuseness" and the impression that the authors seem "isolated rather than members of a social network" (464). For Jacobs, this lack of unity in *Pedagogy in the Age of Politics* came from the editors' inability to tie it all together or explain "the circumstances under which these papers came together" (464), and resulted in a highly inaccurate title that Jacobs argues applies to only one-fourth of the volume (465).

At the same time, others have been critical of the quality of non-anecdotal, more rigorous research in composition. When Stotsky (1997) stepped down as editor of *Research in the Teaching of English (RTE)*, she plainly remarked,

> *RTE* has experienced a documented decline in recent years in the number of high quality manuscripts submitted. . . . I discovered at a

session for editors at the American Educational Research Association that this quality decline is affecting other mainstream research journals as well. (6)

To compensate, Stotsky explained, *RTE* published more reflective essays, "live debates," and other inquiry that Stotsky admitted "helped *RTE* broaden its educational purpose. . . . [and] can serve a vital role in the professional development of English language arts teachers by informing them of the issues under discussion in the research community" (6). But such discussions, for *RTE*, had to be published due to a lack of high quality research (whether qualitative *or* quantitative in nature): "Necessity very much became the mother of serendipitous invention" (Stotsky, 1997, p. 6). Once *RTE* began to accept essays with a personalized bent, the full acceptance of the experiential through debate and anecdote was firmly in place, and our rejection of the quantitative was complete.

Wisely, and perhaps again out of necessity, the new editors of *RTE*, two issues after Stotsky stepped down, published an introductory explanation of what constitutes research, identifying a range of methods that are welcome in the journal (Smagorinsky & Smith, May 1997). One year later, however, in the May 1998 issue of *RTE*, Smagorinsky and Smith again discussed the criteria by which submissions would be accepted to the journal. The editors commented on the need for the "archival significance" of accepted articles— *RTE* is a place for public documents that chronicle the development of a community (121). The editors published three articles that they felt demonstrated what they meant by "significant" in the May 1998 issue of *RTE*. None of the articles presented quantitative data.

In short, the unfortunate rift between "quantitative" and "qualitative" research has not only resulted in a near-abandonment of research that seeks and analyzes numerical data, but it has also divided us further into the more private worlds of personal stories. While such stories can always help illuminate our work and give meaning to our theory, research, and practice, they, alone, cannot be the primary knowledge-making vehicle that defines our field. Given current trends in our scholarship that seem to indicate such a direction, we must consider these (and other) questions:

1. Have we accepted anecdotes as a form of research so much as only to sacrifice other forms?
2. Why has composition gravitated toward the anecdote-as-research so quickly and so strongly?
3. Would our field be better defined by evidence that is personal, social, numerical, or a blend of these? *Can* we blend them?
4. What possible solutions are there to the quantitative/qualitative false dichotomy? What arguments would members of "both sides" listen to?
5. How would a solution change the future of composition research?

COMPOSITION IN A WORD: TRANSFORMATION

To examine research trends in any field is to study its processes of knowledge-making: what logic do we use to arrive at that knowledge? In what contexts do we believe the knowledge we feel we have? What texts comprise what we call our body of knowledge? That body of knowledge, of course, has boundaries that we create to determine what can and cannot be within its scope—boundaries that we choose to maintain or challenge, to accept or reject, to tighten or broaden, and, most importantly, to define and redefine (again and again) in the everchanging context(s) of the world(s) around us.

The long, multidisciplinary history of rhetoric and composition complicates such study of our own field. Our perception of our field and its history and research "in any given age depends on the organic interplay between the disposition of the discipline and the intellectual climate and social complexity of the times" (Johnson, 1991, pp. 6-7). Indeed, Johnson presented a compelling case in *Nineteenth-Century Rhetoric in North America* that "rhetorical theory and pedagogy have displayed a dynamic tendency toward responsive transformation" (7), often due to "shifting social and political conditions" (6). In other words, Johnson outlined rhetoric's heightened sensitivity to context:

> The most conspicuous characteristic in the history of rhetoric has been its responsiveness to the ever-changing nature of certain intellectual and cultural imperatives: 1) governing epistemological assumptions

regarding the relationships between thought, language, and communication; 2) dominant philosophical views of human nature and the nature of affective response to discourse; 3) conventional and institutional perceptions of appropriate modes of formal communication; and 4) the perceived role of the study and practice of rhetoric in the maintenance of social and political order. (4)

The above four imperatives have undoubtedly shaped and reshaped our field: how we teach, how we view ourselves, what and how we choose to research, and what forms of knowledge we deem valuable. Accordingly, we must take note of Johnson's choice of epigraphs preceding chapter one of *Nineteenth-Century Rhetoric*, epigraphs that illustrate an overwhelming transformation has already taken place in our research and in our view of knowledge:

> This is a work of history in fictional form—that is, in personal perspective, which is the only kind of history that exists. (Joyce Carol Oates, *Them*)

> The truth is, I have never written a story in my life that didn't have a very firm foundation in actual human experience—somebody else's experience quite often, but an experience that became my own by hearing the story, by witnessing the thing, by hearing just a word perhaps. (Katherine Ann Porter)

> It is like what we imagine knowledge to be:
> dark, salt, clear, moving, utterly free,
> drawn from the cold hard mouth
> of the world, derived from the rocky breast
> forever, flowing and drawn, and since
> our knowledge is historical, flowing, and flown.
> (Elizabeth Bishop, "At the Fishhouses")

This view of knowledge—personal, experiential, flowing, dark, free, and expressive—has recently and greatly transformed the research of our field. As epigraphs to Johnson's first chapter in a book on nineteenth century rhetoric, the statements above serve to guide readers as they proceed: to frame Johnson's own beliefs about the field, to explain her approach to historical inquiry, to align her, perhaps, with other (women) writers/poets, and to assert what kinds of knowledge our field has ultimately come to value most.

Such knowledge seems best expressed through narratives and poetry rather than scientific reports, through a story rather than data analysis, through the emotional more than the logical, through the specifics of experience instead of the generalizations of probability. The recent "transformation" which Johnson used to frame her text has, indeed, reframed the contexts in which we now do research and publish our work—a new context that has produced research that highlights the personal, the local, the narrative.

A responsive transformation such as this has had, on the one hand, some positive effects: composition has found itself in the more comfortable world of the social, personal, anthropological, political, and literary arenas that have always been of interest to many of us more than the scientific or mathematical; those now being trained as writing teachers and tutors will see more readily than teachers 50 years ago that we teach not so much an impersonal subject, but students alive with personal knowledge they bring to their writing and reading; as writers ourselves, we seem to gain more freedom to contribute to a growing body of knowledge presented in a wider range of scholarship, including the creative; and this scholarship is more accessible to most of us, more understandable—we're in this field, after all, because we've always loved to read "that kind of stuff."

For all we have gained through such a transformation, however, what might we have lost? New trends in our research have taken hold strongly enough to dramatically reduce the same "responsiveness" and "dynamic tendency" for which Johnson had once praised our field: a stronger commitment to one kind of knowledge has made us dangerously less responsive to other kinds and, therefore, less dynamic in our quest to define our field. Peter Elbow's *What is English?* (1990) is the clearest example:

> "What is English?" The title is not intended as a question I can answer with my book, not a slow lob that I can try to hit for a home run. The title *is* my answer, my summing up, my picture of the profession. This book is trying to paint a picture of a profession that cannot define what it is. (v)

Elbow did not pretend to answer the question in his title; instead, he presented his personal reflections on the 1987 English Coalition

Conference, joined by interludes of letters, reflections, stories, and position statements written by conference participants. This book (a picture of a "profession that cannot define what it is") becomes, then, a collage of narratives, experiences—in short, a portrait of a field based on knowledge that is (like the knowledge valued in Johnson's epigraphs) personal, experiential, flowing, dark, free, and expressive. Teachers at the conference shared stories about triumphs and failures with their students, stories about poor (and sometimes violent) conditions in which they teach, questions and reflections about what they did and did not get out of the conference, memories of their own teachers.

By presenting primarily this kind of knowledge, Elbow, while claiming not to define the field, presented a model, perhaps, of what he saw as the best method for getting us there—an anecdotal approach to clarifying our boundaries—and the kind of knowledge to which we should assign the highest value.

I would not be exaggerating if I said, "I *love* Elbow's book!" After all, I, too, am in this field because I like to read "that kind of stuff." Elbow makes me think. He asks hard questions. He makes me laugh. I think he makes us all laugh, especially at ourselves. Every field needs a writer who does those things.

But every field needs more than that, too.

There are, after all, questions that Elbow couldn't ask (or offer as an "answer"), and there are parts of our field he couldn't define (even if he had tried) because of the method he chose for constructing that picture of the field in the first place. While he raised fascinating questions and explored interesting theories, these questions and theories (and the personal, individual stories through which they were raised) cannot help us determine the scope of certain problems he saw in the field (such as how we assign grades); they cannot help us understand the full effectiveness of certain teaching methods; they cannot allow us to compare classroom-wide changes after a school reduces class sizes or installs computers or after a teacher alters her view of testing.

For example, in one of Elbow's interludes, a teacher changed her 8th grade literature tests when a student—and, once, the student's mother—had epileptic seizures after taking those tests. This teacher realized that her exams taxed the memory too greatly and did not allow for investigation or application of principles (higher-order thinking skills, in other words), so she changed the tests to include new features, more essays, and some take-home options. She confirmed through observation that the epileptic student performed far better on the new tests, but she offered no report on whether students who had already performed well were getting more out of the new tests, too (258-259). Here we recognize a teacher who feels she made a change for the better. We have every reason to believe that one student is better off, and we might guess that others are, too. But that's all we can do: guess.

In *What is English?* Elbow presented the "kind of stuff" that is moving. It's "that kind of stuff" that inspires me to stay in this field where everyone seems to learn so much, so much of the time. But it's that kind of guessing (at "dark knowledge") that dangerously draws us further from the kind of research that could shed more light—if only we let it. After all, to allow such "knowledge" to remain dark is, in the end, to accept incomplete knowledge.

To illuminate the assumption that a change for the better for one student is a change for the better for all, the above teacher could have conducted a fascinating study right in her own classroom: to compare student learning of (and, perhaps, attitudes toward) literature before and after her new tests, to explore her test as not so much a test but as another teaching tool, to assess the value of her classroom after the change, perhaps even in comparison to other classrooms.

But such a study takes time and, worse, requires quantifying and analyzing data (numbers, in other words), and Elbow warned us in this book that any reduction of anything to a single number is "untrustworthy" (251). Never mind that Elbow also warned us in the beginning of the same book that his reflections were biased and that he, like Gulliver, was a less-than-reliable narrator (vi). The current climate of our field (one of new favoritism toward anecdotal forms of research) has produced a battle for trustworthiness between a number and a narrative. And the narrative clearly wins—not because it necessarily offers more (or more accurate) information than the other, but because the narrative offers one *kind* of information that we clearly value more.

After all, *that* is English.

But not all narratives and personal experiences are as easily received in composition as those in Elbow's book. Indeed, not one of Elbow's narrative interludes began with "I conducted a study once" or "I was thinking about an experiment I read." When I attend professional conferences in composition, most often on writing centers, and share some of my own narratives, the experiences I now bring to this work, they are often pointed out as "unpopular to say." For example, as an undergraduate, I majored in composition and cognitive psychology. While pursuing these majors, I participated in an undergraduate experimental psychology research group. I once conducted and presented a study on attitudinal similarity and image maintenance between writers and evaluators of writing. I enjoy the challenge of studying statistics and experimental research designs and I wanted to write a dissertation on related issues. My colleagues' responses to these "stories" of mine have ranged from suggesting I'm in the wrong field, to incredulous remarks ("are you serious?") to warnings not to ruin my career, to a simple uncomprehending blink or two.

To me, the defensiveness in these reactions was confusing. My interest in composition began as a peer tutor in a writing center, when I was a sophomore in 1986, about to begin my major in English with an emphasis in composition. At the time, majoring in both English and cognitive and experimental psychology, my studies in these two different areas made a lot of sense to me. When I was tutoring writing, for example, I often kept in mind a principle of human memory from cognitive psychology called the "serial position effect," a notion based on years of research on memory that suggests we remember best what we see last, we remember second best what we see first, and we remember the least the stuff in the middle. Regardless of what direction my tutorials took, I always tried to engage the writers with whom I worked in a summary of what had just happened—a collaborative summary at the *end* of the tutorial, a tutorial strategy based on theories of collaborative learning (as composition had emphasized to me) *and* on principles of cognitive psychology (as research had emphasized). When writers struggled with organization—or with introductions and conclusions—the "serial position effect" was also useful and gave us another language with which to talk about readers and *their* memories and how the writer can help work the brains, so to speak, of their audience.

Studies in social cognition, especially in attribution theory, gave me a lens—not the only lens, of course, but an important one—with which to see a writer's level of confidence, how a writer measured his or her success. Attribution theorists often attempt to answer the question "to what do we attribute our success, our failure, our beliefs, our performance in varied contexts?" Of special interest are attributions to external factors (such as luck or help) vs. internal factors (such as effort or intelligence or ability). I was often struck by the number of students—often those who lacked confidence in their ability—who attributed success to *my help*, rather than to their own effort or intelligence. I was especially struck by the students who attributed success to *luck*, an external factor even more out of their control—or my control as their tutor, for that matter.

Psychologists have found many relationships between attributions to external, uncontrollable factors for success and issues of low self-esteem, low-to-medium success in careers, and poor self-image (especially among women). While tutoring, I would use attribution cues from students—cues that would help me listen for when they needed help seeing the importance of their effort, their ability, the time spent on drafting, their motivation to succeed, their talent and strengths—hoping they would transfer their attributions for their success from others to themselves, so they would become more independent writers, more confident and more proud of their work.

While I often applied what I had learned in my psychology major to my work as a writing center tutor, application often worked in reverse as well. My training as a writing consultant was important to my participation and my learning in our experimental psychology research group. Most of our meetings focused on helping someone design a study. Questions I learned to ask as a writing tutor were important to me and my fellow researchers: questions that tried to determine what the researcher wanted to know, why it was important to know it, and how best to arrive at some answers—questions and guidance that, as a writing tutor, I used all the time in a writing center. Often, my colleagues in the research group would ask me (because I was the only "English person" in their group) for my help wording their arguments, finding the best mode of argumentation based on their data, finding the clearest language with which to express their statistical analyses.

For me, there were all sorts of connections between studies in cognition and tutoring writing, between experimental designs and how we think through a tutorial, between theories of psychology and theories of reading and writing. But when I got to graduate school and began to focus my studies on composition and rhetoric (and writing centers in particular), I would learn a disturbing truth: (some of) the most prominent scholars in composition and rhetoric and writing centers argue that these two worlds—one world of the cognitive, the experimental, the psychologist, and the other world of the composition specialist, literacy theorist, writing teacher and tutor—were not connected at all. (see chapter two)

In my own graduate courses in composition, for example, research methods considered to be more "naturalistic" were often favored over those more "scientific"—favored in student projects, in professors' selections of reading materials, and in course content. In these courses, language we often associate with traditional research was also under fire as other political arenas within composition (especially in basic writing and writing centers) have been ablaze with criticism for terms like "standard," "control," "marginal," "manipulation," and other terms central to an understanding of statistics. And the study and use of statistics, of course, require numbers—numbers that many who are formally trained in a literary tradition find confusing and useless, if not hateful and (for Elbow) "untrustworthy."

FIELD-BUILDING IN A POSTMODERN AGE

Not knowing what evidence to "trust" is natural for any field in a world we now call "postmodern"—but lack of trust seems not only natural but necessary for a field born in part *because* of that world. For Phelps (1988),

> The postmodern world is marked by themes of loss, illusion, instability, marginality, decentering, finitude. . . . Across the disciplines, all of the

old realities are in doubt, placed under radical critiques—critiques that challenge reason, consciousness, knowledge, meaning, communication, freedom. . . . These assaults destroy absolutes and leave us in fear of an ultimate meaninglessness that will paralyze action and thought. (5)

Phelps praised the postmodern consciousness for its attack on scientism—science's belief in its own methods, proof, knowledge—and for questioning the knowledge that scientism has upheld as "permanently valid" and with "absolute authority" (9). In Foucault's (1972) terms, a whole "field of questions" has emerged, seeking "discontinuity (threshold, rupture, break, mutation, transformation)" (5-6).

The modern version of composition studies—though grounded in a long-standing rhetorical tradition—emerged amid such chaos—in the context of a rupture, a transformation, a mutation, if you will, called the "literacy crisis" of the mid-1970s (Harkin & Schilb, 1991). Sommers (1979) had argued that our field lacked an articulated theory at that time *because* of the chaotic response to the literacy crisis, a response that resulted in numerous teaching methods developed without the support of a theory of how students learn.

By 1991, Harkin and Schilb asserted that "composition studies has now become a fully authorized academic field and a site of inquiry in its own right" (3). However, their introduction to *Contending with Words* remained alive with, well, contending words: "tensions," "resistant," "crisis," "refuse," "interrogate." And they didn't quite say *how* this new field became fully authorized, though it seems to me that such a fully authorized field wouldn't need so much contending, wouldn't need to point out that contributors to the volume were those who "refuse to act as the 'window washers of the academy'" (5). Indeed, the culture into which composition was born was one of change, of dissolving boundaries, or, for Phelps, "composition comes to maturity at just the moment when discourse (especially writing) and its interpretation stand at the epicenter of a great change, a fundamental crisis in human consciousness" (4).

Placed "at the epicenter of a great change," then, the field has had to construct its own boundaries in a culture that had just destroyed the old ways of boundary-making and had begun to question knowledge in a new way.

For Hairston (1982), this change was called a "paradigm shift," based on the work of Kuhn (1970). But, in Connors's (1983) reading of Kuhn, our field did not have a paradigm from which to shift in the first place, and was or is, therefore, preparadigmatic, with preparadigmatic elements competing against each other—possibly as a result of our field's history, which Connors called "chaotic, anti-empirical, confused, and at times mindless" (18). In Connors's review of composition scholars' borrowing from Kuhn, he noted that all of those scholars—those who have seen a paradigm shift and those who have argued the field is preparadigmatic—were nevertheless "united in the belief that composition studies can attain a Kuhnian scientific paradigm" of some sort (5).

Regardless of how Kuhn has been applied to composition studies, the quest for a paradigm—for defining boundaries—has been made clear. Currently, composition is defined by a confusing array of ideas. On the one hand, some have said current-traditional rhetoric stemmed from the nineteenth century, and, later, changed, suggesting the widely-accepted notion that our field has, indeed, experienced a paradigm shift of sorts. On the other hand, those who argue that composition studies emerged in the 1970s during the "literacy crisis" suggest that the field possibly emerged because of that paradigm shift, suggesting that the earlier paradigm was quite possibly a very different field, not our own field as we now know it. Currently, the rapid rise of anecdotal evidence, story-telling, and qualitative research, together with a few remaining traditional studies, has multiplied the ways in which the field can define itself. For Kuhn (1970), such a wide range of evidence and its accompanying, competing theories suggests a preparadigmatic state:

> In the absence of a paradigm or some candidate for a paradigm, all of the facts that could possibly pertain to the development of a given science are likely to seem equally relevant. As a result, early fact-gathering is a far more nearly random activity than the one that subsequent scientific development makes familiar. Furthermore, in the absence of a reason for

seeking some particular form of more recondite information, early fact-gathering is usually restricted to the wealth of data that lie ready to hand. The resulting pool of facts contains those accessible to casual observation and experiment, together with some of the more esoteric data retrievable from established crafts. (15)

I agree with Connors that composition was preparadigmatic in 1983. If it is possible for a field to become "more preparadigmatic" as time goes on, composition seems to have done so. In Charney's (1996) words, our recent reliance on individual, personal studies has produced "a broad shallow array of information, in which one study may touch loosely on another but in which no deep or complex networks of inferences and hypotheses are forged or tested" (590). In the absence of a paradigm, as Kuhn noted, our frequent use of random activity and casual observations via the anecdote, together with our struggle to *make* varied kinds of evidence equal to each other, has broadened the scope of our inquiry, certainly in some valuable ways; but such diverse activity has also, unwittingly perhaps, removed the very thing many of our scholars have been searching for: a definition of our field, a paradigm, sensible boundaries in which to contain a seemingly chaotic volume of scholarship.

If we believe that our field emerged in the context of what others have described as a chaotic state, a whirlwind of debate about knowledge, paradigms, and history, it is no wonder that composition has now gravitated toward the heavy use of the personal, individual, anecdotal evidence now seen in much of our scholarship. Perhaps storytelling and experience-sharing allows us a means to join the critique of scientism, or perhaps it binds us to the only part of our knowledge that we believe is still certain and accessible—our personal experience. Perhaps story telling allows us the chance to start over—a new paradigm of sorts that paradoxically favors the absence of one.

Such a shift, for Ward (1995), is reminiscent of Snow's (1965) discussion of the clash of "Two Cultures"—a gap between the sciences and humanities that Snow tried to close even though he saw the gulf as irreconcilable (4-5). In spite of some criticism that Snow's divisions were too simplistic, Ward (1995) has asserted that such a gulf is not only evident, but has actually widened at the close of the twentieth century, dividing not only fields, but subfields and colleagues:

> Often in loosely knit and divisive fields, like literary criticism, philosophy, and sociology, the collective representation of the field itself has not been completely settled and is, therefore, up for grabs. . . . In these settings, cliques and subgroups with competing truth claims and ideologies are likely to exist. (9)

For those fields that reject scientism as a means of organizing themselves, to what do they turn? For Ward, the debate about what constitutes knowledge—what research and inquiry should define a field—is rarely about knowledge itself so much as it is about "ongoing organizational and political struggles" (4). Composition is currently constructing, then, not a Kuhnian scientific paradigm, but what Ward called an "organizational myth"—a "banner or totem around which a social group is internally organizing itself and under which a new political assault on the scientific establishment is being made" (1). Our own "new political assault" advances under the "banner" of the story or anecdote.

Given our field's recent history of doubting traditional research, our current interest in research methods other than the quantitative, our distaste for statistics, and our need to maintain all forms of research in our scholarship, the composition field needs a more accessible analysis of the available research methods and, especially, of the contexts in which we use them. A new look at *research in context* will enable us to understand the potential of diverse research forms, to realize that numbers indeed may tell a story, to accept the terminology of scientific inquiry on its own terms, and to engage in the pleasure of asking wide-ranging questions and seeking their answers.

Such an analysis addresses the nature of research paradigms, the effects of rapid changes in those paradigms, and the power of research to define a field. Scholars in our field currently engage in passionate, sometimes defensive, debates about just those issues, posing arguments and establishing preferences, though unfortunately creating dichotomous language that further divides those same scholars. To achieve common ground, we must avoid the artificial dichotomy (and divisive language) that has naturally and unfortunately emerged from discussions of our research. Others have put forth excellent discussion in an attempt to collapse this dichotomy (Charney, 1996; Hillocks, 1992; Schriver, 1989; Kirsch, 1992) but could do so only through the same dichotomous language and, therefore, have not yet succeeded..

Some of the following terms are central to the debate. A list of definitions for these terms helps condense the conflicts in our field to a concise space—a space in which the language we use to keep ourselves apart is highlighted. Labels we place on our research (and researchers), with their diverse connotations, are, for some, accusations rather than concepts worth defining. Defining such concepts, however, provides a framework in which disputing parties might come together and embrace some of this same divisive language in order to start a discussion toward collapsing the dichotomy from which such language emerges. In the following list, I adopt current usage of some terms as they have appeared in composition scholarship; for other terms, I establish more useful boundaries:

1. *Research*: While many inquiries constitute "research" (I agree, for example, with Miller's (1992) argument that writing about theory can be understood as a form of research), my use of the term in this project is more narrow, focusing on inquiry guided by specific research questions actively explored by a discernible method, such as experiment, interview, survey, ethnography, or case study. Some of the following terms further define different kinds of research as perceived by our field.

2. *Scientific Inquiry/Methods*: I am using "scientific" to describe research methods that engage in hypothesis-testing and employ statistical analyses of data gathered from measurements of identified, controlled variables within the research context. Purposes for such inquiry include description, inference, prediction, and/or explanation as guided by the question being explored in the research context.

3. *Empirical*: For some in composition, empiricism is related to scientism or to extreme positivism (for example, Phelps, 1988). Its relation to the scientific method, to methods of systematic testing and observation (Kerlinger, 1986, pp. 4-5), quite possibly causes this interpretation.

However, a more accurate definition can be found in *Reading Empirical Research Studies: The Rhetoric of Research.* Hayes et al. (1992) included as examples of empirical research in composition "case studies, naturalistic observation, surveys, protocol studies, correlational studies, experiments, historical studies" (5).

4. *Naturalistic Inquiry/Methods*: "Naturalistic" refers to those research methods that seek to describe and/or narrate events, people, phenomena, and experiences as completely as possible by including all variables gained through dialogue and/or observation. Politics of research in composition are such that "naturalistic" is often used in contrast to (and to highlight) "artificial" scientific inquiry; while I object to such distinctions, I will adopt the terms as currently used.

5. *Narrative*: While literary theorists have proposed elaborate definitions of this term, narrative in composition research is synonymous with other terms, such as "anecdote" and "story" or with the kinds of texts that offer full descriptions of events, such as ethnographies and case studies. For composition, then, narrative seems to describe any text that presents a temporal "telling" of some event(s) or phenomenon, a telling that will often have a "personal voice" or personal involvement on the part of the writer. I adopt this use of the term throughout this text.

6. *Positivism*: A view of knowledge "characterized . . . by the use of mathematics, logic, observation, experimentation, and control" such that the "scientific method is the only source of correct knowledge about reality" (Angeles, 1992, pp. 234-235). While this extreme view of positivism does not exist in quite this form in our field, those who define themselves through "humanism" in contrast have argued as if it does.

7. *Humanism*: In composition research debates, humanism is defined in sharp contrast to positivism and is further defined by humanities training, mostly in literary studies. From a research point of view, humanism rejects methods that involve mathematics and that attempt to control variables, preferring instead methods that involve, for example, dialogue and observation in natural settings through ethnography, case studies, and interviews.

8. *Qualitative vs. Quantitative Research*: This distinction is often made in our scholarship, producing a false dichotomy between, for example, a case study as a qualitative work with only descriptive value, lacking quantitative data, and an experiment as a quantitative work with only

numerical analysis, lacking descriptive qualities. I try to avoid these stereotypes except where already used by composition researchers cited in this work.

9. *Objective vs. Subjective Research*: This distinction, too, is made in composition research, and I use these terms only as they appear in our scholarship; otherwise, I avoid perpetuating this distinction as a further division among researchers.

STARTING POINTS AND ASSERTIONS

Such divided language and passions concerning how research is conducted in composition suggest the need for a thorough examination of our research processes and the arguments we construct to defend our preferences for constructing our field. Indeed, Connors (1983) accurately argued, "as a research discipline we tend to flail about" (10).

This book is a response to that "flailing about," and it grows out of my own concern for our growing unwillingness to listen to each other and to create an inclusive research paradigm. While I would never dare suggest that such a work will "cure" all flailing about, I sincerely hope that it helps us (at the very least) flail about less often and (even more importantly) understand why we flail about at all and (most importantly) helps us find new ways to appreciate and engage in not just the kinds of research we like, but also the kinds of research we need.

Many obstacles interfere with this goal, I think. Indeed, for me and for this work, Elbow (1990) captured the most difficult obstacle of all in *What is English?* when he argued that the field cannot define what it is in the first place. Yet, to hold steady, for the moment, the current politics of composition research and the historical forces that have shaped current debates among researchers, the following assertions will guide the remainder of this work:

1. Contemporary composition theorists have erroneously blamed a scientific epistemology for the failed current-traditional paradigm.
2. The current explosion of interest in a social-constructivist epistemology and its accompanying research methods has further shifted

researchers' attentions and questions away from contexts that could benefit from scientific inquiry.

3. Shifting away from scientific inquiry has resulted in newly accepted modes of research in composition that are valuable for answering certain kinds of questions in certain contexts.

4. Formal training in the humanities has not prepared composition specialists for scientific investigations, has constructed a body of knowledge seemingly foreign to and separate from the scientific, and has developed an axiology in which controlled, scientific inquiry is less valued.

5. Most texts that seek to guide researchers in composition are inadequate in their explanations of research design, in their choice of sample studies, and in their treatment of statistics.

6. All research methods are limited in the kinds of questions they can answer and depend on the contexts in which those questions are asked; similarly, all research methods have value within certain ranges of research contexts and questions.

In summary, the goal of *Composing Research* is to collapse the qualitative/quantitative dichotomy in composition research and to construct instead a Contextualist Research Paradigm for Rhetoric and Composition—one that focuses our attention not on form or politics, but on the processes of research that naturally produce varied forms in the varied research contexts we encounter in our work.

2 RESEARCH IN COMPOSITION
Current Issues and A Brief History

[I]n a very real sense, the debate about the relative merits of
qualitative and quantitative research is a distraction,
masking our more basic differences in a rush to argue about
numbers. I want to suggest that it is not whether we use
quantitative or qualitative methods, but the intellectual
stances that underlie the research questions we ask and the
evidence we seek that are at the heart of our differences.

Judith Langer, 1987

Current debates about research methods have often focused on where
and how researchers view reality and evidence. Because we debate the
value of evidence—rather than the contexts from which we gain that
evidence—the rift between different kinds of researchers has resulted
in stereotypes: ethnographers have criticized the rigid, controlled,
decontextualized methodology of the experimental researcher; experimentalists have, in turn, perceived the observations of the ethnographer as loose and error-ridden. In the middle, some researchers have
acknowledged a wide range of methodologies stemming from varied
epistemologies in what is now called "methodological pluralism"
(Kirsch, 1992).

Schriver (1992) illustrated the different perceptions naturalistic
researchers and scientific researchers have had of each other, building
on the debate composition studies began in the 1980s between cognition and writing (equated with scientific studies) and writing-in-
context (equated with cultural studies):

> The stereotype of the researcher interested in cognition is the positivist
> who makes reductive statements about human behavior or who confirms
> the obvious. The stereotype of the researcher concerned with context is
> the naturalistic observer who creates sweeping generalizations about

human behavior or who argues the impossibility of drawing any generalizations at all. (190)

The stereotypes Schriver outlined here are well-documented.
Berthoff (1990), in a most scathing example, criticized the researcher
who seeks numerical data—a quest that, for Berthoff, is devoid of
meaning:

> If meaning is set aside in the search for "data," the findings will not
> then be applicable to the making of meaning. But composition specialists
> who follow psycholinguistic principles of analysis want to have it both
> ways: their empirical research requires that meaning be left out of
> account, but they also want to claim that their findings are relevant to
> pedagogy. (14)

Berthoff condemned cognitive psychologists as researchers who
"deliberately ignore" context (22) and ridiculed psychologists generally for being "usually about a generation behind" (16). Indeed,
Berthoff painted a ridiculous picture of psychology as a field that is
still "awash in Piagetian concepts" (16).[1]

Perhaps in response to (or out of spite for) the so-called positivist
inquiry Berthoff loathes, she proposed her own theory of composing—
a theory that cannot possibly be quantified or analyzed by anyone:

> To teach the composing process entails coming to terms with alla-
> tonceness, learning to consider it not as a source of roadblocks but as a
> resource. When we write, we are simultaneously naming, inferring, refer-
> ring, recognizing, remembering, marking time, wondering, wandering,
> envisaging, matching, discarding, checking, inventing. . . . We need to
> teach ourselves and our students to manage the complexity of allatonce-
> ness, to learn to tolerate uncertainty and ambiguity, to recognize the value
> of *not* knowing what your thesis statement is and thus discovering the
> uses of chaos. (86)

In part, I agree with Berthoff: wonderful prose can emerge from
chaos, and writing is seldom an orderly thing. While we need to be
more tolerant of that ambiguity, however, an ambiguous theory rarely
helps us manage, tolerate, or contextualize ambiguity any better than

we did before. Mysterious theories about mysteries, in other words, keep us where we are—in a complacent acceptance of the unexplainable "that's just the way it is" rather than in an active quest to discover and understand the contexts in which we write and how those contexts affect the processes and products that result. Berthoff succeeded, however, in producing a theory that looks very different from a theory that is "orderly" or controlled or cognitive: her theory of Allatonceness— "everything happens at once or it doesn't happen at all" (86)—is, perhaps, the most "disorderly" and uncontrollable theory composition has ever seen. The "black box theory of composing" leaves questions about context unanswered, unexplored—in spite of Berthoff's criticism for other researchers she felt ignore context as well.

Berthoff, however, was not alone in her criticism of the "reductionist" nature of cognitive studies or in her resistance to methodologies used in such research. Since North's *The Making of Knowledge in Composition* (1987), several debates have emerged with methodology as centerpiece. Because North's work divided the "knowledge-makers" of the field by methodology, new doors were opened for analyses of how we think—as a field, as researchers, as scholars, as teachers—new avenues for debate that perhaps divided us more than North imagined at the time. North's quest was simply to map the field and its *"modes of inquiry*—the whole series of steps an inquirer follows in making a contribution to a field of knowledge—as they operate within *methodological communities"* (1) and "to characterize—and indeed, value—each brand of knowledge on its own terms" (5). North's work provided, in other words, a look at the questions we ask, who asks them, and how we go about answering them—a valuable contribution to the field in its own right at the time.

Since then, however, North's divisions among our researchers have been expanded and sometimes redivided in other terms—a division healthy for the sake of debate but dangerous for a field still attempting to define itself. As Langer (1987) argued, our field "has been using our methodological differences to keep ourselves apart" (117). Indeed, since *The Making of Knowledge*, tensions in our field have provided some of the most popular dichotomous topics in our scholarship: between the social and the cognitive (Berkenkotter, 1991), between theory and practice (Phelps, 1991), between cognition and context (Flower, 1989), just to name a few.

Rose (1988), however, reminded us that difficulties in cognitive studies do not always lie in the methodologies used or in the questions asked. In small part, Rose saw weaknesses in some cognitive studies, but to a greater extent, he blamed our own application of such studies and theories for the disaster he called "cognitive reductionism":

> My intention in this essay is not to dismiss these thinkers and theories but to present the difficulties in applying to remedial writers these models of mind. For there is a tendency to accept as fact condensed deductions from them—statements stripped away from the questions, contradictions, and complexities that are central to them. . . . This reductive labeling is going on in composition studies at a time when cognitive researchers in developmental and educational psychology, artificial intelligence, and philosophy are posing more elaborate and domain-specific models of cognition. (294)

In contrast to Berthoff, then, Rose saw research findings "stripped away" from context not by the researchers, but largely by the readers of that research: ourselves.

In spite of his analysis, however, most scholars in composition through the late 1980s and early 1990s have seen themselves as irreconcilably divided by methodological and epistemological differences. These tensions come from the perceived differences among research methods and the epistemological stances on which they are based, resulting in a much greater preference for research we call "naturalistic," often rejecting research that looks "quantitative"–a tension that scholars such as Irmscher (1987) have summarized in generalized statements: "scholars in the humanities characteristically distrust quantitative measures, even for linguistic or stylistic studies" (85).

In a 1987 review of composition's struggle for a place in the academy, Irmscher blamed Richard Braddock, the first editor of *Research in the Teaching of English* (the NCTE journal most likely to present studies with numerical data) for a misdirection in our research:

> Braddock, whose degree was in Education, was undoubtedly instrumental in shaping prescriptive, positivist standards for research in composition, encouraging a model that has prevailed in composition studies. . . . Research

in composition has become identified with one kind of research—controlled experimental studies producing statistical evidence. (82)

Further, Irmscher blamed what we've come to call the "Braddock Report" of 1963 (*Research in Written Composition*) for why our field had yet to gain "academic respectability" (82) by the late 1980s; Irmscher was in full agreement with Hagstrum's 1964 review of the Braddock Report:

> These are undoubtedly the five best "scientific" studies ever conducted on written composition—virtually the cream of the cream. It is therefore extremely disheartening to have to say that 1) none of them strikes a layman as definitive or persuasive and 2) there is very little promise that, without rigorous antecedent thought, the "scientific" method applied to composition will yield better results in the future than it has in the past. (qtd. in Irmscher, p. 83)

Interest in methods that downplay the role of numerical evidence, as North (1985) reminded us, is natural for "people who are trained as humanists" (89); or as Irmscher argued, composition specialists have much in common with literary colleagues, "with critics, textualists, historiographers, bibliographers, linguists, novelists, and poets, each of whom differs in approach, but all of whom represent the tradition of humane letters" (85). For example, Ede (1992), who has considered herself open to a range of research methods, admitted that her training as a graduate student in Victorian Studies made her realize "the distinction between quantitative and traditional humanistic research" and that her training taught her "to do, and to value, the latter" (317). Beach (1992) agreed: meaningful research comes more often from ethnographers, and he has made a distinction between artificial environments—environments Irmscher (1987) called "foreign" (83)—created by the experimentalist vs. the natural (i.e., more meaningful) environments studied through ethnography (219).

In a discussion of research on writing centers, Neuleib and Scharton (1994) have argued that since writing centers already engage in observations of students, "the most suitable methodology for [research in writing centers] is some variation on an ethnographic model," discounting the possibility of other kinds of research in the writing center (55). Neuleib and Scharton argued that we must reject the "dispassionate distance of scientists" (55) immersed in "some kind of animal research based on generations of selective breeding" (54): "student writers are not laboratory rats, with genetic and behavioral constants we can manipulate experimentally" (55). Similarly, the 1990 CCCC Roundtable, "The Writing Center as Research Center," condemned "Research with a capital R"; this roundtable called for more case study and ethnography in writing centers—research that is more "beneficial," "pragmatic," "dynamic": "The best method for writing center research ought to mirror the daily activity of tutoring" (Bushman, 1991, p. 34).

In spite of the clear popularity of "naturalistic" methods, Schriver (1992) was hopeful when she commented on her own summary of research stereotypes, noting that the most extreme stereotypes might be fading (190), and for a few scholars, they are. Kirsch (1992), for example, explored the potential of methodological pluralism in our multidisciplinary field, but Kirsch's questions suggest that a strong polarity—a climate of difference—still remains within the field and among its researchers:

> What philosophical and epistemological assumptions guide different research methods? How are different methods related to each other? Do multiple methods build upon one another, producing cumulative knowledge? Or do various methods stand in conflict with each other, producing contradictory results? (247)

Central to this debate about different methods has been the question of evidence rather than the question of varied contexts from which we gain evidence. As Hillocks (1992) has written, "This distinction divides us over questions such as what counts as research, what counts as evidence, and what the principles are by which we connect evidence to our claims" (57).

In summary, our research, our claims, and our principles have been governed recently by a growing preference for certain kinds of evidence, most of it personal–not governed by full analyses of research contexts or guided by a clear understanding of and training in a wide range of methods and research principles.

GUIDES TO RESEARCH IN COMPOSITION: A CRITIQUE

Although several texts in the last decade have attempted to train composition researchers in the procedures and concepts of research (or have invited us to explore research paradigms and epistemologies), their success has been clearly limited. Lauer and Asher attempted to guide composition researchers in *Composition Research: Empirical Designs* (1988). Lauer and Asher began with a valuable goal and with an argument similar to the one I am making here: composition researchers, trained in the humanities, either reject scientific inquiry or "consume" it indiscriminately (ix). According to Lauer and Asher, "adequate study of the complex domain of writing must be multidisciplinary, including empirical research" (ix). In the end, however, Lauer and Asher look at only the many puzzle-pieces of design as "obstacles to understanding for the humanist" (ix), obstacles that remain for the humanist due to other difficulties in the text: they offer examples of studies that are far too complex to be used as tools for teaching and are not well designed, present statistical analysis out of the context of the research process (by relegating statistical analysis to an appendix), and removed the method from the context of the research question (by focusing only on the mechanics of each method, ignoring the questions that method could answer).

For instance, Lauer and Asher included as an example Pianko's (1981) study of students' writing processes. Pianko's study had more dependent variables (twenty-two) than students (seventeen). Lauer and Asher stated that the high number of dependent variables was a problem (84), but the study was used anyway as one of three examples of quantitative description—a research method described in a short twenty-page chapter, of which nearly one page (87) was the listing of Pianko's twenty-two dependent variables.

Unfortunately, it is in this context that Lauer and Asher introduce the concept of independent and dependent variables:

> We identify the terms *independent* and *dependent* here because they are used by many composition researchers. The distinction between them, however, is rather imprecise in descriptive research. Researchers often call those variables independent which constitute differences in subjects prior

to research—e.g., class level, age, or gender. Dependent variables are often those introduced by the researcher for the analysis, e.g., prewriting time, planning behavior, or number of pauses. (86)

Such definitions of independent and dependent variables (especially for those who are new to such concepts) are confusing and unfortunate. First, Lauer and Asher suggested that they used these terms only because other composition researchers use them, not because they are important concepts for any researcher to know. Second, the distinction between the two kinds of variables was noted as "rather imprecise," when in the context of most research tasks, researchers make very precise distinctions between dependent and independent variables in the attempt to understand the differences and the relationships among them. Third, readers of Lauer and Asher's text should be confused by their suggestion that independent variables are only those that exist prior to research (such as gender) and that dependent variables are "introduced by the researcher for the analysis." Researchers "introduce" both independent and dependent variables (as long as they are the ones designing the study), but it would be more accurate to say that dependent variables are "measured" rather than introduced—they are, in a sense, the "resulting differences" among independent variables (variables that may or may not exist only prior to research). Finally, Lauer and Asher listed a few examples of dependent variables—such as prewriting time—that, depending on the full context of a study, could be *either* independent *or* dependent variables. Prewriting time, of course, can have an effect on a later process (such as revision) or a feature of a product (such as organization) and, thus, would be an independent variable (a common sense notion, given that prewriting obviously comes before other kinds of writing/revising/editing). This is where Lauer and Asher's inattention to context (and heightened attention to only mechanics of research design) fails to help readers become better researchers—indeed, might do more harm than good.

But problems inherent in *how* we teach research concepts (and, especially, statistical concepts) pose difficult questions about research-in-context. If we teach research methods as merely *methods* and procedures devoid of context, such principles are difficult to grasp and are often meaningless without some grounding of purpose. On the other hand, research methods introduced in particular contexts potentially draw attention to the intricacies of the context itself (past research, politics of an area of study, formal knowledge of the specific area of expertise, etc.) such that discussions of method become secondary. To equalize the interplay of context and research method for beginners, we would do well to choose concrete everyday contexts in which to demonstrate research procedures.

Effective training in research methods and statistics is often based on the outlines of simple, hypothetical, yet realistic contexts in which we might want a question answered. Demonstrations based on television programs, movies, recreational activities, and daily living often begin an introduction to research concepts, especially in courses attended by students from several disciplines, carrying with them different kinds of formal content knowledge.

Starting with simple contexts enables students to expand later into contexts more closely related to their areas of study. While some everyday, humorous, simple contexts might seem a bit corny at first (my favorite and most effective statistics professor had a fondness for Blondie and Dagwood and *The Sound of Music*), such contexts allow the explanation of research concepts and statistics to gain clarity while the humor in them aids our memory. Hence, the following simple context–the test of a lucky bowling ball–will be inserted throughout the next three chapters.

SOME BASIC RESEARCH CONCEPTS: A TRIP TO THE BOWLING ALLEY

So somebody gave you a new bowling ball for your birthday—a new, shiny red one. You put your old green one in the closet, and suddenly your game improved. Now you think your new red bowling ball, even though it's the same size and weight as the old green one, is responsible for improving your game. Somehow, the red ball is making a difference in your scores. Your friends, however, laugh at your superstition. "Prove it," they say.

So we need to design an experiment to see if your red bowling ball is as lucky as you think. We'll take your old green ball,
your new red ball, and we'll steal that pretty purple one with
glitter (also of equal size and weight) from the next lane. We'll
let the bartender bowl in one lane, trying each color, testing
your prediction that the red ball is luckiest. (We don't trust you
to bowl—you might *cause* the red ball to win because that's
what you hope to find.)

We'll keep score, of course, to see which color does the
best. And because we're testing the luckiness of your red bowling ball, we'll make a chart to organize scores by the color variables: red, green, or purple. By the way, these are the
"variables," because we are varying or manipulating them in
our study. Colors will be the "independent variables," because
they have the freedom and power (independence) to cause a
change in your bowling scores. We are seeing if the difference
in score *depends* on the color of the ball, which is why we'll call
the scores the "dependent variable." It, too, varies, but its
variation depends on the color of the bowling balls, the
independent variable.

Therefore, we have three levels (red, green, purple) of one
independent variable (color), and we'll see if the variation in
colors has an effect on your scores. Our research question,
then, is this: Is there a difference in bowling score (dependent
variable) with changes in bowling ball color (independent
variable)?

To help answer the question, we've controlled for two potentially "extraneous variables": 1) the bartender bowls in only one
lane to ensure that a difference in lanes doesn't affect the
score; 2) only the bartender will bowl to ensure that other
bowlers' skills do not affect the difference in scores.

While we will not be able to make any grand claims from
such a small study, this *context* will enable us to play around
with some research concepts. In other contexts, we would not
want to gather data from just one person, so our ability to
generalize this study to others will be limited. In other words,

we've enhanced "internal validity" by controlling for the
extraneous variables. Because only the bartender is bowling
(and in only one lane), we have limited "external validity,"
preventing us from making generalizations to other bowlers or
other lanes. But that's not our purpose here. Our purpose is to
provide some information and a way to think about something
that interests *you*.

If you're worried about how the lucky red ball will do here,
we should stop the study now so your superstition can remain.
But you strike me (ho, ho) as the type who wants to be a more
informed bowler. Getting this information (or knowledge) isn't
hard at all. And learning about independent and dependent
variables doesn't have to be, either.

Lauer and Asher's text had other problems for those desiring to
learn research methods. For example, the treatment of statistics was
too brief to be especially accurate, it had very little context, and it
could be confusing in the complicated formulas designed to
"enhance" their explanations. Lauer and Asher discussed the null
hypothesis (the hypothesis that asserts "there is no difference" in variables being measured) as a hypothesis we "accept" or "reject." In more
accurate terms, we only "reject" or "fail to reject" the null hypothesis.
There is a reason for this: accepting the null hypothesis would con-
note that "there is no difference" among or between variables being
studied, when the study itself did not test all possible differences
and/or might have failed to show the specific difference sought. Lauer
and Asher here provided not only simplified information worthy of
more discussion, but also potentially misleading language with which
to relate our research.

In a way, we teach a form of hypothesis-testing to our freshman composition students all the time. In research writing
especially, we advise our students to 1) formulate a research
question to guide their library work and other research, 2)
guess or hypothesize about what they'll find, and 3) later
construct a clear thesis to guide their texts that convey their
research. We as researchers construct a research question

first and then recast the question into a claim: a hypothesis (proposed thesis). Our later write-ups, too, will be governed by our "answer": the thesis.

At the bowling alley, remember, our research question is, "Is there a difference in bowling score with changes in bowling ball color?" Recast as our hypothesis, it would look something like this: There *is* a difference in scores achieved by different bowling ball colors. You, of course, hope the red ball achieves the highest score. However, every researcher is accompanied by a skeptic (which is why you took us along), and the skeptic's job is to say, "I doubt it,"— in other words, "the difference will probably be null." The skeptic's null hypothesis is this: There is *no* difference in scores achieved by different bowling ball colors—that is, any difference you have obtained among the different colors has been obtained by chance and, therefore, do not reflect "real" differences.

If your scores show that the difference is unlikely to be due to chance, you can *reject* the null hypothesis, because it only takes one good piece of concrete evidence to argue that a skeptic is wrong. If, however, the scores show *no* difference (just like the skeptic predicted in the null hypothesis), you can argue effectively that one trial cannot demonstrate the skeptic is probably right. While we have gained an interesting piece of information, we have no proof yet that another trial won't produce different scores or that other variables we haven't talked about yet didn't interfere with the red ball's performance. Therefore, we can't fully *accept* the null hypothesis, either (that there is never, ever a difference in these scores). At this time, we simply *fail to reject* it.

The skeptic (being a skeptic) will understand this. Further demonstrations (replications) will help us answer our question more fully in the future. Later in this study, we will test our hypothesis and discuss the role of chance.

In a text with a different purpose, *Understanding Research in Reading and Writing*, Kamil, Langer, and Shanahan (1985) attempted to help reading and writing specialists "come to terms with many of the techniques and perspectives of reading and writing research" (ix) and to "encourage nonresearchers to understand and use research" (x). In short, this text focused on helping readers become more critical "consumers" of research: "Our purpose is not to explain how to *do* research. Doing sophisticated research takes time, effort, and experience" (x).

While bowling alleys may not be the most sophisticated place to do research, our task is complicated and will, of course, take time and effort. For instance, we need to decide how many trials each ball should have. And because only the bartender is bowling, we must consider the bowler's potential fatigue.

In addition, we'll need to decide in what order the balls should be bowled: they should not, for example, be bowled always in the same order (red first, green second, purple third, for instance). The last color bowled may achieve a low score because of the bowler's fatigue, and the first color bowled may score the best because our bowler will be "fresh." On the other hand, our bowler might not get fatigued at all; instead, the more the bowler practices, the better the bowler might get, so later balls bowled might score higher. Either way, we introduce a potential bias into the study if we don't mix up the colors somehow.

Therefore, the colors should be systematically rotated through a procedure called *counterbalancing*:

red, green, purple
green, purple, red
purple, red, green
purple, green, red
green, red, purple
red, purple, green

Counterbalancing ensures that each color will be first, second, and last an equal number of times so that fatigue or practice will not influence a difference in scores per color.[2]

Counterbalancing helps answer the question about how
many trials we should ask our bowler to bowl. Since there are
6 possible combinations of the three colors (see above), we
could have our number of trials for each ball be in multiples of
6 (6, 12, 18, etc.). Now we have to ask a harder question: how
much time do you want to spend at the bowling alley?
OK, we'll just do 6 trials for each ball, for now.

Even though *Understanding Research in Reading and Writing* was
aimed at nonresearchers, it curiously assumed a background in basic
statistics (x). Therefore, the authors' treatment of statistics is brief,
but it is always (wisely) within the context of research questions. The
authors gave examples of various research questions and how they
have been explored by reading and writing specialists, and they
offered sage advice to readers of this research. For example, the
authors wisely warned us against inferring causation from correlation
studies; they reminded us to articulate our data clearly in our texts
and not to let an extremely high number of variables complicate our
studies.

In other words, *Understanding Research in Reading and Writing* has
given us just what the title suggested and what the authors promised:
a consumer's guide to research. It has not, however, (as the authors
also acknowledged) provided a guide for *doing* research, a guide our
field greatly needs. As a result, such wise advice as theirs has often
gone unheeded. Hillocks (1986), too, provided general criticism for
how researchers unknowingly destroy their own results by not presenting and articulating their data clearly enough, not establishing
clear criteria for what we wish to know, and for inferring cause and
effect too readily (often assuming, for example, that observed behavior causes observed writing). In addition, in spite of Kamil, Langer,
and Shanahan's warning against allowing too many variables to complicate a study, Lauer and Asher's text (three years later) provided as
an example, remember, Pianko's study, which did just that. (See also
Ferris, 1994.)

Another text for researchers in our field, *Multidisciplinary
Perspectives on Literacy Research* (Beach, Green, Kamil, & Shanahan,

1992), offered a collection of papers from the 1990 National Conference on Research in English. While the title suggests "multidisciplinary" perspectives on research, authors of most individual essays obviously favored some perspectives over others, fueling an already-growing debate about our research and research methods.

Harste, for example, set the tone in the "Foreword" by sharing a story in which an international student asked him about his use of the phrase "nauseous positivism" during a debate about research methods in a graduate seminar at Indiana University (ix). Harste shared the story in order to illustrate his own position in the debate and to highlight the passion of the debate itself. Further stating his position, Harste argued that researchers in literacy should find their own method and stop pretending to be cognitive psychologists or anthropologists and stop borrowing from their methods; he responded negatively to "the illusion which the volume gives that all research methodologies are equal. . . . I have trouble with this. . . . [N]ot all methodologies are equal for me. Some violate what we know" (xi). For Harste, the methodologies that "violate what we know" are those that stem from what he called "nauseous positivism."

In their introduction to the text, the editors reiterated the perceived paradigm shift in English Studies and examined its effect on our research:

> shifts in conceptions of literacy have resulted in a shift in the kinds of methodological approaches employed. . . . Many of the experimentalist approaches employed in previous literacy research, which attempt to "control" for factors shaping literacy events, have been seen as artificially constraining the ways in which readers and writers construct knowledge. (5)

These editors equated our changing notion of research with, not surprisingly, our previous rejection of "traditional, formalistic textbook models of composing" (2); similarly, they forecasted the future of research in reading and writing by equating an outdated view of literacy as a controlled, scientific, and objective series of "cognitions" with the controlled and scientific methodologies that attempt to provide "simple answers to a complex problem" (3). While the editors of the volume attempted to create an "open dialogue between a range of perspectives" (8) in research and acknowledged that criticism among all perspectives exists, their own criticism for only one end of that range continued:

> Cognitive psychologists often prefer controlled experiments . . . while sociolinguists or cultural ethnographers often prefer ethnographical observations. This latter approach assumes that the meaning of literacy events could only be understood by studying these events as they occur in authentic settings, rather than as "controlled" in an experiment. And it assumes that quantitative analysis of literacy practices strips away the rich meanings available from observational analysis. (9)

Again we see authors *and* editors valuing the kind of personal knowledge that Elbow used to construct *What is English?* and that Johnson used in epigraphs to chapter one of *Nineteenth-Century Rhetoric in North America.* While composition *should* value this kind of knowledge, we now do so by *devaluing* other kinds that, in spite of being "controlled" or quantified or "cognitive," could also be of great value in the varied contexts of our teaching and our research. We are teaching and researching in a field that claims to have "multidisciplinary perspectives," while clearly designating which perspectives are welcome and which ones are not.

Similar in purpose to *Multidisciplinary Perspectives on Literacy Research* was *Methods and Methodology in Composition* (1992), edited by Kirsch and Sullivan:

> Because this collection aims to expand our understanding of research methodologies, [the editors] decided to present reflective essays that examine procedures, assumptions, and issues relevant to a broad range of research methods, and not to only a few well-established methods. (4)

The essays in this volume explored, for example, how ethnography unfolds in language studies, how writing about theory is a form of research, in what ways historical inquiry contributes to our body of research, how to code data, and how competing epistemologies come together in methodological pluralism. Most of the essays, in other words, do not so much offer research procedures as they examine the politics of research, reflect on some research topics, and debate the value of varied research methods. In chapter ten, for example, Beach also paralleled our current shift in research strategies with the earlier paradigm shift we perceive in teaching strategies, reminding us again of that previous era of current-traditional rhetoric:

> The textbooks of the era were filled with model essays and endless grammar exercises. . . . It was assumed that if teachers in all classes taught the "five paragraph theme" and grammar rules, that students would learn to write. Given the teacher-centered nature of this approach, researchers therefore were primarily interested in determining whether certain kinds of direct instruction worked.
>
> Traditional method A versus method B experimental research reflected the limitations of this prevailing paradigm. (217)

Here again we see the dichotomous tension among our researchers, augmented by the perceived parallels to an earlier paradigm shift in teaching. The "once that, now this" approach attacks one set of well-established empirical methods; at the same time, such a "paradigm shift" approach forces *choices* such that multi-modal research becomes discounted as well.

Fitting well with the editors' promise to explore methods other than the "few well-established methods," Sullivan, in her chapter ("Feminism and Methodology in Composition Studies") in the Kirsch and Sullivan volume, argued that "methodological underpinnings of modern science . . . have developed according to male prescriptions and proscriptions of knowledge" (56) and described the current research debate in composition in terms of feminist response to male dominance:

> [feminist approaches to research] do not represent a wholesale rejection of empiricism by feminists but only of the positivist elements that still linger in the dominant paradigm of scientific inquiry. . . . Many are drawn, for example, to the cluster of methods that fall under the rubrics of qualitative and naturalistic inquiry. (57)

Here, Sullivan (as I will discuss more fully in chapter three) drew further distinctions among researchers that, again, encourage us to seek research methods that fulfill certain ideologies rather than seek methods that adequately answer our research questions that emerge naturally from varied contexts—questions that vary in form and procedure within and among varied ideologies *because* of shifting contexts and, therefore, require varied methods to seek their answers.

In the newest book available as this work goes to press, *Strategies for Empirical Research in Writing*, MacNealy (1999) addresses several issues similar to ones I explore here. MacNealy admirably devotes space in her text to "calming the nerves" of her readers, addressing anxieties about numbers, research, and terminology through a calm voice that speaks directly to readers and asks gentle questions. MacNealy explores the need for research, the need for theory, and the relationships and tensions between research and lore. Most importantly, MacNealy stresses the importance of valuing *all* research methods and provides an excellent model through her own text, which is fleshed out by research of all kinds, including her own personal anecdotes, to help readers gain a conceptual understanding of research as well as an introduction to some research procedures.

In fact, I liked MacNealy's approach so much, I wished that she had continued beyond the introductory level this text provides. Her introduction to some concepts, such as kinds of data (nominal, ordinal, interval, and ratio) and some statistical procedures, is necessary to a new researchers' understanding. But what next? Our field still has not produced a comprehensive series of texts that will help us advance in our research capabilities beyond a fairly modest level.

GEORGE CAMPBELL AND THE NATURE OF EVIDENCE

The current-traditional rhetoric that flourished in the nineteenth century, supposedly defining "truth" as external, objective, and empirically verifiable, has been displaced in favor of other theories of composition that view "truth" either as residing "within" (as internal and subjective), or as stemming from, the transaction between the external and the internal (as now evident in the popularity of social-constructionist theories). In other words, current-traditional rhetoric has been rejected because of its view of reality, which, for some, reeks of positivism, an argument that extends to our use of scientific methods in our research.

As composition researchers argue the value of diverse research methodologies, we can learn much by returning to George Campbell's *Philosophy of Rhetoric* (1776), in spite of the fact that Campbell has taken much of the blame for the current-traditional approaches we now reject.

In chapter five of *Philosophy of Rhetoric*, Campbell, linking forms of evidence to forms of logical truth, presented two kinds of evidence. The first, *intuitive*, relies "on a bare attention to the ideas under review"; the second, *deductive*, emerges "by a comparison of these with other related ideas" (174). Intuitive evidence is much like evidence gathered by the ethnographer: that which is readily observable. Deductive evidence is much like evidence gathered by an experimenter: that which is compared, measured, altered, and tested.

Campbell gave us three kinds of *intuitive* evidence, presented as "basic" forms of human knowledge, easily observable by the seeing, thinking person:

> *Intellection*: mathematical axioms, such as "two plus two is four."
> *Consciousness*: concerning only the existence of the mind, requiring basic thought.
> *Common Sense*: an extension of basic, logical thought; knowledge such as "there are other intelligent beings in the world besides me" (174-81).

For Campbell, then, intuitive evidence includes the kind of basic knowledge that something is irrefutably true ("such as two minus one does not equal three" or "humans need water to survive") or the kind of knowledge *that* something exists: if I'm in a bad mood today, for instance, I am aware of it through Consciousness; through Common Sense, I extend that knowledge to realize that being in a bad mood also means I am not in a good mood or that being in a bad mood might affect others around me. To ask *why* I'm in a bad mood, however, asks a different question, calling on a different kind of evidence, that through which we can deduce meaning and speculate on an answer.

Campbell divided *deductive* evidence into two types: moral and demonstrative (or scientific). Moral evidence is divided into four kinds: *experience, analogy, testimony,* and *calculations of chance.* These types of evidence involve, as their names suggest, critical thinking and reflection. For instance, I note through *experience,* perhaps, that I had skipped breakfast this morning, and the last time I was in a bad mood, I skipped breakfast, too, allowing me to deduce that breakfast might have something to do with my bad mood. For me, the *analogy* of a car running out of gas or of trying to bake bread without enough flour helps explain how I feel and suggests how essential breakfast might be to my moods. *Testimony* from a friend might add that she, too, experiences bad moods after skipping breakfast. *Calculations of chance* allow me to speculate on the probability that I will be in a bad mood the next time I skip breakfast. For Campbell, that calculation is mathematically possible if, for example, we're in a coin toss or rolling a pair of dice (a calculation that can be done prior to any trials), but speculation of chance can also be based on experience. If I've noted twice that I'm in a bad mood after twice skipping breakfast, I could speculate that the probability I'll be in a bad mood after skipping breakfast again is high.

While much of this moral evidence seems to make sense—seems to suggest, for instance, that I'll be in a bad mood whenever I skip breakfast—conclusions drawn from such evidence are premature. This kind of moral evidence is valuable in the absence of other evidence—if impossible to obtain. But in order to arrive at any meaning through this series of moral proofs, I must impose order upon it. I now see only the connections I *can* see and, possibly, connections I *want* to see. For instance, my friend provided testimony that she, too, is in a bad mood whenever she skips breakfast, testimony that seems to lend credibility to my claim when added to my own experience. But what if I'm ignoring other observations I've made that she will also be in a bad mood whenever a traffic light turns red, whenever her favorite parking spot is taken, and whenever a vending machine rejects her dollar bill? I am guilty, then, of assigning too much credibility to her single testimony about skipping breakfast.

And what if I focused on the wrong variable in my own personal experience, ignoring other variables in the full context? Sure, I skipped breakfast twice, but a colleague who joined me for lunch both times reminds me that I ate two Big Macs to make up for skipping breakfast and that, perhaps, such indulgence in fast food has something to do with my mood? To complicate matters, the same friend reminds me that my bad moods, too, are not unique to the days on which I skip breakfast.

Concluding from this moral evidence alone that skipping breakfast has something to do with my bad mood, then, is a mistake. For help, we need the second of Campbell's two kinds of deductive evidence: *demonstrative*. Campbell outlined four differences between moral and demonstrative evidence:

1. Difference in subject: moral evidence concerns independent truths; demonstrative concerns the relationships among ideas [*The analogy, for instance, of having enough flour to make bread is not directly related to the fact that I'm in a bad mood; the testimony of my friend's bad moods is independent from the fact that I, too, am in a bad mood*]

2. [M]oral evidence admits degrees, demonstration doth not [*Unable to "measure" what a bad mood is or how bad a mood I'm in, the determination of my bad mood is, in part, based on opinion and is debatable— i.e., in terms of degree in relation to other kinds of bad moods, other people's bad moods, etc.*]

3. In moral evidence, truths cannot be contrary because they are independent of one another; in demonstrative evidence, future demonstrations can contradict earlier demonstrations, creating new truths [*My speculation on future bad moods does not contradict the fact that I am in a bad mood now; testimony of anyone else's bad mood will not contradict my own experience*]

4. Scientific evidence is simple, consisting of only one coherent series, . . . moral evidence is generally complicated, being in reality a bundle of independent proofs [*The series of moral proofs in determining the relationships between bad moods and skipping breakfast comes from four different kinds of evidence that must be linked through the imagination because they are not actually related to one another*] (182-183)

These differences between moral and demonstrative evidence should not surprise modern composition researchers. Campbell presented the perceived difference between "naturalistic" and "experimental" research, between ethnography and experiments:

observations cannot be replicated, whereas demonstrations can be; observations rely solely on one's own memory and cannot be refuted, tested, or measured; the subject of one's interest may determine which forms of evidence should be trusted and sought; observations have degrees, room for memory error, whereas demonstrations do not.

Less surprising, then, is Campbell's admiration for scientific (or demonstrative) evidence. Based primarily on his concerns about error of memory, Campbell warned of potential error in moral reasoning: "though the procedure of the mind were quite unexceptionable, there still remains a physical possibility of the falsity of the conclusion" (197). At the same time, however, Campbell seemed to value equally all forms of evidence and to understand the additional potential of multi-modal inquiry. For example, Campbell believed that mathematical axioms form the basis of revolutionary discoveries and that testimony provides us with history. All forms of evidence, for Campbell, create "the foundation of all conviction, and consequently of persuasion too" (197).

Scientific evidence, for Campbell, also has room for error, much like moral evidence does. The difference, however, is that errors made through demonstrative evidence can be identified and corrected through later demonstrations. This type of evidence is in the realm of logic, rather than rhetoric, for Campbell, perhaps because of its scientific nature. Rhetoricians must pay attention to scientific evidence, however, as Campbell argued, "for though he may be an acute logician who is no orator, he will never be a consummate orator who is no logician" (197).

Indeed, Campbell saw both kinds of evidence—though separate and different from each other—as necessary to each other because of their unique contributions to a greater understanding of *the full context* for any inquiry:

> if [scientific or demonstrative evidence] is infinitely superior in point of authority, [moral evidence] no less excels in point of importance. Abstract truth, as far as it is the object of our faculties, is almost entirely confined to quantity, concrete or discrete. The sphere of Demonstration is

narrow, but within her sphere she is a despotic sovereign, her sway is uncontrollable. Her rival, on the contrary, hath less power but wider empire. Her forces, indeed, are not always irresistible; but the whole world is comprised in her dominions. . . . By [demonstrative evidence], we must acknowledge, when applied to things, and combined with the discoveries of [moral evidence], our researches into nature in a certain line are facilitated, the understanding is enlightened, and many of the arts, both elegant and useful, and improved and perfected. (184)

For Campbell, then, the interaction of moral evidence (and its complexity) with demonstrative evidence (and its simplicity) is the most powerful and persuasive of all intellectual inquiry. Unfortunately, today's scholars in rhetoric and composition not only separate demonstrative and moral evidence, but argue that they *must* be separated because they stem from seemingly different epistemologies. And, perhaps, the deceptive simplicity of demonstrative evidence is at the core of our criticism for some inquiry being "artificial" or out of context. The complexity of moral evidence, after all, helps place demonstrative evidence in context, but it is increasingly preferred by our field even when stripped of *demonstrations* that also give meaning to the same contexts.

At the bowling alley, we'll be much more careful not to infer causation from correlation. In other words, we'll better understand that just because two things exist somewhat side-by-side, one does not necessarily cause the other to happen. In fact, it's just that kind of belief that we're hoping to test at the bowling alley. Every time you bowl with your red bowling ball, you get great scores, so you think it's lucky (as if it being red causes a high score). We're going to explore that issue.

At the same time, a red bowling ball could indirectly influence your score (even if it doesn't directly cause your scores to be high): for instance, if red is your favorite color, you might simply enjoy the look of the ball and, therefore, be in a better mood because of it; therefore, *you* might be influenced by the color of the ball, but the color of the ball didn't directly cause your *scores* to happen. Once we leave the bowling alley, we should continue to be careful with this.

The simplicity of scientific evidence mentioned by Campbell (and the notion that it is often quantified) is, perhaps, what Elbow (1990) responded to when he warned, "All those valuable perceptions and data are rendered less trustworthy and less useful when they are reduced to a single number" (251). However, Elbow's view ignores, here, first, that when joined with the "complexity" of moral evidence, scientific evidence adds information and helps make sense of the complexity of moral evidence, and, second, that the "single number" never *replaces* the "valuable perceptions and data"; instead, the number *summarizes* the perceptions and data, which remain very much intact and are even enhanced by the new language given as a summary: the number.

Elbow's distrust for the "single number" brought forth by demonstrative evidence resulted in his reliance on moral evidence in *What is English?* a book that is, in Campbell's terms, "a bundle of independent proofs." And while that bundle is valuable because of the diverse experiences offered in it, readers must provide their own coherence to it and bring their own memories, interpretations, and at times, misinterpretation (or no interpretation at all) to such a text. Moral evidence, then, is malleable, subject to reshaping in a reader's mind; in other words, we find moral evidence to have a certain beauty we easily recognize: it is quite literary.

As composition researchers who today argue the value of diverse research methodologies, we can learn much from Campbell. Because Campbell presented a range of evidence that encompasses all of humanity, his analysis of evidence fits well with modern composition concerns. As modern composition researchers seem close to the day when they abandon "traditional" methods entirely, I argue that these methods must be kept a part of our available tools of research for four reasons.

First, as Campbell noted, the selection of research methods—or a decision about admissible evidence—depends on our subjects and the contexts in which we pursue them. In other words, a method should be chosen based on one's research question and the context from which that research question comes. To choose a methodology based only on "what we already do" (as Neuleib and Scharton suggest in writing centers) is to choose a methodology for the wrong reason. Imagine someone who chooses travel destinations based only on locations covered by a certain airline. Such a person limits travel possibilities by adhering to only one way of getting there. I am reminded of a graduate student researcher who set out to examine the effectiveness of a particular program but designed her research only to define the scope of the program and to observe its daily activities because she decided on her method first (participant-observation, because it's "in") and her research question second (a question that demanded rigorous measurement, the "effectiveness" of a program): fine destination, wrong transportation. Campbell reminded us to understand our question-in-context first—to find out where we want to go, why and when, and then decide the best way to get there.

Second, as Campbell reminded us, demonstrative evidence can be replicated—can be held up against other demonstrations, inviting contradiction or confirmation, even testing demonstrations in new or varied contexts. In other words, demonstrative evidence allows a community of researchers to test each other, to communicate with each other, to refine each others' theories and methods, and, together, to establish the greatest amount of knowledge with the least amount of error, applicable to the most contexts. This, ironically, relates well to an idea that composition now greatly admires: the social construction of knowledge.

Third, Campbell also reminded us that rhetoricians should be good logicians. In other words, composition researchers should remain open to a variety of research methodologies with their varied ways of thinking, with their varied epistemologies, with their varied logic—as these elements shift in varied contexts. To study experimental design and statistics would make an ethnographer, for example, a better ethnographer, as exercise in identifying variables, watching for extraneous factors, and recognizing where error exists should inform any researcher's endeavors.

Finally, composition is quite proud, I think, of having realized the limitations of current-traditional models. Old and useless, current-traditionalism is now studied with other embarrassing histories of our field. The scientific thought that is supposed to have formed the basis for current-traditional rhetoric may soon follow. My fourth reason, then, for urging composition researchers to maintain the availability of (and to improve our understanding of) all methodologies is that we should not abandon what is old simply because it's old or somehow automatically connected to other old, rejected ideas. Even inquiry that relies on numerical data should remain with us and be more carefully studied and used to help us examine our community of knowledge, achieve our research goals, become stronger thinkers and theorists, and embrace all kinds of knowledge we have created—both old and new.

SUMMARY

The debate about what kinds of evidence we should value has been a harmful one for our field, resulting in decontextualized arguments that seemingly center on numbers vs. narratives regardless of the research contexts that naturally produce both. As a result, those who argue that only naturalistic methods are sensitive to context paradoxically ignore the contexts in which numerical data are readily avail able, useful, and necessary. In our effort, perhaps, to extend traditional forms of research guided by the scientific method, the evidence associated with that tradition has come under fire in spite of its necessary place in our scholarship. Attempts to draw parallels between this shift in research and an older shift in pedagogy has resulted in greater distaste for an older research tradition, erroneously placing blame on the one common element of both "old paradigms"—the scientific method. Such conclusions persuade us to dismiss a theorist like George Campbell, who was influenced by scientific developments of his time, when such a theorist—if we were willing to read him well—would have warned us against such a faulty conclusion in the first place.

In Campbell's terms, our review of "Paradigm Shift #1" and "Paradigm Shift #2," the scientific features they appear to share, and the testimony on which we often rely in our arguments against scientific methods are rich in "bundles of independent proofs," and we cannot draw clear conclusions or connections among them without the help of demonstrative evidence that can add power to the moral evidence we've come to prefer. Further, our preference for what Campbell called moral evidence not only divides our field in terms of "qualitative vs. quantitative" research but divides us further *within* our qualitative preference: moral evidence, in Campbell's terms, does not attend to relationships among ideas so much as it is composed of independent ideas (such as personal anecdotes).

Before we proceed to the need for joining moral and demonstrative evidence (and all research methods) in composition research (the focus of chapter four), we must address another force that spurs our growing distaste for numerical data–one of audience. In an age of passionate arguments favoring the opposite(s), how does one "sell" an argument for valuing numerical evidence more equally? The following chapter will address three issues I see driven by audience concerns: feminist responses to traditional research, math anxiety, and a preference for storytelling as a genre more literary than the traditional research report. Addressing such issues of audience, of course, is necessary for us to articulate and explore the full rhetorical context of the perceived (and false) quantitative/qualitative tension.

NOTES

1.   I'm not sure of Berthoff's information here. In my own studies in cognitive psychology (including developmental psychology), taken during the 1980s, when the essays in *The Sense of Learning* were originally published, Piaget was presented as merely an historical backdrop to more advanced, later theories and methods. The most I had read of Piaget at that time was in a history of psychology course. In applications of psychology to composition, for some reason, we find Piaget frequently. My professors in psychology in the 1980s were amazed by this. Therefore, our own application of psychology to composition is a "generation behind" active psychological research, not the reverse, as Berthoff suggested.

2.   For an example of the results researchers must contend with when they do not properly counterbalance, see Chiste and O'Shea (1988), "Patterns of Question Selection and Writing Performance of ESL Students" in *TESOL Quarterly*. The researchers tried to determine how ESL students chose placement test questions: on length or on position in a list of four? However, there was "a statistical tendency on the 20 exams [in the study] for the short question to be positioned at the beginning of the set and the long ones at the end" (682). In other words, the authors had to admit, "This correlation hinders any attempt to attribute primary responsibility to either of these factors [length or position]" (682). These researchers 1) reviewed previous placement tests they had readily available and then 2) asked a question that the study (and the chosen tests) was not designed to answer. Designing a new study that would answer their question would require counterbalancing: questions of different lengths should be equally rotated among the four positions in a list. Such care in a designed study would prevent the unsupported conclusions these authors drew: "Questions that seem most accessible to ESL students should be positioned at the beginning of the set, where they are most likely to receive attention. . . . To prevent selection by length alone . . . questions should be comparable in length" (683). Such conclusions cannot be supported by this study because the authors could not determine the separate effects of either length of prompt or its position.

3 NUMBERS, NARRATIVES, AND HE VS. SHE
Issues of Audience in Composition Research

> Whether "knowledge" gets noticed at all is partly a matter of whether the community is ready and willing to listen.
> *Karen Schriver, 1989*

> It must be assumed that the objecting audience has the epistemic goals of truth and the avoidance of error. If they were not critical truth seekers, they would not raise appropriate objections.
> *David Annis, 1978*

Our growing defense of qualitative research and storytelling in composition is accompanied by passionate arguments against the older, traditional research paradigm—a passion that, as conversation with others in the field has made clear, makes some of us look the other way or lash out at the "old school" whenever conversation turns to the older tradition. That paradigm, for many, has grown out of a male-dominated tradition, places too much value on mathematics, and is written in a stifling, disinterested style that is unpleasant to read (and write).

More importantly, our abandonment of "traditional" research has been praised for allowing more diverse researchers to express their voices, voices that—as women, people of color, and practitioners—have been relatively silenced until recently. Such shifts bring into focus new epistemological stances that question the traditional ways of knowing, and this epistemological shift has produced attacks aimed at the old research paradigm on two levels: the broader issue of epistemology and the more narrow issue of research methods. Before we review how and why research methods relying on numerical data should remain potentially valuable depending on context, it is important to address that part of the audience that wants nothing to do with such research.

I focus here on three particular sources of arguments against the traditional research model. While this chapter is divided into three sections, readers will see features and arguments that overlap among the sections: 1) our general anxiety about mathematics and statistics, 2) feminist responses to that older model, and 3) our preference for writing that is more creative and literary than the standard research report. These arguments often relate to each other, but for my purposes here, each deserves its own treatment.

DON'T MAKE ME DO MATH: MATH AND STATISTICS
AVOIDANCE AND ANXIETY

If I could steal a dedication from someone else's work and use it for my own, I would steal from Paulos's (1995) *A Mathematician Reads the Newspaper*, dedicated "To storytelling number-crunchers and number-crunching storytellers." Paulos briefly shared some childhood memories, joked about using Pythagoras and Pulitzer in the same sentence, and speculated on the relationships between mathematics and our daily lives. In the plainest of language, Paulos explained, "The misunderstandings between mathematicians and others run in both directions" (4), but Paulos argued that "number stories" can enhance our understanding of economics and environmental predictions, illuminate our understanding of "crime, health risks, or racial and ethnic bias," and even eliminate myths surrounding sports figures (4).

For Paulos, mathematics provides insight into popular culture and scholarly pursuits and should not be separated from either, but he understands where much of our anxiety comes from:

> [B]ecause of the mind-numbing way in which mathematics is generally taught, many people have serious misconceptions about the subject and fail to appreciate its wide applicability. . . . It's time to let the secret out: Mathematics is not primarily a matter of plugging numbers into formulas and performing rote computations.It is a way of thinking and questioning that may be unfamiliar to many of us, but is available to most of us. (3)

Indeed, in composition studies, quantifying data is rarely seen as illuminating what Paulos called "people stories" (3) and is seen instead as a separate world, often having nothing to do with people at all, certainly nothing to do with anything pleasant. Phelps (1989) called scientific research "distanced and neutral, sometimes employing elaborate statistical apparatus" (40), suggesting that statistics play a role in separating such research from people stories. Charney (1996), in "Empiricism Is Not a Four-Letter Word," strongly objected to such distinctions but accurately captured the distaste often expressed toward numbers and the unfortunate stereotype of researchers who use them:

> [N]o one likes the way scientists seem to privilege numbers and disparage words—the way numerical and graphic evidence is treated as clean, precise, and solid. . . . misrepresenting the world as manageable, fully determinate, and reducible to clear and accurate formulas. (571)

And if we believe Shea's (1996) comment in an article on statistical significance in the *Chronicle of Higher Education*, we would think that everyone in higher education trembles at the mere mention of statistics:

> No subject makes the eyes of graduate students in social science glaze over faster, and even many professors view statistics as a necessary bit of drudgery. (A12)

When we bring that "bit of drudgery" into composition research, we sometimes apologize for its presence in people stories, as Lerner (1997) did in "Counting Beans and Making Beans Count," an analysis of grade improvement among students who visited his writing center and students who did not:

> First a caveat: I know that numbers can obscure (and what I'm about to detail does reduce those complex human beings who come to our writing centers down to manageable integers). My own research into writing center settings has primarily used qualitative methods because it's the processes of interaction, goal setting, teaching and learning that make our work so fascinating. (2)

As if aware of his "anti-bean-counting" audience, Lerner carefully walked his readers through the process of his data gathering and comparison, providing excellent explanations for his choice of methods. He presented his "bean counting" with humor, especially in headings like "Full of beans" and "Bean counters unite." Lerner praised the "exciting prospect" of numerical data gathered on the National Writing Centers Association website as added proof that "writing centers can and do make a difference" (3). But Lerner captured what many see as the necessary evil of numbers when we direct writing programs or writing centers. After all, we have, for Lerner, a tougher audience to please:

> [I]nstitutional mandates, bean-counting administrators, and, ultimately, our professional standing often call for answers. . . . I've learned about a whole new level of accountability. . . . I need to anticipate my audience's needs. College administrators often want numbers, digits, results. (1-2)

Lerner's justification illustrates Charney's (1996) assertion that "Compositionists readily assume that disciplines that adopt scientific methods do so for reflected glory and access to institutional power" (576). When we adopt such methods—and their accompanying numbers—for ourselves, then, it is sometimes due to the pressure to gain that same protective power or simply because we feel, apologetically, that we have to. Especially in writing centers, for Kail and Allen (1982), research is necessary for many reasons in writing centers: one reason is to "educate your administration," and "like it or not, administrators need numbers" (233).

At the bowling alley, we're gathering numbers to please no one but ourselves. We're here because we really want to know if your red ball is as lucky as you say. Now that each ball has been bowled 6 times, we have our scores, our data set, showing how many pins out of ten each ball managed to knock down:

Just by eyeballing the raw scores, we note that the red ball seems to have come in second. But don't panic yet. Thankfully, we have more ways of looking at numbers that can help us out.

TABLE 3.1

	Green	Red	Purple
	9	9	10
	8	9	9
Scores	6	8	8
	5	7	8
	5	5	7
	3	4	6
Totals	36	42	48

For now, you've taken the first step: gathering, organizing, and presenting the information you found.

In addition to apologies for numerical data, we have examples of research that gathered such data but surprisingly did not share it. For example, Fitzgerald, Mulvihill, and Dobson (1991), in their work on graduate writing groups in writing centers, conducted a survey of graduate students at their university. They asked graduate students about their preferences for working on theses and dissertations and about the kinds of services the writing center could offer them. The authors referred to the survey (attached as an appendix to the published article) but did not report any of the quantitative data they worked so hard to gather.

The survey asked, for example, if graduate students would prefer multidisciplinary writing groups or discipline-specific writing groups if the writing center offered such services to graduate students. Instead of reporting the answers to that survey question, the authors stated, "the students told [the director], almost unanimously, that they preferred to be in groups with people from other disciplines" (137). Here, the authors preferred—and have given more value to—the testimony of the few students who participated in graduate writing groups, when much more data were readily available about their graduate population generally (data that readers would undoubtedly find useful).

Hunzer (1997) also conducted a survey in a writing center to explore gender stereotypes. After observing that female students preferred working with female tutors because male tutors were "intimidating" and that male students preferred working with male tutors because female tutors "were not aggressive enough" (6), Hunzer mailed a survey with twelve questions to seventy-four students. She printed three of those questions in her article but did not share any of the responses. While she noted the number of students who responded (39 total, 16 male, 18 female, and 4 anonymous) and the age range of her sample (17-30), she shared results only from the five students who volunteered (and kept their appointments) to be interviewed (7). Responses in these five interviews—not responses on thirty-nine surveys—formed the entire data analysis. While student responses here are interesting to consider in relation to gender stereotypes and student expectations of writing center tutors, more data were available but not given.

Now that you've gathered the scores at the bowling alley, we need a way to talk about them. It's a bit bulky to discuss your raw scores: the red ball scored a 9 and then another 9 and then. . .

Averages or means help us share information with others. We can easily figure the average scores for the bowling balls by dividing the total score by the number of trials each ball had (6).

TABLE 3.2

	Green	Red	Purple
Scores	9	9	10
	8	9	9
	6	8	8
	5	7	8
	5	5	7
	3	4	6
Totals	36	42	48
Avgs	6	7	8

You still shouldn't panic. After all, the average, or mean, is only one way of looking at these data. The mean is a *measure of central tendency*, or a number we can use to summarize the data somehow, to capture its "flavor," so to speak, or describe the data in some way—which is why we call it a *descriptive statistic*. Like adjectives, these numbers describe what we see, so we can more clearly share them with others. Here, "7" is the best descriptor of the red ball's overall performance.

But there are other measures of central tendency that can describe what we see. Stay tuned. I know you're going to like one of them.

In "Students' Reactions to Teacher Comments: An Exploratory Study," Straub (1997) did present his data, but only descriptively: in a study of 142 students' ranking of forty teacher comments on a four-point scale (1=definitely prefer, 2=prefer, 3=do not prefer, 4=definitely do not prefer), Straub presented the average score students gave for each teacher comment and some average scores for categories of comments (such as "praise" or "advice"). Straub made comparisons among students' responses by "eyeballing" the average scores. For example, Straub concluded that

> These students were generally receptive to questions, but they were particularly receptive to open questions. . . . The average rating for open questions was 2.08, the third-most preferred mode of commentary in the study, behind advice (1.76) and explanations (1.56). The average rating for closed questions was considerably less favorable: 2.24, only a notch better than imperative comments. (109)

Eyeballing the data to determine differences resulted in Straub's loose phrasing, such as "generally receptive," "considerably less favorable," and "a notch better"—loose comparisons that significance testing would have clarified. Overall, Straub concluded that students "seemed to be influenced far less by the *focus* of teacher comments than by the *degree of specificity* of the comments and the *modes* of commentary" (100). Even though these three variables—focus, specificity, and mode—were a part of this study, Straub presented only one table of data: for mode of commentary.

Statistically, "mode" has a different meaning. While the mean determines the arithmetic average of a set of scores, the *mode* describes the same set of scores by looking at the most frequently-occurring score. The mode, of course, does not contradict the mean. It simply gives us another angle from which to view the same thing, as all researchers converge on their data in as many ways as possible to learn as much as possible about it.

Since you want the red ball to win, presenting the mode might help you. Even though the red ball placed second in overall raw score (and, therefore, the mean), you win when it comes to the mode. Of the three balls, the red had the highest mode, or most frequently occurring score: 9. The mode for the purple ball was 8, and the mode for the green ball was only 5.

At this point, the red ball still has hope. While the purple ball achieved the highest average, you could argue that the red ball appears to achieve the highest score more consistently. If you argued only the mean vs. the mode, however, you would never get anywhere. So the difference here between the mean and the mode illustrates two more important points: the mean is not the only number that can describe our data, and we need to look at our data set in other ways in order to understand all of the information it contains.

If Straub crunched his data beyond simple averages, he did not share it. Certainly, looking at the means for each comment helps us describe students' preferences, and anyone would know that a mean of 2.1, for example, seems different from a mean of 3.1. But how different were they? How much variation is it, exactly? And, for an item that achieved a mean of 3.1, for instance, how varied were students' responses *within* that item? Straub didn't elaborate on his data by discussing or presenting the standard deviation, another descriptive statistic that gives us more information about the averages, except for one comment in a footnote:

> The extent of students' agreement about their strong preference for advice is indicated by the standard deviation on their ratings for the eight advisory comments. It is .84, the lowest in the study, indicating only a minor variation in the students' preferences for items in the group. (114)

Readers should also be interested in the highest standard deviation in the study, a number that would tell us the extent to which students might have disagreed about their preference for a certain comment, but Straub did not share it. Here, we have a study in which data are presented, but only in part—and data will always contain more than just averages.

At first glance, *standard deviation* looks like an oxymoron, but it is, actually, a very descriptive term. Here, "deviation" refers to how far an individual score deviated (or varied) from the mean. When the green ball scored a 9, for example, we can see that it deviated 3 points from the mean (6.0). Knowing how far each score varied from the mean gives us additional information about those scores and about the mean's ability to describe the whole data set. But to talk about each individual score, again, gets bulky, so we'll instead determine the "average" deviation among the individual scores in each set: the standard deviation.

To do that, let's see how far each score varied from the mean by subtracting the mean from each score. You'll notice, though, that subtracting the mean from each score will result in some negative numbers. How do we get the average deviated score when we have to add negative numbers? If we add the numbers we get when we subtract the mean from each score, we'll have zero, as the second column below shows. We solve the problem by squaring that score (multiplying two negative numbers gives us a positive number). Think of it as grammatically correcting a double negative. Later, we'll have to remember that we squared these numbers.

For now, let's label our columns to help keep them straight. Let's work with the red ball as an example, and label the raw score "X," the deviated score "x," and when we square that x, we'll label it x^2.

Once we've squared each deviated score, we can determine their mean by adding them (22.00) and dividing by the number of scores (6), just like we compute any average.

TABLE 3.3

Standard Deviation for the Red Ball

X	subtract the mean	x	x^2
9	-7.0	2.0	4.0
9	-7.0	2.0	4.0
8	-7.0	1.0	1.0
7	-7.0	0.0	0.0
5	-7.0	-2.0	4.0
4	-7.0	-3.0	9.0
Totals 42		0.0	22.0

The average (mean) turns out to be 3.67, but remember we had to square each deviated score to correct for negative numbers. The average, 3.67, then, is the standard deviation *squared*, not the standard deviation for the green ball's scores. We can take the square root of 3.67, however, and get that number: 1.91. The scores that the red ball achieved deviated from the mean of 7.0 by an average of 1.91 points.

calculating the mean of X: 42/6 = 7.0

calculating the mean of x^2 : 22.0/6 = 3.67

standard deviation: $\sqrt{3.67} = 1.91$

You can do the math for the green and purple balls.

Similar to Straub's study, in which he gathered data but did not share a full analysis, was Radencich's (1998) summary of research done by four of her masters students (coauthors, Eckhardt, Rasch, Uhr, & Pisaneschi). In one of the four studies, which tried to determine a difference in word count in students' journals when given either teacher-provided or self-selected journal topics, Radencich articulated the data analysis as follows: "Becky computed word counts per journal entry per student and then used an ANOVA to compare those of boys and girls for teacher-provided and self-selected topics. The only difference she found was higher word counts for self-selected than for teacher-provided topics" (88). Here, mere mention *that* an ANOVA was done seemed sufficient, rather than a full detailing of the analysis and results. In another of the four studies —one that attempted to measure the effects of different background music (including a no music control) on students' journal writing— Radencich also ignored numerical data, sharing only the teacher's observations and students' commentary. While Radencich's purpose was to examine her graduate-level course on research, such vague summaries of the research done in the course cannot help us understand the full context in which that research was conducted or what that research might mean.

While other researchers certainly publish the data they find, the above examples illustrate that it is possible to publish research that relies on data without reporting all of that data–or any data at all–or to convert numerical data to a qualitative report. This is a surprising notion, considering how difficult it is to gather that data in the first place: why wouldn't a researcher want to share the results of such hard work? But perhaps we shouldn't be surprised to see some researchers ignore the math when research textbooks in our field do the same. Lauer and Asher (1988) explained statistics and measurement in an appendix to *Composition Research: Empirical Designs*, referring to a list of other suggested readings "for someone without extensive statistical background" (232). In a more comprehensive, sophisticated text, Hayes et al. (1992) reviewed strategies for reading research reports, including the statistics/results section, but suggested to readers who "have trouble reading graphs" that they, too, refer to the list of "additional readings" that can help with such matters (15): "Our objective is not to give you extensive knowledge of subject matter or of statistical methods" (11). And while MacNealy's *Strategies for Empirical Research in Writing* (1999) was "intended for novices: those with *no* background in empirical research and even those who are afraid of math" (ix), MacNealy acknowledged that her introduction to statistical procedures was insufficient: "As you begin to think about possible statistical procedures to use in analyzing your data, you should consult one of the many books on statistics" (x).[1]

While none of these texts purported to be a statistics textbook, each reviewed several studies and research methods that relied on statistical analysis in order to provide meaning to that research. All referred readers elsewhere to learn more about statistics on their own, as if it is not the place of the composition researcher to teach stats, or as if readers wouldn't mind that omission. While these texts offered definitions of statistical concepts, none walked readers through the intricacies of basic procedures to help them understand the logic behind them, in the full context of investigating a research question. Without such help, mere definitions often remain confusing, vague. While these authors acknowledged that some of their readers would need help with (or, perhaps, would have anxiety about) statistical analysis, none took the opportunity to offer full procedural and conceptual help that would ease anxiety or clarify confusion.

Such anxiety is not uncommon in a field more concerned with words than with numbers—with literacy rather than numeracy (Steen, 1990; Snyder, 1990). Steen (1990) argued that, even in careers requiring mathematics, some must overcome "insecurity brought on by their school experience with mathematics" (216). Still others, though often well-educated, "are virtually innumerate; others become 'mathophobic,' avoiding tasks or careers that require any use of mathematics" (216) (see also Tobias, 1978, 1987). For Steen, lack of confidence in math or statistics naturally leads to avoidance.

Other forces, of course, have shaped our response to numbers. A Nike advertisement for women's athletic shoes, printed in popular women's magazines in the early 1990s (and available now on several websites), captured both a public and a scholarly awareness of the potential harm in a number:

> A woman is often measured by the things she cannot control. She is measured by the way her body curves or doesn't curve, by where she is flat or straight or round. She is measured by 36-24-36 and inches and ages and numbers, by all the outside things that don't ever add up to who she is on the inside. And so if a woman is to be measured, let her be measured by the things she can control, by who she is and who she is trying to become. Because every woman knows, measurements are only statistics and *statistics lie.*

We have to be careful, especially in rhetoric and composition, if we believe that statistics lie. Our own field has had to justify rhetoric as an honorable pursuit, refuting charges that often come with phrases like "mere rhetoric" or "empty bombast"—phrases that suggest rhetoricians, too, can lie. And let's admit it: words tell more lies than numbers do. After all, we have another way of pointing out liars: "you're just telling stories."

FEMINIST RESPONSES TO THE TRADITIONAL RESEARCH PARADIGM: IN SEARCH OF OUR MOTHERS' VOICES

Science and scientists—and the numerical data and scientific thought accompanying them—have been criticized for years by feminists fighting the combined effect of male domination in science (and in higher education generally) and society's general acceptance of science as power. There is widespread discussion, of course, of the high number of men over women involved in the sciences, of numerous fields (especially medicine) studying men far more often than women, of differences between men's and women's ways of knowing, and of long-standing social expectations of women to engage more fully in the arts or humanities than in the "bolder," more analytical sciences, often remaining assistants to the men who "do real science."

Before I proceed, I feel the need to make my own stance clear here. I include a review of feminist arguments about research and research methods only to caution against choosing research methods based only on political ideology or against choosing research methods only because they do not have a male-dominated history. At the same time, several feminists have posed perhaps the most valuable arguments about our research at the epistemological level (producing great changes, of course, in what we hope to know, how we can come to know it, and, most importantly, who can be a valid knower). Still, several others have pushed a feminist ideology stripped of epistemological discussion that could and should include everyone.

Feminists and non-feminists alike may ask feminist or non-feminist research questions, and, of course some questions may be neither. I agree with Harding (1987) that both men and women can engage in feminist inquiry and that research without loyalty to either gender is possible and can be helpful (Harding, 1986). At the same time, however, gender neutrality in research does not always help us understand women and men when gender is not an explicit variable, and feminist researchers still run the risk of being perceived as "persons who 'stir up trouble' over nonissues" (Carter & Spitzack, 1989, p. 1) when they move from gender neutrality to gender studies.

We would make a big mistake if we understood feminist contributions to our research as contributions by and for women only. In spite of some arguments to that effect, I hope instead to present feminist inquiry as aiding our understanding of both women and men and, especially, the unwritten rules of the power structure in which we live. Of special interest here are the arguments put forth about traditional methodological preferences for research. An even bigger mistake than always choosing one method would be to reject a research method *only because* of its male-dominated history or to prefer some methods because they appear to suit women better. For some, this might sound like an anti-feminist argument that requires more defense.

Like many women, I first came to feminism for survival and for tools for fighting back. In my first semester of graduate school, I had the opportunity in an advanced composition class to write about my own experiences as they relate to a larger social issue. In my essay, I told my favorite shaping stories in an exploration of sexism: my stories about raising pigs when I was in high school so that I could go to college—only to be voted "prettiest pig farmer in town"; about bringing those pigs to market—only to be asked if I was "keeping Dad company"; about working at a farm supply store for a couple of years in college—only to be doubted that I even knew where things were; and about driving a forklift in a freezer during the summer between my undergraduate work and graduate school—only to be told too many times, "let one of the men get it". (Often, the men who challenged me in these ways "got theirs" eventually, especially when I worked in that freezer—like the men who wouldn't take my advice to put their tailgate up to hold the 100 pounds of ice they just purchased: I was told not to worry my little head, but I laughed that "little head" off when the ice didn't make it out of the parking lot, when it started to melt immediately and slid off, and the men were too embarrassed to come back.)

And in my first week as a writing center director, the male professor who asked me if our new furniture arrangement came out of that same "little head" reminded me yet again that women's battles—and my own personal ones—are far from over.

I share these stories not only to demonstrate my own fondness for stories and my understanding of what they can reveal, but also to illustrate that my life does not allow me to be anti-feminist, in spite of some questions I have of feminist arguments about our research. Especially in composition, many women are now in positions to make a difference, and we do—for the present and the future. Active research of all kinds will move us forward so that no more histories of male domination are needed to assert our right to the present. Such research will require that we use all available tools to make necessary changes. With this in mind, several texts are well worth reading—with a critical eye for what they mean for all of us.

While I hope we're ready to move beyond discussions of our male-dominated history, I cannot deny that we still live within the culture that such a history shaped. Go back to the bowling alley and ask yourself if you assumed our bartender to be male or female. Be honest. In the actual text, the bowler has no gender. Your vision of male or female was imposed on the text. If you assumed neither sex, good for you. If you assumed male, it doesn't mean you're sexist: you simply live in the same world feminists have been trying to expose and change for decades.

For many, research that relies heavily on numerical data embodies a set of stereotypically masculine values. Relating her experiences as a biochemist, Shepherd (1993) speculated on "the emotional" more often associated with the feminine and "the rational" more often associated with the masculine. In her quest to "unveil the feminine face of science" (as the title of her book suggests), Shepherd traced the male domination of science—as have numerous feminist scholars[2] — and blamed such domination for a decreased public interest in science, for scientific language that has become increasingly cryptic and more separate from the public, and for "the intentional repression of one such approach, that representing the feminine viewpoint, which has been ignored from the outset" (2).

Science without feeling (in other words, science without the feminine) if taken to its extreme, Shepherd argued, is akin to Nazi scientists conducting experiments on Jews (249)—the extreme result, for Shepherd, of masculine thought that looks only at the objective, at the data and procedures, and ignores what the feminine attends to: the interconnectedness of people and of social responsibility (250). This absence of emotion or of personal involvement in the sciences was addressed immediately by Shepherd's first sentence of her "Acknowledgments": "This book is a personal journey, embarked upon to discover and honor the emerging Feminine in myself and in our culture" (vii).

For some, the inclusion of women and women's issues involves a change not only in research questions and the researchers themselves, but also in research methods. Railing against a male-dominated tradition and its favored research models, we now seek different methods that seem able to embrace and reveal what Shepherd called the "personal journey" and what has become a new epistemological stance. For example, Hawkins (1989) argued that "participant observation, unstructured interviews, and use of personal documents" should be emphasized in research on (in particular) sexual harassment and (in general) any research that recognizes the "reactivity of human beings" (61). Langellier and Hall (1989) argued for interviews as the best method for understanding women's communication, rather than "sex as a variable measured against male-as-norm" (202), in their research involving women's personal narratives about food and food preparation.

In composition, Sullivan (1992) also favored such methods for advancing feminist inquiry. While she praised composition for the large number of women who have been pioneers in our field and for not being guilty of studying male populations only (38-39), she curiously proclaimed that women students who enter the male-dominated academy still must learn "modes of discourse that [women] have had little voice in shaping" (40). Sullivan, like Shepherd and others, lashed out at the male dominance in higher education and in the sciences:

> Taking gender as the starting point of inquiry . . . is a necessary but not a sufficient condition of feminist methodology, for feminism has as its ideological goal the overturning of patriarchal assumptions and practices that render women's experiences invisible and undervalued. (50)

For Sullivan, this feminist ideology leads feminist composition researchers to prefer "the cluster of methods that fall under the rubrics of qualitative and naturalistic inquiry" (57), arguing that "traditional methodologies—the research practices and assumptions—of our discipline" continue to allow "men's discursive practices to define the standard against which women's writing is judged" (58). Sullivan was highly critical of two texts in particular that have attempted to contribute to composition's quest for a firmly established research paradigm:

> The dominant paradigm, reflected throughout works such as Lauer and Asher's *Empirical Designs* and in parts of North's *The Making of Knowledge in Composition,* dictates that the researcher must detach herself from the object of inquiry and keep personal bias and values from influencing her observations and analysis if she is to paint an objective and undistorted picture of reality. (55)

Sullivan relied heavily on Harding's (1987) work, in which Harding questioned the existence of a "feminist methodology" but proposed three important characteristics of feminist inquiry: 1) it should be based on women's experiences; 2) it should examine phenomena important to women; and 3) it should involve the researcher and his/her experiences and assumptions rather than pretend objectivity through a disinterested stance.

Highlighting the voices of women (including the researcher) seems to be the most important contribution feminist scholars can make to composition. To achieve this goal, Sullivan argued for research methods she called "qualitative and naturalistic"—research that invites a prose style related more to narrative than to the traditional research article:

> Techniques such as open-ended interviews and case studies enable researchers to generate descriptions of composing from the point of view

and in the language of the writers they are studying. Participant observation, a defining feature of ethnomethodology, allows researchers to reflect
critically on their own subject position, both as researchers and as
authors, in the twin sites of the study—in the field and on the page. (57)

While Sullivan concluded that these particular methods would
suit a feminist researcher best, she admitted in the same piece that
previous case studies—even those on (and by) women writers—have
upheld the male-dominated prescriptions of good writers, especially
in graduate work. She criticized a case study in her own 1988 dissertation and another presented by North (1987, pp. 37-42) in *The Making
of Knowledge in Composition*; both case studies focused on women
graduate students who were struggling to succeed. Sullivan illustrated
how the lack of a feminist research question and feminist research
principles created studies that she later seemed to construe as anti-
feminist—in spite of methodologies she argued were naturally suited
for feminist inquiry. Both studies, for Sullivan, drowned the voices of
the women being discussed and never considered socialization of
gender as a potential reason for difficulty in either woman's writing.
In short, while Sullivan argued for case study methods as a means of
revealing women's voices and as an appropriate tool for feminist
inquiry (or for inquiry in composition generally), she illustrated how
case studies can also distort—through the very subjectivity of the
author—that same inquiry.[3] In other words, Sullivan inadvertently
demonstrated that method alone cannot determine good or poor
feminist scholarship: in spite of her argument that qualitative and
naturalistic methods are more suitable for such scholarship, she illustrated two cases in which this was not true. And in spite of her
reliance on Harding's work, which is open to a range of research
methods and styles, Sullivan suggested, though indirectly, that any
study involving women must be done in a certain way or it will not
make a valid contribution (or, conversely, that other, different ways
are still acceptable for studying men, with or without their "voices").

Also relying on Harding's (1987) question of feminist methodology, Kirsch (1993) constructed and defended her research method in
Women Writing the Academy according to Harding's three principles

of feminist inquiry: focusing on issues important to women, grounding inquiry in women's experiences, and being personally involved as
a researcher. Kirsch presented valuable case studies that examined
women's views of authority and audience in their writing for various
disciplines, but, like other researchers, Kirsch defended her method
politically and ideologically *rather than via her need to answer a particular research question.* Even though Harding doubted the existence
of a feminist research method, Kirsch adopted Harding's principles in
"method form" and apologized for how traditional that method
appeared when written out in chapter two:

> The feminist research principles described by Harding informed the
> design of this study. . . . Although the subheadings of this chapter appear
> to indicate a rather traditional research report, the discussion within each
> section, the last section of this chapter, and the overall organization of the
> book (e.g., the portraits of writers between chapters) all indicate the
> extent to which this research is shaped by a feminist methodology. (30)

The apology for such a traditional-looking research report suggests the extent to which composition researchers have established
their distaste for such research, even for how it looks. In her defense
of her chosen method, Kirsch also implied that research in traditional
form is never based on experience, never involves the researcher personally, and never examines feminist research questions. Of course,
Women Writing the Academy contributes greatly to our inquiry about
gender issues and writing and is enlightening and readable. On a less
positive note, however, it contributes also to the tension of a false
dichotomy–separating (and elevating) one kind of research from
(and over) another.

Preferences for case studies and other qualitative forms of research
have often been contrasted with what has been called the "masculinization of thought" that requires objectivity, mathematics, and distance on
the part of the researcher. A stronger defense of personal narratives and
case studies, then, has been developing among several scholars in our
field—a field said to be highly feminized (Lauer, 1995; Enos, 1996;
Connors, 1995, 1996; Healy, 1995) and, therefore, in a position to be
naturally opposed to such masculinization of thought—especially for

feminist scholars who use gender issues as a means of defending such a growing preference. Much in our field has been determined feminine: student-centered and collaborative pedagogies, the nurturing environment of writing centers, and the staffing of most first-year writing classes and writing centers. Changes in the field brought on by women, I believe, are the strongest and most productive new features of our field. It seems natural, then, that preference for research methods mirroring these features—case studies, narratives, interviews, ethnography—are now rapidly following suit.

Even when narratives are combined with numbers in multi-modal research, narratives are sometimes assigned more weight. In *Gender Roles and Faculty Lives in Rhetoric and Composition*, Enos (1996) presented an extremely valuable study on composition faculty in English departments that gave special attention to gender issues. Enos's blend of demographic data, survey results, and interviews provided a strong picture of the scope of gender bias in our field, and the stories from many women (and a few men) illustrate all too clearly the often combined struggles that composition faculty still face against literature-dominated departments and that women face in a male-dominated hierarchy. In spite of a large amount of numerical data presented with these stories, however, Enos believed the stories clearly carried more weight: "I believe our stories, more than statistics, tell who we are" (2).

> I believe the "power" depends on something besides "reasoned discourse" or statistical analysis. I believe this book's most powerful use of "data" is the narrative, in the *stories* that help us define our places in academia so that we can better trace our future. The stories you will hear, more than the "hard data" you will read, use the power of the occasion to make our histories more compelling, more true. (1)

Of interest here is that Enos presented the stories as more true than the statistics she gathered to show the scope of the problem. Without those numbers, however, some value in the stories would be lost (though they would not be "less true"): the numbers and the narratives support each other too well; one without the other would collapse their mutual support on which the power of Enos's book depends.

PREFERENCE FOR NARRATIVE-AS-GENRE: ARE WE STILL THE STEPCHILD OF LITERATURE?

Like Enos, who argued that stories are more true for us than statistics, Elbow's *What is English?* (1990) demonstrated a clear hunger for stories among teachers of writing. Sharing his notes from one session at the 1987 English Coalition Conference, Elbow captured a discussion in which Janet Emig asked other participants, "What are the conditions that all teachers need?" Some participants gave standard responses, such as "smaller classes" and "more time." Then, according to Elbow's notes, "Rosalinda Barrera suggests stories" (197).

Stories. Indeed, the blurb on the back cover of Elbow's book praised its storytelling nature, especially for being "very personal" and for having been written in "a lively and accessible style"—features we would rarely assign to even the best of traditional academic theory or research. Writing teachers naturally gravitate toward methods that not only relieve us of the need to crunch numbers or count beans, but also allow us to share the things we like best: Stories. Stories with style.

For some, stories have provided the foundation for teaching philosophies. Carroll (1997) argued, "English I is about telling stories, about the stories we tell students and the stories they tell us and the stories we construct together. At the same time, *it's all true*, not because stories map a unified reality but because stories do have consequences" (932). Welch (1997) articulated the role of stories in her own teaching philosophy:

> I approach composition with the belief that rhetoric and poetics are intertwined, that arguments are underwritten by stories, and that these stories work powerfully as forms of persuasion. . . . I learn from stories. (939)

In a positive review of five books on storytelling and teaching writing, Welch argued, "All five can teach us about the shapes and uses of stories in our field" (940).

Perhaps this passion for stories is what made Rose's *Lives on the Boundary* (1989) so popular. The subtitle gave it away: "A Moving

Account of the Struggles and Achievements of America's Educationally Underprepared." For me, the book was, indeed, moving, especially in those places where I saw stories much like my own. Rose relied on stories—stories from his own life and from others—and, for Rose, there was a reason for that:

> The stories of my work with literacy interweave with the story of my own engagement with language. *Lives on the Boundary* is both vignette and commentary, reflection and analysis. I didn't know how else to get it right. (xii)

Other researchers also attempt to get it right through stories. For composition studies, storytelling serves as the primary selling point of methods such as ethnography; as Brodkey (1987) so concisely articulated, "All ethnographies begin in stories":

> [O]ne needs *more*, not fewer, ways to narrate experience, for the value of ethnography inheres in neither analysis nor interpretation, but in the researcher's decision to examine lived cultural experience—to conceptualize it, reflect on it, narrate it, and evaluate it. (32)

Relying on Foucault's (1977) discussion of authorship ("What Is an Author?"), Brodkey explained that ethnographers, not the method, tell the story. In contrast to experimental replications or repeated explications of the same poem (works that "display methodologies" more than their "authors"), ethnographers are in charge of their "candidly authored" works and construct narratives anew; they are, therefore—for Brodkey and in Foucault's terms—authors (27).

For those who have explored the place of stories in our scholarship, a new focus on the author (and on authorship) holds power in other ways as well. Gannett (1995), for example, explored the story as not only a means of sharing our lives or reflecting on our lives, but, more importantly, as a means of *making* our lives, as the title of her essay (in Phelps and Emig 1995) explicitly stated: "The Stories of Our Lives Become Our Lives." In part, Gannett reviewed, as others have, a male-dominated history that once prevented women from engaging in academic discourse, a restriction that attracted (forced?) women to the set of genres known as journals and diaries (114), a set of genres that Gannett argued is now entering university discourse: "In the university, women have begun to valorize and reclaim the discourse traditions they have historically found empowering" (124), a discourse tradition based on the personal and social meanings found in stories.[4]

Storytelling also has the power to construct our identities as classroom teachers. Royster and Taylor (1997) explored the identity of the basic writing teacher through Taylor's teaching journal[5]—an identity often lost in the scholarship that attends more to constructing instead the identity of the basic writer. Of importance to Royster and Taylor, however, was not only storytelling, but also a critical look at the nature of storytelling as an inclusive tool with the potential to construct identities for a diverse group of teachers:

> In one way, this article is yet another call to story as a very useful methodology for sharing classroom experiences—this time with the gaze on the teacher. Our call, however, is also for a critical step back from our narratives to make them reach out more inclusively and more meaningfully for the general landscape of our work. At this point, our view is that we need to think, not only about ourselves in classroom space, but also about the art of storytelling in terms of its theoretical and political implications. What have we learned about the telling of stories? How do we assign meaning and draw value for the classroom cultures from which our telling comes? (42)

In addition to constructing academic identities, storytellers and authors of ethnographies are able to connect their personal lives/identitites to their academic identities, to "bridge . . . a rather large gap between academic research and real problems" (Moss, 1992, p. 153). For Moss, ethnography and its focus on the everyday activities of communities allowed her to take a personal approach to her research on literacy in the African-American church, an approach in which the story had clear value for Moss:

> [Ethnography] was the only research method I had been introduced to that allowed a researcher to tell a story about a community—a story told jointly by the researcher and the members of the community. (154)

Here, Moss reminded us that the author of an ethnography not only constructs the narrative, but she is also a part of the study itself "in more than some abstract 'researcher' way" (154; see also Radencich, et al., 1998).

Authorship in research was also important for Newkirk in "The Narrative Roots of the Case Study" (1992). Critical of those who justify case study research by "straddling paradigms" (132)—defending case studies as scientifically rigorous and generalizable while upholding the individualized narrative at the same time—Newkirk presented the need for a case study paradigm that he understood could be perceived as "dangerous" because it is not one "of methodology and objectivity, but of authoring and the cultural values embedded in various narrative plots" (133). Newkirk argued that we have not yet embraced such a narrative-based paradigm because of "the consistent warning in the educational research textbooks. . . . The great god of Methodology is invoked to protect the researcher from charges of storytelling" (133). The value of storytelling rests, however, as Newkirk argued,

> . . . on a core of mythic narratives—deeply rooted story patterns that clearly signal to the reader the types of judgments to be made. . . . As readers of these studies, we find them true or convincing, not because of careful methodology (important as that is), or because of wealth of detail, but, I would argue, because of the gratification we get from seeing cultural myths being reenacted. (135-136)

As these cultural narratives are reenacted, the author, more than the method, controls the text, and while Newkirk did not say so, such a shift from method to author allows one important feature to be revealed that authors have and methods apparently do not: emotion. Storytelling, more than statistics, allows our emotions to emerge, an act that, in Newkirk's terms, brings us gratification.

Paulos (1995), intrigued by the popular need for gratification, pointed out the popularity of emotional appeals (rather than evidence) in the media, law, and business. And while our own scholars put forth their own reasons for storytelling and for the emotional involvement of the researcher, Paulos proposed his own (less favorable, more dangerous) reason for that natural desire:

It's easier and more natural to react emotionally than it is to deal dis-
passionately with statistics or, for that matter, with fractions, percentages,
and decimals. The media (actually, all of us) frequently solve this problem
by leaving numbers out of stories. . . . [W]e all tend to be unduly swayed
by the dramatic, the graphic, the visceral. (80-82)

For Paulos, we avoid the mathematical/rational/statistical in part
because it is difficult and because the emotional is easier and feels
more natural. We can find numerous examples of such emotion in
composition scholarship. As Newkirk, for example, shared his own
experience with case study, he related his struggle to find the narrative
thread on which his final product would ultimately be based:

I had to "intensely consult and intensely ignore," keeping the data I
needed, putting aside the rest, grieving a bit for all I had to leave out.
It is a lonely feeling, and for a while an empty feeling. But I was not
totally alone because I had patterns of other narratives to draw on. I could
make new stories out of old ones. (150)

Shifting our attention from the method to the writer greatly
enhances the emotional side of our research while increasing variability in texts, audiences, and the subjects or stories themselves; indeed,
such attention to authorship and narratives, for Newkirk, has been
seen as "radicalism" in composition research, going against the grain,
so to speak, of traditional research methodologies, when, paradoxically, case studies and ethnography are based on equally long-standing traditions of "enduring narratives" such as the tragedy (136). This
radicalism, however, is demonstrated by other scholars who believe
that allowing the method and data to speak through experiment or
other standard, traditional methods is to allow the traditional genre
of academic prose to remain unquestioned, undisturbed.

Indeed, for most storytellers in composition, the value of a story
rests mostly in its potential for political resistance to academic tradition. In *Narration as Knowledge*, Trimmer (1997) explored the
subordinate role that stories (and the English teachers who love
them) have held in the academy:

We became English teachers because we loved stories. We loved reading them, writing them, and talking about them. . . . But as we worked our
way into our professional lives, we slowly, almost imperceptibly, changed
our attitude toward stories. We lived in a world that did not trust them.
Stories were not true. Stories were not reliable. If we wanted to keep stories in our lives, we had to convert them into something else. Something
more serious. More scientific. (x)

For Trimmer, English teachers have compromised their love for
story under pressure from an academy that values science: we ask students to write stories only to diagnose their errors; we teach them to
"dissect plots and theorize themes," to be analytical rather than creative (x). The analytical dissection of text is expected in traditional
academic prose.

Kirsch (1993), too, resisted such traditional academic prose when
she refused to traditionally conclude her work on women writing in
the academy:

Conclusions demand that an author summarize and unify, make
coherent what might be otherwise fragmented, impose order and control
on material that might be otherwise out of order, out of control. . . .
[C]onclusions can lead to erasing differences, and erasing differences can
lead to the silencing of voices. . . . It is that kind of silencing, that kind of
concluding I would like to avoid here. (125)

Instead of a traditional conclusion, then, Kirsch reminded us that
the stories in her volume were presented without interruption so they
may speak for themselves, to "become audible" (126) in an academic
system blamed for drowning those voices and stories. For some scholars, then, stories contribute to our scholarship by throwing in a
wrench that reminds us that academics and academic research come
from anything but a well-oiled, efficient machine. Trimbur (1993)
praised this value of stories in his "Foreword" to Kirsch's work:

The stories women tell about their lives writing in the academy are
worth listening to in part because they challenge the conventional view of
academic publication as a seamless meritocratic system that recognizes

significant work, rewards talent, and ignores the rest. . . . Their stories also call into question the genres in which academics write and the reasons they write in the first place. (x-xi)

The same kind of "breaking free" from traditional academic prose also formed the foundation for Sullivan and Qualley's collection of essays, *Pedagogy in the Age of Politics* (1994) in which

> authors locate their inquiry in their own practices as teachers, scholars and theorists, writing from their own narratives and not merely from (or about) the master narratives currently circulating in academe. (xii)

Here, stories allow the individual to "come forth" and combat traditional modes of inquiry we somehow find limiting or constraining to our individuality.

In a review of *Pedagogy in the Age of Politics*, however, Jacobs (1997) warned that such diverse, individual narratives "contributed to the diffuseness of the volume and the sense that contributors are isolated rather than members of a social network" (465). Indirectly, then, Jacobs warned that such narratives could lead to a collapse of community: stories are often given value for the sake of the individual telling a story or for the flavor of the story itself, rather than the story's relationship to other stories, to other storytellers, to the field, or to other kinds of inquiry. Jacobs perhaps sensed the potential for stories such as these being told outside of a larger context—specific criticism often reserved for quantitative research (as many scholars have condemned data-gathering as devoid of context).

SUMMARY

Our researchers have, on the one hand, successfully highlighted the voices of marginalized groups as valuable contributors to the field, have critically questioned the status quo of university and departmental hierarchies, and have produced scholarship to which the majority of the field can personally relate. On the other hand, some proposals that "the rubrics of qualitative and naturalistic inquiry" (Sullivan, 1992) are best suited for such goals have stemmed from a desire to be different from a male-dominated history and male-only research and research communities. In addition, other arguments and preferences for these methods have expressed the relief we feel when not required to do math or to write or read those old-fashioned, boring research reports.

We must be careful not to dismiss particular methods–especially those that rely on numerical evidence–as anti-woman, anti-humanist, or anti-creative, for to do so would be to blame the vehicle for having had a lot of bad drivers. Research relying on numerical data is still a dependable vehicle for getting us to some of the places we need to go, and we need all possible vehicles in order to convey the most valuable and diverse body of knowledge possible. Such a vehicle need not be so strangely driven, however: instead, we should all become the best drivers we can, ready for any road.

All research methods and how we teach those methods to others can be done in such a way to include the feminist, to understand math as a storytelling language in its own right, and to include the narrative as a foundation for and an extension of that research in relation to experience and practice.

Chapter four will construct a means through which such an inclusive view of our research might occur. Letting go of dichotomous language, bypassing debates among competing epistemologies, and returning to the roots of a long-standing rhetorical tradition—a Contextualist Theory of Epistemic Justification will help us begin to understand our research needs in the contexts from which they arise, provide us with a more inclusive language, and enable us to further our training in even more diverse research methods.

NOTES

1.   In a 1998 survey of subscribers to consortium-l@mtu.edu (a listserv devoted to graduate studies in composition), none of the respondents (N=8) indicated that their composition program included a statistics course. While some graduate programs in composition (such as my own program at Ball State University) require statistics training for their graduate students, such requirements are clearly

unpopular. Permission for this survey is on file at Ball State University, IRB Protocol ID #98-160.

2.   See, for example, Harding & O'Barr, 1987; Harding, 1986, 1987, 1991; Noble, 1992; Schiebinger, 1993; Wells, 1996.

3.   Another case study that drowned the voice of the student in question was "The African-American Student: At Risk" (Gill, 1992) published in *College English*. Gill argued that African-American students face situations that are unique. She proceeded to describe an African American male who lived in poverty in a fatherless home with his mother supported only through welfare; he needed to work full-time in order to supplement his family's income, and he was the family's only hope for a college graduate since his older sister had become an unwed mother (225-226).

While the problems this student faced have been frequently associated with the African American community, not all African American individuals have faced situations similar to this student's, and non-African Americans face similar problems. Gill chose an extreme scenario to illustrate her point and did not include the student's voice or texts.

Unfortunately, Gill's primary purpose for sharing such a scenario was to argue the benefits of giving African American students positive feedback and praising strengths and improvements in student writing (226). However, she did not illustrate how that kind of reinforcement enabled the student in her case study to succeed, nor did she examine why such reinforcement is uniquely successful with African Americans.

For a strong case study, see DiPardo's (1992) "'Whispers of Coming and Going': Lessons from Fannie" (*Writing Center Journal*, 12.2, pp. 125-144). DiPardo focused on a Navajo female student (Fannie) for whom English is a second language and an African American female tutor (Morgan) in her second semester of tutoring. DiPardo's case study is informed by a sensitivity to language, culture, class, and gender: she related passages from interviews with both the student and the tutor, portions of Fannie's essays, and excerpts from taped tutorials. She wove these voices with her own and with scholarship on language, culture, and tutoring/teaching with a unique blend of sensitivity and authority.

DiPardo's case study included as much writing and talking produced directly by the women she was studying as passages that were her "own." Further, DiPardo's case study did not purport to generalize about Navajo students or African American tutors; instead, she used this case study to examine effective and ineffective tutoring strategies and the need for strong tutor training. DiPardo's case study won the 1993 Outstanding Scholarship Award from the National Writing Centers Association, and the piece was reprinted, most likely for its tutor training value, in Murphy and Sherwood (1995), *The St. Martin's Sourcebook for Writing Tutors.*

4.   While it might be true that the stories women have historically told in diaries and journals ultimately became empowering, Gannett also admitted that men's diaries were published far more often than women's and that diaries and personal writing that women managed to publish were most often for the purpose of illuminating the life of some famous man (125). While much discussion and research might portray personal narratives and journals as uniquely feminine, we must not forget that many stories of historical importance were uniquely masculine. For instance, we have few slave narratives from women (Gates, 1987), and most slave narratives were introduced by white abolitionists who attested to the credibility of the slave's authorship.

Gannett's argument that personal narratives (especially in journals and diaries) are, by their very nature, empowering requires more discussion. I tend to agree more with bell hooks (1989) that diaries and the personal stories in them have the potential to serve as another silent place where women, especially young girls, are "holding and hiding speech" (7) that does not necessarily empower them so much as it maintains their silence and their status as "seen but not heard." Indeed, what makes a story empowering is not always the story itself or the nature of narratives, but the changing culture around the narrative that changes how those narratives are perceived.

5. Taylor's journal, excerpted in Royster and Taylor's article, serves as
    an interesting illustration of the connection between our literary
    training and our desire to tell stories. Most of Taylor's headings for
    her journal entries/stories were framed with literary references:
    "September 25: Great Expectations," "September 29: The
    Outsiders," "Late October: Invisible Man," "The Grapes of Rap,"
    and "Final Portfolios: Grim Fairy Tales," to name a few.

4 FROM EPISTEMOLOGY TO EPISTEMIC JUSTIFICATION
Toward a Contextualist Research Paradigm

> I know that nothing pleases an academic more than a
> defense of the indefensible, an affirmation of the value and
> truth of what all had come to agree was worthless and false.
>
> James L. Battersby, 1996

As rhetoricians, we have a long history of debate and verbal banter-
ing. From Plato's attack on Gorgias, to Aristotle's criticism of contemporary handbooks, to Ramus's arguments against Quintilian, to the
nineteenth-century "art vs. science" debate, to our own time in which
we debate the kinds of knowledge we value and the kinds of research
we should conduct, the very foundations of what we believe is accurate in our field have seemed to shift rapidly from the start. *How* we
see those foundations, however, how we frame our debates, both past
and present, is at issue here. On the one hand, diversity within our
field is necessary: diverse theories and scholars work for and against
each other in a way that is necessary for our field to enrich our knowledge, to gain a respectable place among scholars in other fields, and to
invite new scholarship of the future. On the other hand, especially
regarding research methods in our field, we seem to adopt an opposite view: our field is simply divided by different ways of knowing,
and we argue which ways are better and which are worse. This latter
approach has fueled our debates about research practices in our field,
highlighting a perceived incompatibility among them.

In order to progress beyond such divisions in the future, we must
first understand why they are false, harmful, simplistic, and limiting.
So far, for example, several scholars under review here have seen a certain "truth" in narratives and a certain "falsehood" (untrustworthi-
ness) in numbers (e.g., Charney, 1996, p. 582): there is an established

tendency to see information that is mathematical as somehow automatically decontextualized and reductive, while information that is story-like is seen as somehow able to capture context naturally and automatically in a narrative. The quest for context and our sensitivity to it has advanced our preference for the narrative, a form that we claim has the power to reveal the full complexities of the contexts in which we teach and conduct research—contexts in which we have dialogue, feelings, and problems to solve.

In spite of our tendency to believe that narrative forms capture context better than numbers do—or that narratives are contextualized by their very nature—we must understand that "context" and "narrative" are not synonymous.[1] While numbers might give us only *some* information, we must reframe our praise for the narrative with the understanding that narratives, too, give us only *some* information.[2] And, depending on context, the kind of information we seek *must* vary: when stories are readily available and are informative (or, perhaps, are all we have), we should, of course, share them; when numbers are easily obtained and are informative, we should share them, too (and share them completely and, certainly, without apology). To argue instead that narratives, anecdotes, and stories are *always* more true than numbers, that numbers are *always* for some reason out of context and narratives are not, that it is *always* appropriate to share a researcher's personal voice ignores the very thing to which we claim to be rhetorically most sensitive: context.

Instead of discussing our research with a sensitivity to the contexts from which our work emerges, we have developed a sensitivity to a more simplistic element: form. The narratives we share *and* the numbers we show are *products* of inquiry that emerged from some natural *process*, a context in which we had the desire to know something. When we argue, as we have been, that some *forms* of research *products* are more welcome, more interesting, more "true" than others, we ignore the full contexts of research that would naturally produce other valid forms or, especially, contexts that would naturally produce a mix of forms.

When we publish our research in traditional scientific-looking forms, the process of that research often seems to be hidden—never ignored, but assumed to be understood by the trained eye—and is, therefore, misunderstood by the untrained eyes of our field. The narrative form, in contrast, is readily understood—literary training has enabled us to easily grasp it, relate to it, and extend its meaning. In other words, we forget our own advice that the process of learning and process of writing cannot always be seen in the product alone. As *teachers* of writing, we are trained, and continue to train ourselves, to look at products from our students as clues to their processes, knowing the process is there and how to look for it. As *researchers* of writing, we do not look at our research with nearly as much care—or with as much sensitivity to context as we claim to have.

A greater sensitivity and attention to form has instead produced a body of scholarship in composition that defends our preferences for certain forms. Theories of knowledge, as we have come to frame them in our field, have been artificially divided as much by form as by "thinking"—a division that also ignores the varied contexts in which we learn and know. Worse, we sometimes argue that some theories of knowledge, or epistemologies, are sensitive to context while others are not. The context (usually ideological) in which such arguments are made, however, is often ignored.

Because our response to quantitative research methods has been, in part, emotionally and politically driven(as argued in the last chapter), the epistemological arguments we make to defend and to theorize our positions often leap widely from the local to the global. On a daily basis, we don't live at an epistemological level; we live in the immediate, emotional, political, social world of things we like or are good at (such as form) or things we need to get done at the present moment—that is, for academia, our teaching, researching, and publishing. We construct epistemology abstractly as a means of defending our world—defending our preferred teaching methods and, especially, preferred research methods—but we can't always "get there from here" without dismissing other worlds, other methods.

As a field of composition, we need to "get there from here" in a more inclusive manner, but a discussion of only competing epistemologies would erroneously make the same leap while maintaining the artificial dichotomy we have already created. Therefore, the competing epistemologies we have outlined for our field will be briefly reviewed in this chapter—but only for the purpose of illustrating the decontextualized arguments they represent. The remainder of the chapter will present a Contextualist Theory of Epistemic Justification (Annis, 1978), a theory that allows for what Hobson (1992) called an "epistemological mix," a template for rethinking our research and one that (re)grounds us firmly in the rhetorical principles that have guided our field from the start and that should always guide our research questions, whatever they may be—as shown in the Contextualist Research Paradigm proposed later in this chapter.

Instead of arguing, in other words, about *which* research method or *which* epistemological stance is sensitive to context, we must ask instead: In what context does that sort of argument make sense? In what context does such division naturally occur? In what contexts do divided ways of knowing serve us well? In what contexts in other areas of our lives do we make such distinctions?[3]

Divisions among theories of knowledge construct context artificially, after the fact. As a result, we are often coerced by our own field's scholarship now to reject traditional research methods, opting instead for other methods, regardless of what we want to know, regardless of how best to come to know it. Simultaneously, we propose misguided arguments that only certain methods are sensitive to that same context—contexts we either ignore or construct artificially after our chosen method is comfortably in place. Inattention to the contexts in which we construct such arguments, and ultimately choose one research method over another, has created the unfortunate illusion that the range of research methods available to us somehow stems from incompatible systems of thought—incompatible and, therefore, competing epistemologies.

COMPETING THEORIES OF KNOWLEDGE IN COMPOSITION

Berlin (1987) once noted that

> [R]hetoric refers to a diverse discipline that historically has included a variety of incompatible systems. . . . [E]very rhetorical system is based on epistemological assumptions about the nature of reality, the nature of the

knower, and the rules governing the discovery and communication of the known. (3-4)

The notion of epistemological assumptions was captured by Emig's (1982) articulation of "Inquiry Paradigms," in which she asserted the need for five elements in such a paradigm:

> 1) a governing gaze; 2) an acknowledged, or at least conscious, set of assumptions, preferably connected with 3) a coherent theory or theories; 4) an allegiance to an explicit or at least a tacit intellectual tradition; and 5) an adequate methodology including an indigenous logic consonant with all of the above. (65)

In Emig's words, "there can be no more than three governing gazes, so it is easy and almost inevitable to regard most of us as one of three kinds of gazers: positivistic, phenomenological, or transactional/constructivist" (65) (see Figure 4.1). In other words, as Emig defined a governing gaze—"a steady way of perceiving actuality" (65)—there can be no more than three, there can be no overlap among the three she has outlined, we can adopt only one of them, as the three are clearly incompatible with each other. For Emig, the most "diametrically different," and "most fundamentally opposed" (65) were the positivist and phenomenological governing gazes: the positivist focusing on phenomenon stripped of context and ignoring individual interpretation, and the phenomenological focusing on context and the perspective of the individual who is perceiving the phenomenon.

Emig connected the phenomenological gaze, as others have, to Polanyi's (1964) concept of "personal knowledge," a concept Emig praised as "steadily useful" (67). Kerlinger (1986), too, found Polanyi's concept of personal knowledge to be useful, though as a behavioral scientist, in a different way. Borrowing Polanyi's phrase, "passionate commitment," Kerlinger outlined the role of personal knowledge for the scientist (those often accused of the narrow, useless governing gaze of positivism). Though the following passage from Kerlinger is quite long, it is this very passage—the first page of his Preface to the third edition of *Foundations of Behavioral Research*—that helped me begin to rethink our own debates about how we conduct research in our own field—a rethinking that, in part, inspired and formed the context for this work.

>Some activities command more interest, devotion, and enthusiasm than do others. So it seems to be with science and with art. . . . It seems a far cry from science to art. But in one respect at least they are similar: we make passionate commitments [Kerlinger cited this phrase as Polanyi's] to them.

>This is a book on scientific behavioral research. Above everything else, it aims to convey the exciting quality of research in general, and in the behavioral sciences and education in particular. A large portion of the book is focused on abstract conceptual and technical matters, but behind the discussion is the conviction that research is a deeply absorbing and vitally interesting business.

>It may seem strange in a book on research that I talk about interest, enthusiasm, and passionate commitment. Shouldn't we be objective? Shouldn't we develop a hardheaded attitude toward psychological, socio-logical, and educational phenomena? Yes, of course. But more important is somehow to catch the essential quality of the excitement of discovery that comes from research well done. Then the difficulties and frustrations of the research enterprise, while they never vanish, are much less signifi-cant. What I am trying to say is that strong subjective involvement is a powerful motivator for acquiring an objective approach to the study of phenomena. It is doubtful that any significant work is ever done without great personal involvement. (vii)

In contrast to the many in composition who see the subjective and the objective as fundamentally opposed to one another, Kerlinger invited his students, readers of his text, to bring their own personal commitment to their reading and offered two pieces of advice: First, "I would encourage students to discuss, argue, debate, and even fight about research. Take a stand. Be opinionated" (viii). This is the part that composition has done quite frequently, though not in the context of Kerlinger's second piece of advice: "Later try to soften the opinion-ation into intelligent conviction and controlled emotional commit-ment" (viii). In the end, for Kerlinger, "It is doubtful that students can learn much about science, research design, and research methods without considerable personal involvement" (vii-viii).

Such emotional commitment and personal involvement, for Emig and others in composition, are often perceived as absent in what we have framed as "objectivist" or "positivist" epistemology—a perception that has fueled our passionate defense of the personal as more valuable than the scientific. Such a perception has narrowed, especially recently, our potential channels of scholarship: in the current climate of composition research, the personal commitment that brings us to our research must result in an equally personal text/product. Often citing critics of science (as Emig did), rather than scientists (such as Kerlinger), we have latched onto that criticism of science before we have firmly grasped what science is,[4] what a scientific method is.[5] Thus, what Emig called governing gazes and what others have called epistemologies remain artificially contrasted, divided, and separate in our field.

Berlin, especially, outlined a simplified division among epistemological assumptions in our field—three theories of rhetoric (see Figure 4.1): *objective theories* based on a positivistic epistemology that locates truth in the external, measureable world; *subjective theories* based on truth residing within the individual, a notion eloquently captured by writers such as Emerson and Thoreau; and *transactional theories* based on the assumption that truth arises from the "interaction of the elements of the rhetorical situation" (7-17), the basis for current theories regarding the social construction of knowledge.

Berlin outlined three kinds of transactional theories: the cognitive and the classical, which, Berlin argued, virtually ignore the role of language; and the epistemic, which involves language "in every instance of its manifestation" (16). We could rebut Berlin's assertion that language was not significant in the classical tradition or the cognitivist (16), and we should have difficulty with his use of "truth." Gradin (1995), for example, found Berlin's simplification of epistemological stances in our field troublesome, and, frankly, I've always been confused that some epistemologies are "epistemic" and others are not. This classification, however, has provided language and frameworks that we have used to solidify the divisions within our field ever since.

Lunsford (1991), for example, went on to identify three kinds of writing centers (see Figure 4.1): the garret center (expressivist) where writers go to think individually and be inspired, the storehouse writing center (objectivist) where writers get information on rules and so on, and the collaborative center—a center based on a social-constructionist point of view and a center that Lunsford argued was best.[6] Murphy and Sherwood (1995) applied a similar three-paradigm model for writing centers in their Preface to *The St. Martin's Sourcebook for Writing Tutors*. While Murphy and Sherwood argued that "tutorials are rarely, if ever, exclusively the product of any one paradigm" (4), they point out limitations and criticism of only two of them—the current-traditional/objectivist and the expressivist—while upholding the social-constructionist as "dominant" (3), pointing out the strengths of only this model.

Using a collaborative/social-constructionist model, Murphy and Sherwood articulated four "principal ideas" governing the rest of their text and, generally, the tutors' role: 1) tutoring is contextual, 2) tutoring is collaborative, 3) tutoring is interpersonal, 4) tutoring is individualized (1). Of course, all tutoring is contextual, but the last three principal ideas decontextualize the tutor's role: not all tutoring is automatically collaborative when direct instruction is sometimes necessary, online tutoring has brought into question our definitions of "interpersonal," and small-group and in-class tutoring creates contexts in which tutoring might not be individualized. Unfortunately, only the first principal idea can be supported, and in the context of the first, the other three cannot, *because* they ignore the first—context. Construction of these principal ideas was based on the dominant social-constructionist model of rhetoric, ignoring other theories.

Such divisions among theories of rhetoric have been of concern to some in the field. Gradin (1995), for instance, argued that Berlin's three-part division for theories of rhetoric was too simplistic (see also O'Donnell, 1996). Of concern to Gradin, however, was the separation between expressivist and social theories, two stances she combined in *Romancing Rhetorics*. Gradin offered a new look at romantic rhetoric through which "we can continue to embrace social theories while retaining what is most valuable about expressivist doctrine" (165), an argument that rests on the field's current acceptance of social theories. Of the three-part division that Berlin offered, Gradin, here, sought to join only the transactional and the expressivist. Evidently, the objectivist is dead and buried.

LIMITATIONS OF THE COMPETITIVE EPISTEMOLOGICAL FRAMEWORK

Such artificial divisions among theories of knowledge have led to the artificial dichotomy we have perpetuated in our research. When debating the merits of qualitative and quantitative methods, we connect that debate to competing epistemologies, as our field has outlined them (Figure 4.1), in order to defend our preferences.

Such competitive theories of knowing, however, are stripped from the context of the need to know and are, therefore, false lenses through

Figure 4.1

Governing Gazes (Emig), Competing Theories of Rhetoric (Berlin), Competing Models for Writing Centers (Lunsford), and Current Research Models

	Positivist	*Transactional*	*Phenomenological*
Emig 1982	focus on phenomenon outside of context; quest for absolute truth	knower and known interact; mutual transformation	focus on personal reality in context; quest for multiple individual truths
	Objectivist	*Transactional*	*Expressionist*
Berlin 1987	relying on external, scientifically verifiable proof	relying on group dynamics and collaboration	relying on one's internal interpretation of the world
	Storehouse	*Collaborative*	*Garret*
Lunsford 1991	writing center features handbooks, drills, modules, handouts	writing center features dialogue; meaning is negotiated by the group	writing center features individual expression, inspiration
	Quantitative	*Social*	*Personal*
Research Models	relying on numerical data, controlled methods, and statistial analysis	relying on case study, observation and dialogue/interviews	relying on personal narrative, reflection on experience, anecdotes

which we attempt to define our research, accepting in the process only limited parts of what it means to know something fully. How we see our research has suffered from this self-imposed near-sightedness—a near-sightedness that threatens to move our research even further from the contexts of other work in our field, such as our teaching.

For all of our attempts to construct such competitive theories of knowing, after all, composition teachers and tutors are already keenly aware that elements of all of them, in spite of the competitive nature we have assigned to them, are *at work* in our field at every moment. Any writing teacher who takes attendance, gives grades, and teaches students how to correct grammatical or structural errors works in the so-called outer, measurable, objective world. Any teacher who has individual conferences with students, small-group work in the class-room, or interaction with a writing center, operates on transactional theories. The same writing teacher who incorporates journals, freewriting, and expressive assignments allows for the subjective to work, too. And when students attend writing centers, the best tutors will know that sometimes students need dialogue to generate ideas, sometimes they need to vent or "talk out" an idea, and sometimes they need direct instruction on writing skills that can't be coaxed into their minds through questions or discussion.

On a day-to-day basis, experienced and successful teachers and tutors do not flail about when all of these "competing" elements enter our teaching, our offices, our writing centers, our classrooms—as they so regularly do. On the pages of our scholarship, however, pages on which we construct our theories and present our research, we divide these same elements and defend our stances passionately, as if the elements have nothing to do with each other. Appropriately, Connors (1983) specified our research rather than our teaching when he noted, "as a research discipline, we tend to flail about" (10).

Especially for those who advocate qualitative research on the grounds that quantitative methods/researchers ignore context, the decontextualized three-part epistemological structure of our field must be revised and recontextualized. (It should also be blamed in large part for the flailing about that currently plagues us.) To construct competing theories of knowing, as we see them operating in our research, does no more than suggest that we are incapable of embracing all ways of knowing, and that we refuse to acknowledge the truth of our field: we *live* in all worlds, in all modes of knowing, but we are trained to understand only some, unable to discuss the "other," and unwilling to see the narrow channels of scholarship we have imposed upon ourselves.

And what, ultimately, are we saying about ourselves when we construct such arguments? Consider, for example, arguments that support socially-constructed models of knowing because they are more collaborative (feminine) than competitive (masculine): these arguments are also based, directly or indirectly, on a competitive (masculine?) model of epistemological difference (after all, "collaborative *vs.* competitive" is, in itself, a *competitive way of thinking*). Indeed, we embrace one epistemological stance by acting through another.

Further, our distrust of numbers—or our misunderstanding of them and our own poor training in how to use them—has led us to distrust the researchers who use them as well. I agree with Charney (1996, p. 583) that we have fallen into a most destructive and inaccurate view of quantitative researchers: if the traditional researcher focuses the context of an experiment in such a way that does not reveal the "gut feelings" that led to the study, does not articulate the full process and trials and tribulations of that research, and does not share emotion, that researcher will be criticized not so much for *not sharing it*, but for *not having that process at all*. Add to that our anxiety about statistics that inhibits our understanding of that text, that makes our "eyes glaze over," and we fall victim to another all-too-human phenomenon: to blame the "other" for what we cannot understand: It is wrong to use numbers (because I don't like reading them, and I've never understood them); it is wrong to use an experiment (because I've never conducted one myself).

In the context of our experiment at the bowling alley, we are motivated by your personal belief that your red bowling ball is lucky. Luck, of course, has much to do with "chance," so it is only fair (and necessary) to determine mathematically the extent to which the data we have gathered are due to only chance. We have noticed differences in the average scores for each color (green=6.0, red=7.0, and purple=8.0). By eyeballing these means, remember, we could guess that the purple ball is actually "luckiest," but we also remember that individual scores *within* each color group varied, too. Chance, then, could be operating in two places: between colors (each color achieved a different mean), and within colors (the 6 scores within each group were not consistent). To determine the extent to which the color differences are *not* due to chance, we can determine the ratio of the two places where variation occurs: between colors and within colors.

This is what an Analysis of Variance (or ANOVA) does. Stay tuned and relax.

Our anxieties about numbers, experiments, and the statistical analyses they require have moved our field to construct epistemological stances abstractly, as a means of defending our own anxieties, our inadequacies, our lack of training—epistemological stances from which we attack "the other"—in an uncomfortable contact zone (Pratt, 1991) in which two cultures (Snow, 1965) collide, miscommunicate, and remain by our own contention irreconcilably different. Perhaps epistemology does not "construct us" as strongly as we suggest, at least as such inquiry appears on the pages of our scholarship: after all, we were researchers and teachers long before epistemological inquiry appeared in that scholarship. *We* constructed *it*. If we created these false divisions and a false theoretical security through our epistemological inquiry, we, too, can *change* it.

Though we have successfully broadened the scope of our research potential to include more than the older tradition of the quantitative, we swing too far, dismissing the value of that tradition for reasons that do not serve any of our research endeavors well, whatever the contexts might be.

For simplicity here, let's look at only the red ball and the purple ball. Of course, your red ball was the reason for this experiment, but the purple ball scored a higher average. To see if the difference between the purple score and the red score was due to chance, we need to determine three kinds of variation among the scores achieved by each ball:

1. What is the total amount of variation in the study?
2. Of that total amount of variation, how much of that variation can be explained by a difference in color (the variation that occurred between the color groups)?
3. Of the total amount of variation, how much *cannot* be explained by a difference in color (the variation that occurred within each group)?

This mathematical procedure will look similar to the procedure for the standard deviation described in chapter three.

First, let's review the raw scores and the group averages we're looking at:

TABLE 4.1

	Red	Purple
	9	10
	9	9
Scores	8	8
	7	8
	5	7
	4	6
Totals	42	48
Avgs	7	8

To determine how much variation was due to differences in color and how much was due to differences in individual trials/scores, we first need to calculate the total units of variation and then we'll determine how many of those units were due to the color of the ball and how many were due to differences in individual scores within each color group.

To do this, we'll first need to calculate the grand mean, the mean for all scores in this red/purple comparison, by adding all 12 scores and dividing by 12: the grand mean (or M) is 90/12 = 7.5.

Now we return to the three places where we determine how many units of variation we have:

1. the total units of variation will be determined by subtracting the grand mean (M) from each raw score in the study (Y), or: Y-M.
2. the units of variation due to group differences (between colors) will be determined by subtracting the grand mean (M) from each group mean ($\overline{Y}$g), or: $\overline{Y}$g-M.
3. the units of variation due to individual differences (within groups) will be determined by subtracting the group mean ($\overline{Y}$g) from each individual score (Y), or: Y-$\overline{Y}$g.

This process determines *components of differences*, allowing us to look at each different score in different ways. To look at these individual scores in the overall study, however, we'll need to compute in a similar fashion the *components of sums of squares*.

This computation is similar to the procedure for computing the standard deviation. We'll need to square each difference we find through subtracting and then sum (Σ) those squares.

Our overall formula for Components of Sums of Squares looks like this: total variation = variation between groups + variation within groups $\Sigma(Y\text{-}M)^2 = \Sigma(\overline{Y}g\text{-}M)^2 + \Sigma(Y\text{-}\overline{Y}g)^2$

The chart below will help clear up confusion. We'll subtract as outlined above, but remember from computing the standard deviation: if we add up all the results of our subtraction, we'll always have zero (because we're subtracting using the mean, and it makes sense that the mean will have an equal amount above and below it). Therefore, we'll square each result like we did for the standard deviation. Our computations for total units of variation (Y-M) will look like this:

TABLE 4.2

	Y-M		$(Y-M)^2$
Red	9-7.5=	1.5	2.25
	9-7.5=	1.5	2.25
	8-7.5=	0.5	0.25
	7-7.5=	-0.5	0.25
	5-7.5=	-2.5	6.25
	4-7.5=	-3.5	12.25
Purple	10-7.5=	2.5	6.25
	9-7.5=	1.5	2.25
	8-7.5=	0.5	0.25
	8-7.5=	0.5	0.25
	7-7.5=	-0.5	0.25
	6-7.5=	-1.5	2.25
Total Units of Variation			35.00

You can practice your own computations to determine how much of this total variation (35.0) is explained by differences between colors ($\overline{Y}g$-M, and then square the difference) and how much cannot be explained because it's due to differences among individual scores within groups (Y-$\overline{Y}g$, and then square the difference).

I'll give you the answers: the units of variation explained by difference in color is 3.0. That is, of the 35.0 units of total variation, 32.0 cannot be explained by difference in color because they were due to differences *within* colors. Does that mean your results are not statistically significant—due merely to chance and not differences between colors? Stay tuned for the significance testing and find out.

THEORIES OF EPISTEMIC JUSTIFICATION: META-EPISTEMOLOGY

All epistemological inquiry, of course, focuses on the nature of knowledge, how we go about finding or creating it, how and where it exists in the first place, and what can even be known. Alston (1989), however, distinguished between epistemology and epistemic justification, asserting that there "is a distinction between what we may term *substantive epistemology* and *meta-epistemology*":

> Meta-epistemology is concerned with the basic concepts we employ in epistemology, concepts of *knowledge, truth, belief, justification, rationality,* and so on, and with the methods, procedures, and criteria to be employed in determining how to apply those concepts. Substantive epistemology, on the other hand, consists in our endeavors to use these concepts to arrive at results on such matters as the conditions under which we have knowledge or justified belief of one kind or another, and on what knowledge or justified belief we have. (1-2)

In other words, a meta-epistemology focuses on all of the parts that are at work in an operating epistemology and conducts analyses of how those parts work and definitions of the terms we need to discuss epistemology. Substantive epistemology puts those parts in motion (in practice, so to speak) and prepares us to share our beliefs and knowledge with others. Alston's book, *Epistemic Justification,* then, focused on meta-epistemology through an analysis of epistemic justification theories, a look at all "the parts" of our justification for beliefs or knowledge and how those parts work.[7]

Theories of epistemic justification, when properly understood, will aid a researcher's understanding of a research process grounded not so much in competing epistemologies, but in an epistemological dynamic that allows us to find the best available means of knowing at a given time, in a given place. Alston explored the nature of justification as both (and necessarily) objective and subjective. The notion of justification, especially epistemic justification, is, on the one hand, subjective and personal:

> What confers justification must be "internal" to the subject that she has a specially direct cognitive access to it. It must consist of something like a belief or an experience, something that the subject can typically spot just by turning her attention to the matter. (4-5)

At the same time, epistemic justification involves and seeks the objective, the external world we hope to justify, to know, or to believe:

> We typically turn our attention to justification and the like when we
> fall prey to doubts about the possibility of knowledge, about our capacity
> to get beyond our own thoughts and experiences to the real objective
> truth about the world outside our minds. . . . For nothing else would lend
> a belief some rational credibility when we are radically questioning our
> access to anything beyond our own consciousness. (5-6)

Alston warned against seeing only the "internal," personal view
here as the driving epistemic force in our inquiry. The interplay
between the subjective and objective—the interplay between our own
doubts, our own experience, and our world—moves us beyond an
"egocentric position" (6).

Our development as researchers who are able and willing to pursue the wide range of research questions we naturally encounter
requires a movement beyond an egocentric epistemological state.
Though our work is often personal, individualized, and based on
experience, the natural interplay of both quantitative and qualitative
is necessary for full epistemic justification of our beliefs. We composition scholars, then, could learn much from Annis's (1978)
"Contextualist Theory of Epistemic Justification."

Annis's theory focuses on three "parts" of epistemology in particular—three parts that, for composition scholars, will look remarkably
familiar. Our field has divided itself by competing epistemologies
(objectivist, subjectivist/expressivist, and transactional/social-con-
structivist), but these, for Annis, are not competing substantive epistemologies so much as they are the necessary "parts" that comprise
his theory of epistemic justification based on what Annis called an
"issue-context," as shown in Figure 4.2: 1) the belief sought to be jus-
tified, 2) an appropriate objector group, and 3) a believer's level of
understanding.

Annis's contextualist theory shifts our attention from specific substantive epistemology to a meta-epistemology by asking us to attend
more seriously to context and to examine more fully the "parts" that
exist in that context before we put them in motion. Instead of arguing, for example, that qualitative or quantitative research *methods* are
best, that one *kind* of research is natural or another unnatural, or that

Figure 4.2

Governing Gazes (Emig), Competing Theories of Rhetoric (Berlin), Competing Models for Writing Centers (Lunsford), and Current Research Models

	Positivist	*Transactional*	*Phenomenological*
Emig 1982	focus on phenomenon outside of context; quest for absolute truth	knower and known interact; mutual transformation	focus on personal reality in context; quest for multiple individual truths
	Objectivist	*Transactional*	*Expressionist*
Berlin 1987	relying on external, scientifically verifiable proof	relying on group dynamics and collaboration	relying on one's internal interpretation of the world
	Storehouse	*Collaborative*	*Garret*
Lunsford 1991	writing center features handbooks, drills, modules, handouts	writing center features dialogue; meaning is negotiated by the group	writing center features individual expression, inspiration
	Quantitative	*Social*	*Personal*
Research Models	relying on numerical data, controlled methods, and statistial analysis	relying on case study, observation and dialogue/interviews	relying on personal narrative, reflection on experience, anecdotes
Issue Context	Belief; issue under consideration; observations, proof, data, etc. that relate to the belief in question	Appropriate Objector Group; the culture or community in which beliefs are justified	Believer's Level of Understanding; personal conviction, experience of an individual

Necessary components for epistemic justification,
not competing elements of epistemology

all research must include student and researcher voices, a Contextualist Theory of Epistemic Justification draws us to an analysis of context: *what* do I want to know? *why* do I need to know it? *how* can I frame my question in a way it can be answered? and so on.

Such a framework offers a meta-epistemological reflection *before* the "parts" of the epistemology are put in motion through research—a reflection that might produce surprising answers for those who favor one kind of research method over another, and a reflection necessary for serious inquiry: Annis's theory rightly assumes, as we should assume in our field as well, that those who engage in inquiry through research are "critical truth seekers" (281), not merely defenders of their own preferences, ideologies, or writing styles.

The issue-context is contextually- and socially-driven, based on the *"actual* social practices and norms of justification of a culture or community of people" (282). Because composition studies has become a multidisciplinary endeavor, we have access to numerous cultures and communities, including the scientific. If, for example, I believe that using red ink on my students' papers will cause a negative feeling in my students (a believer's level of understanding), and if other writing teachers around me (an appropriate objector group) believe the same, we agree enough to accept the belief that red ink is "bad." However, if I remember that as a student, I never experienced a negative feeling toward red ink when my own teachers used it, I might begin to doubt the belief our group holds and construct a new belief of my own. I might strengthen that belief by using red ink on my students' papers and then informally asking them for their reactions to it. If the objector group, my colleagues, wish to maintain their belief and reject my new belief, I am now in a position to test or to experiment on my new belief in a way that will either support or refute the objector group. In a final report of this actual study (in chapter six), I will illustrate those rhetorical decisions about events, experience, and data—decisions guided by the context of both *process* and *product.*

The Contextualist Theory of Epistemic Justification is grounded in the assertion that all justification of beliefs is a social act. In a social act, we always have 1) individuals with their own individual experiences and beliefs, 2) other people around the individual who may object to or accept the individual's belief, and 3) issue-related facts, data, demonstrations, and observations that will help refute or confirm both the individual's belief and the group's beliefs. Because justification is a social act, the contexts in which it occurs will vary and, in contrast to how some composition scholars have defined a "social act," some contexts naturally include numerical data or the need to understand probability. Annis outlined an example of a drug being tested to see if it would cure a disease without causing harmful effects. If researchers are testing the drug's effect on animals, their concern for adequate proof will not be as high as it would be if they were testing the drug's effect on humans, so the researcher might require a more stringent significance level in statistically testing the outcome (282). Here, Annis showed the effect that context has on how we analyze data for statistical significance.

For our own test of statistical significance, we return to the units of variation explained by color difference (3.0) and the units of variation not explained by color difference (i.e., Variation due to individual differences in scores *within* color groups) (32.0). Getting the ratio of explained variation to unexplained variation is what we do when we get an F-ratio.

But first, we have to take into account the "size" of the two places where variation occurred. Variation *between* color groups occurred only between 2 colors. Variation *within* color groups occurred among 12 individual scores. It seems unfair, in a sense, to compare 2 things to 12, so we'll have to factor in the size of these comparisons through something we call *degrees of freedom*.

The easiest way to explain degrees of freedom is to play a game: If I tell you that a set of 6 scores must add up to 42, and then ask you to randomly start listing those 6 numbers as you wish, you will have 5 numbers that could be anything. Once those 5 are filled in, however, the 6th will have to be *the* number that makes all 6 add up to 42. Let's say you pick 4, 5, 6, 7, and 8 as your first five numbers. The 6th number must be 12 in order for all 6 to equal 42. In other words, that last number has *no degree of freedom* for you to choose what you want. What you had, however, was 5 degrees of freedom or N-1.

Since we only had two color groups, the degrees of freedom are easy to figure out. N-1 (where N is the number of groups) is 2-1, which is 1. For the 12 scores, however, each set of 6 was in its own group. The 6 red scores had to add up to 42, and the 6 purple scores had to add up to 48. That would leave you with 5 degrees of freedom for each group, or N-k, where N equals the number of scores, and k equals the number of groups (N-k = 12-2 = 10).

Before we get the ratio of between-group differences to within-group differences, then, we'll "even out" the size of those groups by dividing by their degrees of freedom:

$$\frac{3.0\,/1}{32.0\,/10}=\frac{3.0}{3.2} \quad F = .9375$$

In most statistics handbooks, we'll find an "F table," or a table of values where we can find our own F ratio by the degrees of freedom in both the numerator and the denominator in the above equation. An F table looks like a grid, listing degrees of freedom for the numerator (1, in our case) across the top, and degrees of freedom for the denominator (10, in our case) down the side. Like using a map, we find our degrees of freedom and use them like coordinates to look for the critical value required for our F ratio to be statistically significant.

But before we look up our own F value to determine its statistical significance, we have to decide at what level are we willing to accept some error? The F table will give us different critical values for an F ratio having 1 degree of freedom in the numerator and 10 in the denominator, based on levels of probability: Once out of a hundred (.01)? Five times out of a hundred (.05)? Only once in a thousand (.001)?

The standard level of acceptance for statistical significance (especially in the context of a study as harmless as ours) is five times out of a hundred or .05. If we find our F value to be significant at the .05 level, we can confidently say that the probability with which our results were due merely to chance is less than 5 times out of 100.

According to the ratios presented in the F table, if we have 1 degree of freedom in the numerator and 10 degrees of freedom in the denominator, our F value needs to be at least 4.96 to be significant at the .05 level. Our F value is .9375.

While the purple ball achieved the highest average in our study, you can at least argue that such a result could be due merely to chance. At the same time, however, we need to return to the null hypothesis here: there is no difference in scores bowled by different colors. At this point, we *fail to reject* the null hypothesis. This suggests, based on the data we collected and analyzed, that we have no reason to believe that one color is luckier than another.

A Contextualist Theory of Epistemic Justification reframes our current view of epistemology-in-competition and constructs instead an epistemological dynamic that emerges naturally from *the need to know,* from a question arising from a particular context that will, if we examine context fully, lead to the best research method(s) available for answering that question at that moment. If we view our research from this template rather than from one of competing epistemologies, we construct much more than a mere "gray area," a "happy medium" on which we might agree philosophically but continue our debates practically. In the past, others have attempted to achieve such agreement, but strong division among our researchers, dichotomous language that traps us into "camps," and a focus on *method* rather than context has kept us frozen and separate in the same attempts to bring us together.

THE POTENTIAL OF RE-CONTEXTUALIZING OUR EPISTEMOLOGICAL FRAMEWORK

North, in 1987, proposed methodological egalitarianism: the "I'm OK, you're OK" approach to methodological diversity in our field. Practitioners are OK, historians are OK, clinicians are OK. To draw an analogy, imagine an integrated neighborhood of mixed race, one in which no one really interacts. You do your thing, and I'll do mine, and as long as we don't cross boundaries, we can live happily in our neighborhood. In 1992, Kirsch called for methodological pluralism, a call for the children of this neighborhood to play together. After all, they can learn much from each other, share culture and language and values—if only we encourage them to try. But as long as the adults in this neighborhood make the public rules, provide the language, and teach the values, these children might not play together well, might not play together willingly, and might not play together for very long.

Contextualized epistemological pluralism asks that the adults in this neighborhood be willing to play together, too—finding common ground, understanding the wealth of knowledge we have when we put that whole puzzle together, recognizing the contexts in which we naturally share common goals, and changing language to reflect that new value. We must first understand that, though we appear to be different, it is that very difference that makes us *necessary to each other* when we desire to fully examine the contexts in which we work/play/learn—a difference that gives us something to offer each other. After all, if we were all the same, what could we possibly learn when we explore our questions?

A Contextualist Theory of Epistemic Justification forces us to focus not on numbers vs. narratives, but on the questions that motivate us to learn in the first place. A template such as this grounds us in the things we most value as scholars of rhetoric: context, questions, knowledge, and a mix of cultures—and the active quest they set in motion. Much as we teach our students to ask critical questions, to examine all possible points of view, and to find as many sources that help them get to the bottom of their own inquiry, a contextualist theory will help us do the same, will help us practice what we preach, and will ground us again in the rhetorical tradition that shaped the context for our field in the first place.

One final note before we leave the bowling alley (and, yes, we are now leaving). This should not be the only study on which you base firm conclusions. Surely, the results of this study are worth sharing and thinking about, but don't forget the context in which this was done: at only one bowling alley, for only one bowler, with only three colors, and with only 6 trials per ball. The fascinating thing about experiments like this is their sensitivity to context: what will happen when we play with *that*?

And a personal note: *I hate bowling!* I am far from being a bowler or a bowling fan, but I know a good research question when I see one; my feelings about bowling don't keep me from asking those questions. I hope the same is true for anyone doing research in our field, as well.

EPISTEMIC JUSTIFICATION AS RHETORIC: DECISION-MAKING IN CONTEXT

Though Annis never framed his theory as Aristotelian in nature, he could have easily done so (and, perhaps, he should have). For composition scholars, Annis's theory is composed of elements in a rhetorical dynamic similar to what we have come to call the communications triangle, a dynamic inherent in Aristotelian rhetoric.[8] Scholars such as Booth (1963) and Kinneavy (1971) have examined the three-part rhetorical foundation that most of us teach our students in some fashion. How many of us encourage students to examine 1) their persona as a writer in relation to 2) their subject/issue and available information/data related to their subject and 3) their intended audience, all in the rich context of having a purpose or of having a question to explore? How often do our textbooks and our classrooms explore 1) the ethical appeal, 2) the emotional appeal, and 3) the logical appeal, each corresponding to those familiar elements: the writer, the audience, the subject, supported by adequate facts/data/information?

We discourage students' use of purely emotional appeals, calling on them to ground that appeal in solid examples, data, statistics, facts. Aristotle argued, "it is wrong to warp the jury by leading them into anger or envy or pity: that is the same as if someone made a straight-edge rule crooked before using it" ([1354a], p. 30). Our own scholarship, however, has been guilty of the opposite: we have fallen into an odd, imbalanced rhetorical stance that comes from the stories we tell, stories that appeal heavily to audience emotions but stories that are also uniquely personal to the writer, to which an audience may or may not relate.[9] Annis's exploration of the three-part theory of epistemic justification is remarkably similar to Booth's (1963) exploration of why we teach those three parts of rhetoric—together—not to exploit only one or two parts of this human system, but to achieve a natural balance as dictated by context: "the habit of seeking this balance is not the only thing we have to teach under the heading of rhetoric. But I think that everything worth teaching under that heading finds its justification finally in that balance" (145).

A Contextualist Theory of Epistemic Justification not only retrains us to seek that same balance in our research, but also grounds us again in a rhetorical tradition in which such a balance was not only sought, but also was the honest thing to do—an honesty and code of ethics explored not only by Aristotle, but by others who followed him, rhetoricians such as Cicero, Quintilian, and St. Augustine, as well as a few scholars of our own time. To balance our justification of knowledge in composition research, we must understand where and how the rhetorical issues and the research issues in which we conduct our inquiry intersect.

A CONTEXTUALIST RESEARCH PARADIGM

In an effort, then, to bypass the dispute between numbers and narratives, we must return to the notion of context and revise our view of divided epistemologies. Numbers as well as narratives naturally occur in most contexts. A Contextualist Theory of Epistemic Justification is a useful template on which to base a new inclusive paradigm, helping us to decide on research methods for a particular project based not on politics or on personal preferences, but on the contexts in which our research questions arise.

Numerous forces shape our research questions and decisions. Those decisions are guided by the contexts in which we work, contexts in which must ask several questions and solve several problems—about method, form, ourselves, our audience, and our evidence. Figure 4.3 presents a Contextualist Research Paradigm for Rhetoric and Composition—a matrix that shows the intersection of the rhetorical issues and the research issues that form varied research contexts. Our use of this matrix should be guided by three simple principles.

1. There are no predetermined answers for any of the questions in the matrix. Researchers must answer these questions in the specific contexts of their own research.

2. Each cell in the matrix, though focused on a particular kind of question, cannot be explored without the others. In other words, no question in any cell can be asked and answered without all of the others

Figure 4.3

A Contextualist Research Paradigm for Rhetoric and Composition

Rhetorical Issues

	The Social: Audience	The Personal: Researcher	The Factual: Evidence
Question / Issue	What types of readers or listeners will value this study (students, teachers, tutors, the field, my department, myself, funding sources, administrators, etc.), and how do I prioritize those potential readers?	What intuition, observations, or experience have driven me to ask this question? What do I hope to learn? Why am I curious? Do any ethical concerns bother me?	How should I word my question such that I can answer it with the resources available to me? What is the most accurate portrayal of my task? Does my question have ethical problems?
Purpose	Whom will my research benefit? How will my research benefit them?	Where would I ""fit"" in the available literature? When I read related literature, with what points do I disagree? Agree?	What evidence will most fully help me answer this question? What types of data should I explore?
Method(s)	How does my audience usually discuss this question? What methods, if any, could I borrow from others? Do scholars in my field call for new methods to be applied to this question?	Do I have resources, access, and expertise necessary to accurately and ethically explore this question? What are my strengths and weaknesses in this project? How is my research question different?	What methods and/or literature will help me find and evaluate the data I am seeking? Which data are readily available? What instruments will I need to borrow/construct?
Publication	What is the best form and language for presenting my research, given the audience I envision?	How do I want to be perceived as a researcher in the final presentation? What voice would best enhance what I'm trying to say?	How do I articulate my evidence accurately, persuasively and ethically? What conclusions can I ethically draw?

(Left margin label: Research Issues)

being asked and answered as well. Such is the relationship of evidence, method, form, writers, and audience—dependent on each other.

3. The questions presented in the matrix do not have to be asked in any particular order, as all research could potentially have any starting point, depending on individual contexts.

The questions I've placed in each cell of the matrix are general enough to be asked by any researcher. Specific answers and further questions must be provided in context and will, of course, vary. Each question, however, ties the researcher specifically to the context of the initial research question being asked in the specific context from which the question emerged. Such a matrix, then, keeps us focused on the issue at hand, rather than letting us become embroiled in arguments about competing epistemologies, political defenses of research methods, and an avoidance of quantitative measures that do enhance the knowledge of our field.

In Alston's words, a matrix such as this helps us move beyond our own consciousness, embracing the interplay of the subjective and objective—an interplay necessary for discovery, for constructing our identities, and for sharing our discoveries. Such a matrix helps us break free of our current anxieties and debates about different research methods so that we are better able to conduct more of the research we—and our students—need, research that will explore what we feel is the truth and what we do or do not believe. Aristotle reminded us, "things related to truth [are greater] than things related to opinion" ([1365a], p. 74).

In this matrix, we see rhetoric and dialectic unfold in Aristotelian terms. In his translation of Aristotle's *Rhetoric*, Kennedy (1991) retained the original Greek *antistrophos* in the first sentence: "Rhetoric is an *antistrophos* to dialectic. . . . All people in some way, share in both; for all, to some extent, try both to test and maintain an argument [as in dialectic] and to defend themselves and attack [others, as in rhetoric]" ([1354a], pp. 28-29). While current interpretations of *antistrophos* vary (see Green, 1990), the interplay of rhetoric and dialectic was, for Aristotle, determined by context: "Let rhetoric be [defined as] an ability, in each [particular] case, to see the available means of persuasion" ([1355a], p. 36). The pursuit of any research question, then, is based on the dynamic interplay between rhetoric and dialectic and guided by an understanding of contextualist principles.

Phelps (1988), too, applied "contextualist principles" (219) in her own quest to reconstruct "composition as a 'discipline,' a human science" (205). Phelps drew heavily from varied theories in an effort to illustrate the potential of drawing together the eclectic epistemic foundations of our field. For instance, Phelps explored the role science plays when testing our experience but also discussed science-as-background that we fold into our experience. While I agree with much of Phelps's exploration—and certainly admire her goals—her own context seems unclear, because the text is purely theoretical.

Though Phelps addressed briefly the notion that teachers often object to theory (207), her text doesn't address that objection directly through concrete examples–an important task in light of her argument that teaching/praxis should be a central issue in our field. Indeed, Phelps's text is far removed from the contexts of our day-to-day teaching and inquiry. Phelps acknowledged that she gave limited attention to "the fact that students are themselves human subjects in the classroom and the further complication that they are themselves *learning to reflect* via written language" an element seemingly crucial to her argument. One might argue that Phelps's reconstruction of composition as a human science—teaching, praxis, integrating varied forms of knowledge with our practice—cannot succeed outside of the context of what we most wish to research: our teaching and our students' learning.

In contrast, a Contextualist Research Paradigm that focuses on questions (rather than just theory) and that demonstrates *how* eclectic forms of knowledge could work together in varied contexts (rather than just theorizing that they *could*) is able actually to release the power of the research process and the actions of the researcher within the specific contexts that produce them.

APPLYING A CONTEXTUALIST RESEARCH PARADIGM

A Contextualist Research Paradigm allows us to see not only the process of our research, but also the products of that research differently. A new lens such as this will enable us to see more clearly the bridges that already exist in the qualitative/quantitative dichotomy. Quite naturally, narratives and numbers often coexist in some fashion in most research contexts. If we truly embrace a wide array of research methods, we will see especially the narrative undercurrent of traditional-looking studies and begin to understand better why researchers make the decisions they do, guided by their understanding of the intersecting rhetorical and research issues present in the context of their work.

To illustrate the matrix at work, chapter five will re-present Eileen Oliver's (1995) study published in *RTE*, "The Writing Quality of Seventh, Ninth, and Eleventh Graders, and College Freshmen: Does Rhetorical Specification in Writing Prompts Make a Difference?" Inserted throughout the reprint of Oliver's study are sections of an online interview in which Oliver articulated the story behind her study and her reasons for choosing her methods—a description of decisions made in the context of her desire to answer a research question and to share her discovery. To the traditionally trained eye, such a description will not be a surprise. To those trained only in narrative methods, however, I hope the presentation of these two texts together begins to show how a traditional study can also reflect a "thick description" and—as the matrix illustrates—a natural product of the research and rhetorical processes at work in a scholarly context.

NOTES

1. Consider, for example, Enos's (1996) *Faculty Lives and Gender Roles in Composition*. Enos outlined carefully how she gathered her demographic data—where the numbers came from, how she gathered them, and what they might mean. In other words, she carefully articulated the context from which those numbers emerged. In contrast, not all of Enos's narratives were so carefully presented. While most stories clearly revealed moments of discrimination, several stories are vague and hard to understand—were out of context—partly because Enos kept the storytellers and their institutions anonymous. Enos, in her introduction, remember, argued that narratives more than numbers tell us who we are (and are more "true"). However, because her numbers are more consistently contextualized, we might find them more "true" than the narratives sometimes taken out of context.

2. The notion of "partial truths" in narrative was articulated by Clifford (1986) in *Writing Culture: The Poetics and Politics of Ethnography*. Clifford argued that ethnographies are fictions in "the ways they are systematic and exclusive. Ethnographic writings

can properly be called fictions in the sense of 'something made or fashioned.' . . . Interpretive social scientists have recently come to view good ethnographies as 'true fictions.' . . . Ethnographic truths are thus inherently *partial*" (6-7). Clifford introduced the essays in *Writing Culture* by emphasizing their attention to the creation of form. Something is always excluded from our stories because "one cannot tell all" (7).

3.   In *A Mathematician Reads the Newspaper*, Paulos (1995) outlined numerous contexts in which the average American pays attention to mathematics, including policy-making in the courts, fat grams in food items, personal finance, presidential polls, and health reports. In other contexts of our lives, in other words, we make numbers important.

4.   In a review of five books on science, Selzer (1998) noted that only one of the five, Toumey's *Conjuring Science* (1996), "renders science as a benign, trustworthy, liberal, liberating, and admirably self-regulating enterprise that deserves public support" (450). In contrast to the other four books reviewed, "Toumey takes as his given that science is a part of culture, and as such is both a product and producer of it . . . that science is indeed open to humanist scrutiny" (450). Selzer's complaint about two other books under review, Taylor's *Defining Science* (1996) and Gates and Shteir's *Natural Eloquence* (1997), revealed our misguided expectations of scientific inquiry and our attention to form: "there is too little textual analysis to satisfy someone like me who understands English studies primarily as the investigation of written discourse" (Selzer, 1998, p. 450).

5.   Emig called the scientific method 'mistakenly named' (66). Other scholars have similarly doubted the phrase as well: Shapin (1996), Phelps (1988), Ray (1992), to name a few.

6.   Bushman (1998) articulated a "Social-Expressivist" writing center based in part on Lunsford's (1991) three-part division for writing centers. Though Bushman also cited criticism for such divisions, such as Hobson's (1992) examination of epistemological debates in varied writing center contexts, he defined his terms, as Lunsford and Berlin did, with three ways of knowing—the transactional, expressivist, and objectivist. Like Gradin (1995) and O'Donnell

(1996), Bushman attempted to join only two: the transactional and expressivist.

7. Alston noted that many theories of epistemic justification are not a unified set of theoretical explorations. Indeed, Alston pointed to some epistemic theories' potential for justifying beliefs even in the face of that belief being clearly incorrect and to some epistemic theories that do not allow for intuition or experience on the part of the knower (3). This, of course, poses a problem for theories of epistemic justification generally, but Alston's warning here is one of common sense or, perhaps, what happens when common sense is lacking.

8. See especially, *On Rhetoric,* (1356a): "Of the *pisteis* provided through speech there are three species: for some are in the character [*éthos*] of the speaker, and some in disposing the listener in some way, and some in the argument [*logos*] itself, by showing or seeming to show something."

9. In spite of the popularity of personal stories and anecdotes in our research, we must examine those times when stories fail to communicate. While I was finishing the first draft of this project, for example, I had numerous conversations with a friend of mine (who has given me permission to relate this), a woman approximately my age who had just started the doctoral program I was then finishing. For reasons I cannot fully understand, she had felt an overall sense of powerlessness in her coursework. She had shared stories with me, trying to give me examples of the lack of power she felt. In turn, I had given her stories in which I tried to share numerous (and similar) times when I have not felt powerless in the same program. Eventually, however, she gained a new sense of power—not through stories, but through reading theories of critical pedagogy. When I asked her why my stories didn't help her (and why abstract theory *did* help her), her conclusion was simply that "You're not me, and I'm not you." My stories and hers, though they *appeared* to be contextually similar, were, in fact, different—because they were so personal and could not cross boundaries that two individuals would naturally have.

Briggs (1998) outlined a similar use of narrative—as a writing center director/tutor, Briggs shared a past tale of her own frustration with academic norms (an M.A. thesis) in order to help a freshman confront her own frustration in a freshman composition class. Briggs explored why this "narrative as response" worked here, and I have also made such storytelling work with my own students, both in a writing center and in a classroom. But I have more stories that did *not* work with my students, and in their own words, "But you're the *teacher*, I'm a student!" or "You're an *English* major!" or, more simply, "Yeah, right, like you can compare your writing to mine!" As much as I might see those connections and try to make my students see them, too, their unwillingness to find what we have in common makes the storytelling fail *because* the stories are personal and, therefore, different.

5 A CONTEXTUALIST RESEARCH PARADIGM
An Illustration

My sense is that many put quantitative work down because
they don't know how to do it. Again, it's certainly not the
end all, and I very much believe in and *do* more qualitative
"stuff" these days. But hard data can be very useful coupled
with other means of analysis.

Eileen Oliver (interview)

My M.A. thesis was a cross-cultural learning styles study in which I
tested the applicability of field dependence-independence measures
as a means of assessing cognitive style among minority groups. I fin-
ished the project in the summer of 1993. Traditional in format, my
thesis reviewed the literature from researchers who have asserted that
African-Americans, for example, have a holistic, field-dependent (in
contrast to an analytical, field-independent) learning style based on
instruments and theories developed by Herman Witkin in the 1940s
and 50s. I, too, gave one of those instruments but introduced at the
same time a new instrument that had not yet been used in cross-
cultural studies: the Kolb Learning Style Inventory (LSI). Groups in
my study showed a statistically significant difference on the old
instrument that measures field dependence-independence (FDI) but
no differences on the Kolb LSI, illustrating differences between the
instruments and their cultural assumptions. I also incorporated
interviews in which students upheld the findings of the Kolb LSI and
refuted the findings of the older FDI measures.

While writing my thesis, I enrolled in a graduate seminar (Spring
1993) called "Cross-Cultural Studies and Composition" in which we
focused on ethnography, especially through Clifford and Marcus,
Writing Culture: The Poetics and Politics of Ethnography (1986). I was

hoping the course would provide some insight on my thesis and on my thinking about cross-cultural issues generally, and it did. But the course also produced some tension: our class discussions often focused on the power of ethnography over more rigid, controlled scientific experiments as a means of revealing or constructing culture. Traditional research was limited, we decided, but there I was: neck-deep in my M.A. thesis in which I was doing "traditional" research. Out of frustration, wrestling with my thesis, and partly out of guilt, I asked my professor if I could write the "flip-side" of my thesis for my seminar paper instead of exploring a whole new project. He thought the idea was fascinating, and I thought I'd have a chance to "remedy" the ills of the rigid tradition appearing in my M.A. thesis, thus redeeming myself by studying culture in the way our class decided was best: through narrative.

For my seminar project, then, I wrote the story about how my thesis was constructed: how I came upon the idea, how I designed the study, the problems I encountered with subjects, the difficulties of statistical analysis—but I drew the same conclusions. The project earned an A for that course, and my thesis was completed a few months later, but my curiosity about what had just happened never diminished. On the one hand, I felt I had creatively constructed two versions of the same study—one centered on "context" and one centered on "science"—two worlds that many composition scholars see as fundamentally opposed to one another. On the other hand, both studies described the same conclusions, but without the quantitative measures in the first study, I could not have written the second text, the narrative.

The two texts, in other words, could not have been written in the reverse: if I had done a purely qualitative study for my M.A. thesis, of course, I could not have recreated a second text that would somehow rely on numerical data I had never gathered. The fact that two texts written by the same researcher ended up being very different was, in part, a matter of a choice in presentation (a matter of understanding a genre and an audience), not a matter of "context-stripping" vs. "context-building." More importantly, it was a matter of understanding the full context of the research project and the research questions being explored. That I was able to write a second text describing my thesis in a different way suggested the rich, multiple, and diverse layers of texts that exist in traditional research that relies on numerical data: the "narrative flip-side" that could reveal the context for my thesis was "there" all along. Any well-trained researcher could construct the same text, and any well-trained reader of traditional research could, too.

For example, one sentence that often appears in traditional research interested me in particular: that sentence in which researchers articulate how many subjects participated in the study and how those subjects were recruited. I, too, had such sentences, a few short ones, in my M.A. thesis, in which I stated concisely the number of students in my study and how they volunteered. But in my seminar project for the course on cross-cultural studies, I rambled for more than two pages, explaining how hard it was to get volunteers, that some students who had signed up didn't show up, and of those who showed up, some didn't follow directions, so their tests had to be thrown out.

While it felt good to get all of that "off my chest," I always wondered if it was necessary. After all, don't all researchers face similar problems? Certainly, specific problems with subjects are unique to each research project, but the general notion *that* researchers will likely encounter problems is commonly understood. After all, how did I know to give advice to a classmate when she started her dissertation, hoping to have eight case studies: Aim for more than eight, I said. If some don't show up, don't cooperate, or change their minds, you might end up with eight after all. Researchers know. And I think that's why I never showed my thesis advisor the narrative of my study as the seminar professor (praising its creativity) suggested. Trained in research, my advisor would know, too.

UNDERSTANDING CONTEXTS FOR QUANTITATIVE RESEARCH: AN ILLUSTRATION

How could we *all* be trained to become better readers of research that relies on numerical data or experimental designs, readers who would see and appreciate the context of the study in spite of the numbers? If we asked other researchers who have done such studies to tell the stories behind their research, could they? Could narratives *about* their research assist our understanding of that research so that we can become better producers and consumers of all studies, fully understanding the researchers' decisions in the contexts of their research questions?

To find another study that would help me illustrate how the story behind traditional-looking research can be reconstructed, I searched for authors in the journal most criticized for publishing that kind of research: *Research in the Teaching of English.* Searching issues from two years[1] (Spring 1995-Spring 1997), I chose Eileen Oliver's "The Writing Quality of Seventh, Ninth, and Eleventh Graders, and College Freshmen: Does Rhetorical Specification in Writing Prompts Make a Difference?" (December 1995).

Below is a reprint of that study[2], and inserted throughout the reprint, is Dr. Oliver's commentary on the study—transcribed from my interview of her via email[3]—and, in italics, my own commentary on Dr. Oliver's interview as I see it relating to her published study and to the Contextualist Research Paradigm. Throughout the interview, Dr. Oliver explained the process of her research, the instinct that often guided the study, and her feelings about the project in general: in short, she revealed how the intersections of rhetorical issues and research issues formed the context in which she made her decisions and explored her research questions—a rich, dynamic context in which processes naturally resulted in a "quantitative" product.

The Writing Quality of Seventh, Ninth, and Eleventh Graders, and College Freshmen: Does Rhetorical Specification in Writing Prompts Make a Difference?

Eileen I. Oliver
Washington State University

This study analyzes the influence of rhetorical specification in writing prompts on the writing quality of seventh-, ninth-, and eleventh-grade students, and college freshmen.

Manipulating three composing variables—topic, purpose, and audience—eight assignments were created and administered to college preparatory and college students at four age levels. Trained raters scored 624 essays holistically on a six-point scale. The main and interactive effects of topic, purpose, and audience on writing quality were analyzed using a three-way analysis of variance for all grades together and for each grade separately. Results indicate that students utilized different kinds of rhetorical information at different stages. That is, while seventh graders tended to respond to simpler topic specifications, ninth graders reacted strongly to more elaborated topics. Eleventh graders more frequently utilized rhetorical specification, while college writers less frequently relied on it. Results suggest that specific rhetorical information may be important to students at certain ages for pedagogical reasons as well as for assessment.

As the use of large-scale writing assessments has increased over the last decade (Engelhard, Gordon, & Gabrielson, 1992), researchers have likewise increased their attention to the influence of the assignment on writing quality (Black, 1989; Hoetker & Brossell, 1986, 1989; Huot, 1990; Rafoth, 1989; Redd-Boyd & Slater, 1989; Witte, 1992). Most researchers agree that poorly constructed prompts interfere with writers' rhetorical choices, thereby confounding the problem of fair assessment (Keech, 1982; Murphy & Ruth, 1993; Ruth & Murphy, 1984). But what makes a good assignment? How does an assignment affect a writer's ability to produce good prose in a particular writing episode? And, if rhetorical specification does affect writing quality, when do we implement various specifics in our instruction?

This study explores the effects of assignment variables in order to determine the kind of writing tasks that help students achieve at their highest levels. Further, this study examines these effects for various age groups so that its findings may help us determine the appropriate rhetorical balance for different age groups.

When I asked Eileen Oliver why she chose to conduct such a traditional study relying on numerical data and statistical analysis when qualitative studies are currently more popular, her answer was mixed—partly historical, partly practical, but entirely reasonable. Oliver observed similar research questions and methods being explored by other scholars and colleagues around her, determined a purpose for her own study, and based some of her decisions on her experience and intuition. Here, Oliver answers questions in at least three cells in the Contextualist Research Paradigm Matrix (Researcher x Purpose, Researcher x Question, and Audience x Method).

> *Oliver:* When I collected this data (years ago), qualitative work was just coming in to its own. At the time, the psychometricians were in vogue. This data was collected for my dissertation which I published on only using sample data. The co-chair of my committee (Steve Witte) and many others were doing a lot of quantitative stuff with revision and assessment research so everyone thought this was great. Actually, looking at the results, I did, too.
>
> Years later, when I got a bigger grant and could afford to have the entire data set evaluated, I did. And the findings were pretty significant (at least I and the editor of *RTE* thought so). So what the heck. I submitted the results to *RTE* and they accepted it. Thus, we have a quantitative study reported in the literature a little behind the times. However, I'm glad I did it when I did it. A qualitative treatment would have been much easier, especially with my experience and access to students. What this quantitative study did for me was validate what I thought I already knew about students, writing development, and instruction.
>
> I should also say that this quantitative study was based on my tacit understanding of composition pedagogy grounded in at least fifteen years of experience as a writing teacher at several levels. So you might say that I already had a lot of qualitative information and used this quantitative approach for balance.

THEORETICAL FRAMEWORK

Rhetoricians have long recognized the importance of developing proficiency with discourse forms. For example, Quintilian, the ancient practitioner and teacher of oratory, outlined various types of orations for his students to master (Matsen, Rollinson, & Sousa, 1990). Aside from the requisite good character, "exceptional gifts of speech," and other qualities, Quintilian identified certain conventions of arrangement and style that must be followed by the narrator. He developed graded compositions as little exercises to prepare students to be adept users of language (Murphy, 1990). These *progymnasmata* were then used to perfect rhetorical technique by others. Such strategies later became the model in the Byzantine East and in schools in Western Europe (Matsen, Rollinson, &Sousa, 1990).

Oliver explained the intuitive drive of this study when she outlined more of her experience as a teacher. Notice that the following passage is based entirely on experience and is composed of general "truths" Oliver believes exist in different age groups. It is through this lens/context of experience that she 1) read the related literature, 2) designed her study, and 3) interpreted her results. Here, Oliver answers questions in at least four cells in the Contextualist Research Paradigm Matrix: Researcher x Question, Audience x Purpose, Evidence x Methods, and Researcher x Methods.

> *Oliver:* I have taught ninth and eleventh graders and college freshmen. (No seventh grade.) I therefore have a pretty good idea of what these age levels are capable of. To go into some of the more sophisticated stylistic issues one does with freshmen (if you can call that sophisticated) is simply over the heads of younger students who, albeit very bright, are not developmentally ready to take in certain information. . . . the seventh graders are barely able to generate enough prose (e.g., telling a seventh grader to "vary sentence structure" is less obvious or useful than [telling] a college student).
>
> Revision is another issue. A revision strategy must be very different for 9th graders than for college students in terms of motivation, attention level, and so forth.

Today writing is often judged by one's ability to respond to any number of discourse tasks, and teachers of composition try to attend to the development of many different skills. Yet, as

the 1992 National Assessment of Education Progress (NAEP)
Writing Report Card indicates, student's writing quality is not
consistent over different discourse aims. Thus,

> by grade 12, the majority of students have some under-
> standing of informative and narrative writing, but continue
> to have considerable difficulty with persuasive writing.
> (Applebee, Langer, Mullis, Latham, &Gentile, 1994, p. 3)

Whether or not students have received instruction in
composing, the quality of their writing is affected by the kinds
and amounts of rhetorical specification they are given in their
prompts.

Most studies indicate that assignment effects do exist, but in
what ways and to what extent remain to be learned. As several
studies suggest, determining the influence of prompts on
writing quality is extremely complex, (Greenberg, 1982;
Hoetker, 1982; Huot, 1990; Keech, 1982; Mellon, 1976; 1981;
Witte, 1992; Witte & Faigley). Yet it is important to do so
because

> if assignments are composed carefully so as to assist
> students . . . then their writing should be . . . much easier to
> evaluate. (Farrell, 1976, p. 224)

According to Huot (1990), the research on rhetorical
specification has been "inconclusive" in establishing a
relationship between the prompt and writing quality.
Nevertheless, some studies suggest the importance of
structure. For example, Smith and his colleagues (1985, cited in
Huot, 1990) found that advanced writers did significantly better
than average and basic writers when writing on open-ended
topics. And Hoetker (1982) suggests that well-structured
assignments may be more important for students who are
"unable to intuit the unvoiced assumptions of the topic or to fill
in the gaps as expertly and accurately as the accomplished
student can" (p. 387).

Good writers can handle the demands of the rhetorical situation. However, writers who do not clearly understand the rhetorical question, or see only part of it within the assignment, often cannot solve the rhetorical problem. In an attempt to understand the nature of rhetorical choices in good and poor writers, Flower and Hayes (1981) developed a cognitive process theory of writing in which the "task environment" represented one of three major elements. Defined as "all . . . things outside the writer's skin," the task environment begins with the rhetorical problem or assignment which includes topic, audience, and "exigency" (goals, purpose). We will examine these in more detail.

Though Oliver presented a traditional literature review here, her interview illustrates that her experience "brought" her to the literature in a certain frame of mind, shaping how she interpreted that literature and, later, added to it via this study. The available literature played a large role in Oliver's decisions. Below, Oliver answers questions from five cells in the Contextualist Research Paradigm Matrix: Researcher x Purpose, Audience x Purpose, Audience x Methods, Evidence x Methods, and Audience x Publication.

Oliver: At the time I conducted this study, there were many discussions regarding both writing prompts and assessment (still are). I agreed with a lot of the literature that talked about how discourse purpose affected student response. I also agreed with many who criticized the variety of discourse topics that were used to assess student writing ability. For example, a national assessment might use a narrative prompt one year, a persuasive prompt the next. The results which were used to evaluate student writing ability were disparate because the instrument (writing prompt) was unreliable.

Further, most of the literature targeted small age and ability groups. There were very few which looked at writers at several levels (albeit expert/novice studies are fairly common). Having had experience with ninth- and eleventh-grade students as well as college freshmen, I believed that a developmental component existed that few had addressed. I therefore decided to combine writing prompt variables with age variables with the intention of looking at how particular elements in a writing prompt would influence writers at several levels.

Purpose

Researchers have long believed that different purposes elicit different levels of writing quality and different syntactic features (Moffett, 1968; Odell, 1981; Prater & Padia, 1983). Purpose affects the relationship between speaker and audience (Herrington, 1979). It can also influence syntax (Maimon & Nodine, 1978). Although subsequent studies have questioned the relationship between writing quality and syntactic maturity (Huot, 1990), several earlier findings show that language patterns are, at least, significantly different when students, especially young writers, write with different aims (Bortz, 1962). San Jose (1972) reported highly significant syntactic differences among rhetorical purposes for fourth-grade writing, citing persuasive pieces as the "most mature." Perron (1977) found longer T-units in persuasive pieces than in essays exemplifying other discourse aims. Rosen (1969) identified longer T-units and modifications in referential writing than in expressive discourse. In an attempt to determine the effect of audience specification and mode of discourse on the syntactic complexity of sixth- and tenth-grade writers, Crowhurst and Piche (1979) found "clear and unequivocal" evidence that "mode was significant at both grade levels" (P. 107). They recommended argument assignments (as opposed to narratives) as especially applicable for measuring the development of syntactic skills.

Topic

Looking at the effects of the information given in the assignment topic, Braddock, Lloyd-Jones, and Schoer (1963) recognized more than thirty years ago that the degree of topic abstraction helps determine the caliber of students' writing. However, the small corpus of research on topic choice that does exist has been inconclusive. Interpreting reports of "no effects" from such studies, Hoetker (1982) called them failures by the investigators to utilize methods of analysis sensitive enough to determine statistical and meaningful differences.

In one study to determine effects of information load, Brossell (1983) constructed six topics, each with three levels of "information load:" low, moderate, high. Essays resulting from "high-information-load" topics were much shorter, earned the lowest scores, and proved to be the most difficult for students to begin. Essays produced from "moderate-information load" topics were immediately limited and focused, and received the highest holistic scores. Brossell's research suggested that too much or too little information weakens writing quality. While positing that information load is more important than the topic itself in producing written discourse, Brossell concluded that full rhetorical specification may hinder rather than help the writer in an examination setting and that wording can also affect writing quality. However, Brossell overlooked the actual administration of such assignments and neglected analysis from a writer's point of view. The following examples of Brossell's topics reveal a tremendous difference among the three levels:

Level One
Violence in the schools.

Level Two
According to recent reports in the news media, there has been a marked increase in incidents of violence in public schools. Why, in your view, does such violence occur?

Level Three
You are a member of a local school council made up of teachers and citizens. A recent increase in incidents of vio-lence in the schools has gotten widespread coverage in the local news media. As a teacher, you are aware of the prob-lem, though you have not been personally involved in an incident. At its next meeting, the council elects to take some action. It asks each member to draft a statement setting forth

his or her views on why such violence occurs. The statements will be published in the local newspaper. Write a
statement expressing your own personal views on the
causes of violence in the schools. (pp. 166-167)

Most experienced composition instructors would predict that
students writing in response to Level One would have difficulty
because of the scarcity of information, while those tackling
Level Three would suffer from the length and extent of
instructions, and from the remoteness of the audience (i.e., a
local school council). Thus, Brossell created prompts that as
instruments for his research would seem to have affected his
ability to address the question he proposes to answer. As
Keech (1982) stated:

> the more text testers add to the writing assignment, the
> less guarantee they have that students will read and cor-
> rectly interpret all of the guide lines . . . in the extreme cases,
> students may either ignore a lengthy set of instructions, or
> may become so embroiled in working out exactly what the
> tester wants that they are distracted from their central task of
> trying to generate meaningful, coherent text. (p. 7)

Discussing "thoroughness" of rhetorical specification for
large-scale assessments, Hoetker and Brossell (1986; 1989)
argued for the "frame topic" as the most "content fair" prompt.
Using "a noun phrase consisting of a class name and two qual-
ifying attributes," Hoetker and Brossell claimed that the frame
topic has several advantages: It allows students to control their
topics by "limiting the subject and finding a thesis;" it gives test
makers an enormous latitude in creating prompts; and it
provides raters with a larger variety of subjects and
approaches to read. Such topics look like these: "A character in
a book, film, or TV series who is a good role model for young
people. A book written since 1900 that has had important
effects on society" (p.414).

The researchers concluded that the frame topic-with little
rhetorical specification-does not adversely affect poorer writers,

and thus is an effective writing prompt for large-scale assessments.

Writing topics may also affect students in ways which are often difficult to predict or control. For example, ethnic or racial background may influence the writer's perspective regarding the writing task. However, how writing assessments affect specific groups is not at all clear. For example, White (1985; 1994) found that writing scores for certain ethnic groups were higher using essays than those they received using indirect measures. He thus encouraged the use of essays for all students. On the other hand, Breland and Griswold (1981) found that some members of ethnic minorities "tended to write less well" than an independent measure would predict in a comparison between indirect measures and essays (p. 21). These conflicting findings underscore the need for more investigation of what might be the fairest measures to use for all students.

Audience

Much of the research on audience is also inconclusive. Indeed, even its definition is problematic. Do we mean imagined audience? Real audience? Implied audience? Absence of audience? Some studies show significant audience effects relating to the degree of intimacy the writer had with the audience. Crowhurst and Fiche (1979) found that designated audience affected sixth and tenth graders whose writing was more "syntactically complex" when they addressed teachers than when they addressed friends. Similarly, fifth, eighth and twelfth graders, and expert adult writers composed longer clauses the lower their intimacy with their audience, and more subordinations the higher their intimacy with their audience (Rubin & Fiche, 1979). In another study, the degree of intimacy between writers and their audiences altered the syntactic complexity with which they wrote (Fiche, Michlin, Johnson, & Rubin, 1975).

Two other studies show effects relating to the status of the audience. In examining the effect of audience on language functions (controlling, relational, informing and interpreting, the-orizing and projecting) in sixth and eleventh graders writing to two audiences, Craig (1988) found that essays written for "high-status" readers (teachers) were more "objective and impersonal" than were papers intended for best friends. Analyzing the awareness of audience by fifth graders, Frank (1992) examined their success with transactional writing tasks revised for two audiences-third graders and adults. Though writers successfully communicated to both audiences, they did a better job for their younger readers. Frank identified the importance of "the realistic quality of a transactional writing task" as opposed to the "hypothetical . . . 'pseudo-informative' or 'inauthentic' task' " (pp. 286, 278).

Other studies show the effects of specificity. Investigating the effects of two versions of a writing prompt, Leu, Keech, Murphy, and Kinzer (1982) found no significant difference in the performances of tenth-, eleventh-, and twelfth-grade students. They did find that prompts with specified audience produced 20 alternate mode papers (e.g., letters, journal entries), while those writing with unspecified audience produced only 7 alternate mode papers. Students in this study also reported that they spent more time on prompt versions with the less specified audience.

Analyzing the quality of college-level persuasive writing, Black (1989) reported that writers of "varying abilities may ben-efit from having pertinent information about their audience . . ." (p. 248). Rafoth (1989), in evaluating college freshman writing, agreed with Elbow (1987), noting that attention to audience occurs more in the revision stages of drafting than in the begin-ning writing stage. Roen and Willey (1988), investigating audience awareness in drafting and revising of college freshmen, concluded much the same. Although Redd-Boyd and Slater (1989) did find students writing for a designated audience scoring higher than those without such an audience, their data did not reflect higher scores for real audiences than for imaginary audiences.

Another study shows the effects of the writer's age on rewriting for a specific audience. Looking at the development of audience-adapted writing skills, Kroll (1985) found that, when given the task of rewriting a linguistically complex story, older writers were better able to simplify text for younger readers than were younger writers. Working with fifth-, seventh-, ninth-, and eleventh-grade students, and with college freshmen, he also identified older writers' ability to revise meaning more easily, not staying exclusively with "word-oriented" strategies. Examining "receding" procedures for adapting writing to a particular (young) audience, Kroll chose a wide-ranging age group to "chart developmental trends" of writers, and to "sketch out a more adequate 'map' of audience-adapted writing skills between the end of elementary school and the beginning of college" (pp. 124-125). In his study, older students tended not only to change wording, but also "to retell parts of the story in language more accessible to young readers. . ." (p. 133).

Cherry (1989) warned against unclear audience cues. Describing a writing situation gone awry, he reported on the effects of a writing prompt when the scenario failed to specify audience, thus "placing students both inside and outside" of the writing task. Apparently, in attempts to frame questions as interesting, challenging, and meaningful prompts, teachers and researchers sometimes create problems for writers.

So far, Oliver has articulated why she asked the research questions she did, how her experience played a role in her decisions, and how other colleagues and literature influenced a part of her work. I did not ask her how she worded her questions (the Evidence x Question cell in the matrix) because her study so clearly stated them, as shown below.

THE PRESENT STUDY

The present study examined the effects of varying topic, purpose, and audience specification on the writing quality of seventh-, ninth-, and eleventh-grade students, and college freshmen. Specifically, I asked the following questions:

What relationship exists between writing quality and varying degrees of information about the writing prompt with respect to topic, purpose, and audience?

What relationship exists between students' age level, writing quality, and amount of information in the prompt?

METHOD

Participants

A total of 624 essays were collected from advanced students in seventh grade (127 essays), college preparatory students in ninth grade (196 essays) and eleventh grade (180 essays), and university freshmen (121 essays). Many teachers participating in the study had had previous experience with a National Writing Project affiliate and were already providing strong writing programs for their students. College freshmen were completing the first of two required composition courses at a large university. Thus, all student writers had had some training and experience in composing.

Organizing the 624 essays in this study must have been a formidable task. While Oliver did not detail how she coded her data, she pointed to an important awareness: Know your weaknesses and ask for help when you need it (Researcher x Method cell in the matrix).

Oliver: I coded the data by hand on sheets. It's tedious but not so bad if you're listening to the radio anyway or "watching" the news on tv. I had a small grant to pay someone for the "real" data entry. Then, after the "runs," my friend and I discussed the results. After this "pilot," and several years later, I secured another university grant and had the whole thing entered by someone else. I was very glad for that because it would have taken forever for me to do the whole set.

Assignment

Assignment variables were based on the example and rationale offered by Freedman and Robinson (1982) in their presentation of successful topic design. These researchers created an expository or "transactional" topic based on students' personal experience. To reduce assessment complications while simultaneously increasing reliability, they offered students only one choice. This study adapted the following question from their study. (It was first administered for a writing proficiency test given to juniors at California State University at San Francisco and later used for several other assessments.)

> Everyone has a gripe about the community in which he or she lives. Whether that problem be major or minor, a matter of rising neighborhood burglaries or of inadequate parking facilities on campus, most of us feel that some community need is being ignored by local officials. What's your gripe? How does it affect your everyday life, and how would you suggest correcting it?

Changes were made to make the information less abstract for younger students. In addition, information about audience was added.

Eight combinations were created to include more or less information in the assignment. Assignment #1 (T+P+A+) contains the most specific information about all three variables- topic, purpose and audience- while assignment #8 (T-P-A-) contains the least specific information about all three variables. (See Appendix A.)

Although many researchers agree that a fair test of writing skills demands at least two writing samples for each discourse purpose (Braddock, Lloyd-Jones, & Scheer, 1963; Kincaid, 1970; Odell, 1981), the focus of this study was not to diagnose writing problems of individual students but, rather, to provide a basis for studying the effects of assignment variables on writing quality. Thus, participating students were given one assignment to complete in one class period. Moreover, more teachers were willing to allow their classes to write one essay during one class period than were willing to spend several sessions collecting multiple writing samples unrelated to regular curricula.

Procedure

Sample and Setting. The sample for this study consisted of seventh-, ninth-, and eleventh-grade students enrolled in "advanced" English classes in an affluent community in Central Texas. These students were considered "higher-ability" within their age groups. The choice of "higher-ability" students was based on several factors. First, at this level, students had had at least some opportunity to practice their writing skills prior to completing the writing assignment for the present study. Second, we believed that such common problems as anxiety, inability to generate prose, and the creation of mechanical errors were minimal because each of the participating departments' curricula call for positive writing environments. The target schools are located near a large university, and many of the teachers participating in this research have also been part of other projects reflecting recent trends in composition pedagogy. Because the purpose of this study was to look at the effects of rhetorical specification in prompts on writing quality of students at various age levels, every attempt was made to make the population as homogeneous as possible.

Likewise, the college level students in this study attended the flagship campus of the state's university system, having graduated from high schools comparable to that of the high school students in the study. Each of the eight assignments was given to "advanced English" seventh grade classes, "college prep" ninth- and eleventh-grade English classes, and college freshmen. High school students were asked to consider this writing exercise as an example of a large-scale writing assessment which they would experience in the near future. With no prior knowledge of the assignment, students were given forty-five minutes to complete their essays. Test packets included a cover sheet with the assignment at the top and several lined sheets for writing. Students were allowed to make notes on the first sheet if they wished but were instructed not to write their names anywhere. The tests were coded so that individual teachers could use copies of the tests later for instruction if they wished. For further motivation, instructors told students that their task was adapted from a writing sample used in an actual assessment test and that such practice was important.

Students were assigned to each of the "treatments" by class. That is, each of eight classrooms for each grade received one of the assignment variations. Though random assignment of prompts throughout all eight classes at each grade level was requested, many teachers preferred to give each class a particular question, a process which they perceived would make their task simpler. Because students had already been assigned to their classes randomly, I agreed to this procedure.

Raters. Four high school teachers were selected as raters, none of whom taught in the schools where writing samples were collected. However, each had had experience teaching composition and assessing student writing. These teachers were trained in holistic scoring techniques. The scoring criteria were modeled after general guidelines used by Educational Testing Services (1987). Training sessions began with a description of holistic scoring (see Appendix B), a presentation of Assignment #8 (prompt with least rhetorical information), discussion materials, and the rubric for scoring. The raters completed five sessions lasting about four hours each.

Each essay received two readings using a rating scale of 6 to 1. If an essay received a discrepant score of more than one numerical difference between two raters (e.g., a score of 6 and a score of 4), a third teacher rated the essay. All rater reliabilities were computed using Cronbach's (1970) alpha coefficient. The inter-rater reliability was .82. The main and interactive effects of topic, purpose, and audience on writing quality were analyzed using a 2X2X2 analysis of variance for all grades together and for each grade separately.

I asked Eileen Oliver if she sought help for her analyses of data. Though she felt she might have been able to handle the data analysis on her own, she sought the help of a friend who is an expert, illustrating her own assessment of her strengths and weaknesses in this project (the Researcher x Method cell in the matrix) and demonstrating how a conceptual knowledge of statistics can help us work with research consultants and statisticians more effectively. Further, Oliver illustrates that although this study does not appear to be collaborative, it had collaborative moments, and, as all researchers, she kept learning more about research through the experience.

> *Oliver:* I worked with someone who helped me run the data. I could have done it myself and would have, but we had a friend who did that kind of work all the time. It was great working with him because, as he did it, he explained it so that I'd be able to do it on my own. He was also very valuable to run things by as I looked at my data to try to figure out what I was getting.
>
> I think a lot of people paid graduate students to help them with analyses of various sorts. It depends on the person whether or not it goes well. In subsequent work I've done, I've had some people help with various data analysis. However, if they're not in touch with what you're doing, they're just number crunchers and often crunch the wrong numbers. For example, about three years ago I was looking at the difference that certain variables had on different racial groups. The "consultant" who was supposed to assist me in my analysis suggested that, since my "n" for Native Americans was not very large, I should combine it with another racial group. So you see that if you do not understand what you're looking for, an "analyst" may not be any use to you at all.

Results

Significant main effects and interactions were obtained for seventh-grade essays for topic [$F = 12.46$, $p > .0006$] and purpose [$F = 6.49$, $p > .01$]; for ninth-grade essays for topic [$F = 28.46$, $p > .000$]; for eleventh-grade essays for purpose [$F = 29.22$, $p > .0000$] and the interaction between topic and audience [$F = 4.55$, $p > .03$]; for college freshman essays for interactions between topic and audience [$F = 13.70$, $p > .0003$]; and for all grades together with topic [$F = 5.65$, $p > .021$, purpose [F = 14.02, p>.0002], and the interaction between topic and audience [F = 9.57, p>.002] (see Tables 1-5 respectively).

Generally, the statistical results indicate that seventh graders did better with simpler statements of topic and specific direction in purpose. However, a look at Figures 1 and 2 confounds this evidence because Assignment #1 (T+P+A+) has a high mean, as do Assignments #7and #8 (both with P-). A closer analysis shows that less elaborate topic is

TABLE 1

Analysis of Variance for Assignment Variable at Grade 7

Number of obs =	127	R-square =			0.12
Root MSE =	1.02712	Adj R-square =			0.0912

Source	Partial SS	df	MS	F	Prob > F
Model	17.55	4	4.39	4.16	0.01
Topics	13.14	1	13.14	12.46	0.00
Purpose	6.85	1	6.85	6.49	0.01
Audience	0.05	1	0.05	0.05	0.83
Topic*Audience	3.12	1	3.12	2.95	0.09
Residual	128.71	122	1.05		
Total	146.26	126	1.16		

TABLE 2

Analysis of Variance for Assignment Variable at Grade 9

Number of obs =	196	R-square =			0.1360
Root MSE =	1.03856	Adj R-square =			0.11179

Source	Partial SS	df	MS	F	Prob > F
Model	32.42	4	8.11	7.51	0.00
Topics	30.70	1	30.70	28.46	0.00
Purpose	0.26	1	0.26	0.24	0.62
Audience	1.54	1	1.54	1.42	0.23
Topic*Audience	0.46	1	0.46	0.43	0.51
Residual	206.01	191	1.08		
Total	238.43	195	1.22		

still the major indication of higher scores, while the interaction of
T+ and A+, a significant effect at other levels, may account for
the higher score of Assignment #1. (A discussion of this interaction between topic and audience follows in the next section.)

On the other hand, there is clear evidence that ninth-grade
writers utilized specific information about topic (Table 6 &
Figure 2). Specific information about purpose gave eleventh-grade students an advantage in their writing tasks (Table 6 &
Figure 3). The interaction between topic and audience for all
grades together (Figure 4), for eleventh graders (Figure 5),

TABLE 3

Analysis of Variance for Assignment Variable at Grade 11

Number of obs =	180	R-square =			0.1852
Root MSE =	1.11223	Adj R-square =			0.1665

Source	Partial SS	df	MS	F	Prob > F
Model	49.20	4	12.30	9.94	0.00
Topics	4.35	1	4.35	3.52	0.06
Purpose	36.15	1	36.15	29.22	0.00
Audience	2.19	1	2.19	1.77	0.19
Topic*Audience	5.62	1	5.62	4.55	0.03
Residual	216.49	175	1.24		
Total	265.68	179	1.48		

TABLE 4

Analysis of Variance for Assignment Variable for College Freshmen

Number of obs =	121	R-square =			0.1305
Root MSE =	0.995986	Adj R-square =			0.0927

Source	Partial SS	df	MS	F	Prob > F
Model	17.12	5	3.42	3.45	0.01
Topics	0.01	1	0.01	0.00	0.95
Purpose	0.98	1	0.98	0.99	0.32
Audience	1.04	2	0.52	0.52	0.59
Topic*Audience	13.59	1	13.59	13.70	0.00
Residual	114.08	115	0.99		
Total	131.20	120	1.09		

and four college freshmen (Figure 6) raises interesting questions regarding the relationship between these two variables.

Topic and Audience Interaction

The question of topic and audience interaction is a difficult one. Yet its significance for college freshmen and eleventh graders (and thus for overall significance) makes it worthy of investigation. It appears from these data that assignments which provide complementarity between topic and audience— that is, more specific information about both topic

TABLE 5

Analysis of Variance for Assignment Variable for All Grades

Number of obs =	624	R-square =	0.0489
Root MSE =	1.13232	Adj R-square =	0.0412

Source	Partial SS	df	MS	F	Prob > F
Model	40.71	5	8.14	6.35	0.00
Topics	7.24	1	7.24	5.65	0.02
Purpose	17.98	1	17.98	14.02	0.00
Audience	3.19	2	1.60	1.25	0.29
Topic*Audience	12.26	1	12.26	9.57	0.01
Residual	792.37	618	1.28		
Total	833.08	623	1.34		

TABLE 6

Mean Scores and Standard Deviations for All Assignments

Assignment		1	2	3	4	5	6	7	8
		T+P+A+	T+P+A-	T+P-A-	T+P-A+	T-P+A+	T-P+A-	T-P-A+	T-P-A-
Grade 7	X	3.50	2.93	2.60	2.54	3.50	3.60	3.57	3.60
	S.D.	0.94	1.02	0.82	1.03	0.79	1.78	1.14	0.96
Grade 9	X	3.76	3.71	3.63	4.14	3.00	3.02	2.95	3.13
	S.D.	0.95	1.20	0.97	1.18	0.87	1.06	1.12	0.92
Grade 11	X	4.63	4.27	3.02	3.80	3.75	4.15	3.21	3.29
	S.D.	1.07	0.94	1.14	1.00	1.14	1.17	1.14	1.31
Grade 13	X	4.58	3.58	3.50	4.04	4.00	4.03	4.68	3.33
	S.D.	0.84	1.04	0.81	1.15	1.20	0.95	0.75	0.98
All	X	3.89	4.07	4.80	3.80	4.08	4.50	4.60	4.13
	S.D.	1.80	1.50	0.57	0.83	1.20	0.41	0.65	0.85

and audience (T+A+) or less specific information for both (T-A)—
yielded higher scores than those with differing levels of
specificity (Figure 5). Statistical significance was also found for
eleventh-grade writers (See Figure 6) and for college freshmen
(Figure 7). This interaction is difficult to explain because
audience itself was not significant at any level. Perhaps in these
higher grades, because students have received more instruction
and have matured as writers, they attempted to utilize the rhetorical specifications available to them and found conflicting
amounts of information confusing (i.e., T+A- or T-A+).

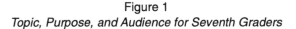

Figure 1
Topic, Purpose, and Audience for Seventh Graders

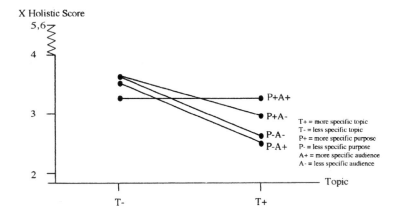

The varied findings regarding audience effect discussed
earlier suggest that we must be careful to craft prompts which
do, indeed, define audience. These results indicate that
students' perception of audience real, imagined, or contrived-
has an effect on their ability to address readers. Perhaps, at
the college level, writers do look for and attempt to address the
demands of the writing task. Results here indicate that a
specific topic with a believable audience, or a very general
topic without audience specification, provided students who

Figure 2
Topic, Purpose, and Audience for Ninth Graders

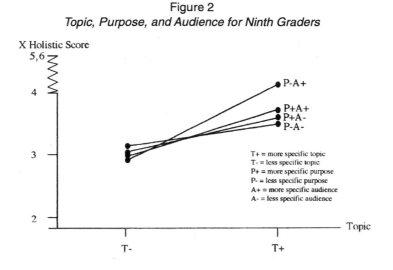

Figure 3
Topic, Purpose, and Audience for Eleventh Graders

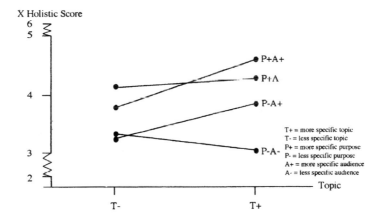

have more experience and who pay more attention to rhetorical cues with a less confusing writing task.

The question remains, however, whether or not the audience variables in this study presented prompts with a clear sense of audience or no audience, or whether, as in some earlier work, the question of authenticity confounded the results.

Figure 4
Topic and Audience for All Grades

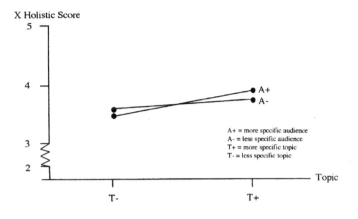

X Holistic Score

A+ = more specific audience
A- = less specific audience
T+ = more specific topic
T- = less specific topic

A+
A-

Topic

T-   T+

Figure 5
Topic and Audience for EleventhGraders

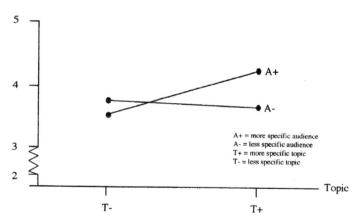

X Holistic Score

A+ = more specific audience
A- = less specific audience
T+ = more specific topic
T- = less specific topic

A+

A-

Topic

T-   T+

Seventh-Grade Writers

Seventh graders seemed to do better with less information about topic (Table 6 & Figure 1). Perhaps at this level, students found the task of analyzing a complete prompt cumbersome, even distracting. Similar to

Figure 6
Topic and Audience for College Freshmen

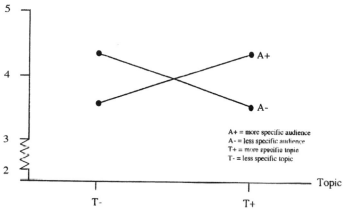

the problem which arises with "high information load topics" (Brossell, 1983), these young writers were not able to make use of so much information. Teachers at this level remarked that though their students had had "lots of writing experience," they were not used to writing in a testing situation such as this one. In fact, some of the teachers said that questions arose from some students regarding their task. I speculate that these questions came from those who were given the more extensive topic assignments. Although assignments with more specific information about purpose were scored significantly higher, Figure 1 shows that only those with more topic and audience information were above the grade level mean (T+P+A+). Although not statistically significant at the .05 level (F=2.95, p .08), this circumstance may be related to the relationship between topic and audience. It may be that at this grade level, students should be given simpler writing tasks for two reasons: they lack exposure to much rhetorical manipulation, and they are not developmentally ready to utilize this information.

These students did not generate long pieces, but their writing was lively and interesting. Results from this study suggest that teachers might want to give students prompts which are more quickly grasped. This may be the level at which the simple "frame topic" (Hoetker & Brossell, 1986; 1989) is useful.

Ninth Grade Writers

More specific information about topic made the most difference with ninth graders (Figure 2). This finding is compatible with what Scardamalia and Bereiter (1986) stated about early adolescents' ability to discuss substantive issues. Also at this age, students have received some formal instruction in writing. They are beginning to organize ideas, elaborate, add, and combine. Operating on a "knowledge-telling" level, they are still able to generate prose from a background awareness that facilitates their work.

Ninth-grade writers were motivated primarily by topic. Unlike the seventh graders, the ninth graders, when given a topic which allowed them to state their complaints, responded emotionally to the topic itself, regardless of other rhetorical components. These characteristics were not only mentioned by their teachers in comments like, "They really loved this topic," and "They 'went to town' on this assignment," but also by the raters who stopped time and again to mention the humor, ethos, and candor of these "adolescents speaking." Perhaps at this level, students take advantage of "voice" as they vent about what for them are emotional issues regarding rules and regulations. Essay #1 (see Appendix C), written in response to assignment #4 (T+P-A+) by a ninth grader, reflects his strong feelings about his school's closed-campus policy.

Eleventh Grade Writers

By the eleventh grade, students seemed to make the best use of rhetorical specification (Figure 3). Not only did complementarity of topic and audience affect their results, so

too did specificity of purpose. This evidence makes sense to
high school teachers who see their eleventh graders emerging
from early adolescence into more serious writers. In these later
adolescent years, college prep students are beginning to look
more closely at college requirements, they have taken the
PSAT, they are starting to research colleges and make applications. As one teacher told me, "By this time, they are beginning
to believe what we've been telling them. They are starting to
see that writing counts. They are listening." Perhaps that is why
so much of a student's rhetorical training in composition takes
place in eleventh grade. At any rate, writers from this
population took advantage of complementarity in topic and
audience interaction as well as specific purpose.

A look at the writing samples themselves illustrates the
importance of rhetorical specification. Essay #2 (see Appendix
C), for example, was written from Assignment #1 (T↓P↓A↓)
which gives the most complete rhetorical information. The
writer states the problem clearly (the need for better physical
education classes), contrasts her subject with another grown
up, develops her thesis with rich detail, and finishes by
suggesting ways to improve existing courses.

Essay #3, on the other hand, is written in response to
Assignment #3 (T+P-A-). Not only does this essay reflect the
consequences for non-specified features, but essays with
specific topic and unspecified audiences combined yielded
lower scores according to interaction effects. Receiving lower
scores (3 & 3), Essay #3's deficiencies become evident examining it from a holistic point of view. One could argue that logically
as well as syntactically, the first writer is more sophisticated.
However, the work of writer #3 is typical of those writing without
specified purpose. That is, instead of stating a problem,
showing how it affects his life, and suggesting a solution, this
writer flounders about and then states several problems with
few, if any, suggestions for improving the situations. Also typical
of these unfocused papers, it begins with an introductory
paragraph which does little to propel the argument. The writer

then launches into a discussion of the price of yearbooks, moving illogically to what the yearbook staff must do with the money. Next he talks about too many clubs, suggesting that admission standards should be raised and the number of members should be limited. He has then, essentially, two topics, not one, a typical modus operandi for eleventh-grade students writing from limited rhetorical specification.

Although Oliver presented her data in a detailed manner, there was more to this study than what we see here. In a part of her interview, Oliver illustrated a researcher's sensitivity to context, especially when trying to decide about the applicability of research results presented in the final report (cells in the matrix: Audience x Publication, Evidence x Publication, Audience x Purpose, and Evidence x Purpose). Further, she illustrated a distinction that all researchers should be aware of—the difference between statistical significance and practical significance (or importance).

Oliver: [T]he other piece of this study had to do with lexical cohesion which was a much more atomistic analysis than even what you see here. The cohesion part is not very useful (or at least I didn't think so)—though it yielded significant results, as well. But this part was so esoteric that I didn't see that it would help the field of composition pedagogy so I didn't pursue it any further.

DISCUSSION

This study investigated whether or not varying degrees of information about topic, purpose, or audience affect the writing quality of students at four grade levels, and if so, in what ways and at what ages? It appears from this research that specification in writing prompts does indeed affect essay quality at certain levels. Thus we should assure that the assignments we give students are carefully designed to promote students production of their best work. Evidence here reflects the important use high school students make of topic, purpose, and the interaction between topic and audience at certain levels. At least in this research, high school students who were given clear rhetorical tasks wrote better essays than did students given less clear rhetorical tasks.

Seventh graders, on the other hand, may also need encouragement for writing. These findings suggest that while the purpose of their tasks should be clear, the prompt might well be simpler. Apparently, these students applied classroom instruction directly in their work. For example, many of their essays had "MAP" written at the top. I asked one of the teachers what this symbol meant. Her response was that she and a colleague had taught students to write this label to remind themselves that they should address "message" (M), "audience" (A), and "purpose" (P) each time they wrote.

Although audience was the only element that did not prove significant by itself, its interaction with topic also raises some concerns. At the very least, we should prevent confusion in audience specification, or we will end up with what Cherry (1989) warned will create problems for writers. And while Redd-Boyd and Slater (1989) did not find a significant difference between a real and imaginary audience, still their results tell us that a target audience is better than no audience at all.

"Inauthenticity," I believe, is the major problem with the variable audience in the present study. That is, those students who were told, "Your essay will be forwarded to a parents' group interested in the welfare of its students," had also been "asked to consider this writing exercise as an example." Thus writers saw from the beginning that their audience was not authentic, a rhetorical element Frank (1992) identified as very important.

Perhaps, too, as Elbow (1987) suggested, utilizing rhetorical information about audience occurs more in the revision stages of writing and would appear in a writing exercise that required more than just one sitting. In any case, the issue of audience relevance has been cloudy and remains so. Continued research in this area should identify real audiences for writers or at least ensure that writers are not encumbered by confusing audience demands.

The importance of providing guidance to writers at certain levels is clarified somewhat in this study. It appears that seventh graders did not utilize information as well as did the more mature writers. They adapted better with simpler topics. These writers (considered high achievers) generated much less prose than did older students. Yet they were still able to come up with lively, interesting pieces. Simple prompts like the frame topic (Hoetker & Brossell, 1986; 1989) might work best. As discussed, however, ninth graders seemed to respond to strong topic cues; their motivation for writing seemed clear in the voices they projected.

Ability of students to write for different purposes is reflected in the results of the NAEP study by Applebee and his colleagues (1994). The most proficient eighth-grade writers in the NAEP study (those judged to be at or above the 90th percentile) responded to narrative and informative tasks. However, while they "seem[ed] to have a growing command of the structural features and rhetorical devices appropriate to narrative and informative writing," they were less successful in developing persuasive essays (p. 94). Though they showed an awareness of how to proceed, their essays were not as well developed. That research, along with the work of Scardamalia and Bereiter (1986), underscores the findings of the present study-younger students were less able than older students to grasp more difficult purpose cues and utilize them. Because in the NAEP study both eighth- and twelfth-grade students wrote better responses when discussing a school problem, it seems reasonable that topic and audience make a difference in student prose.

These findings argue for continued experience with well-crafted prompts, allowing writers to improve with both good instruction and maturation. Though audience was not statistically significant in this study, its significance when interacting with topic in the later grades was important. This research concurs with previous studies that show more mature writers as better able to accomplish the needs of readers both in terms of word-oriented strategies as well as their ability to revise meaning (Kroll, 1985), a phenomenon which "seemed to occur in the junior high school years, roughly between grades 7 and 9" (p. 137). Knowledge of audience did improve the work of college-level writers (Black, 1989; Elbow, 1987; Rafoth, 1989).

Certainly an important area for future research is how "degree of intimacy" influences writing quality (Craig, 1988; Crowhurst & Piche, 1979; Piche, Michlin, Johnson, & Rubin, 1975; Rubin & Piche, 1979). Further examination of "audience" in writing prompts for both junior and senior high school students is needed.

Statistical results as well as comments by teachers and raters of ninth-grade essays indicate that these early adolescents respond positively to topics that engage them. Clearly, this group showed the importance of choosing topics that are relevant to their lives. As their teachers pointed out, these writers were sensitive to issues in their environment, and they loved speaking their minds. Pedagogical implications are obvious: more practice writing about relevant topics.

Eleventh-grade writers took advantage of rhetorical cues and produced high quality pieces when given clear purpose. When topic and audience were in complementarity, they wrote without confusion. Results of this study show that high ability high school juniors are able to produce good persuasive discourse. Testimony to the capability of these high school juniors came often from raters' comments. In fact, there were many times that one or the other remarked that these essays were, on the whole, as good as some of the college students' work. From a pedagogical standpoint, eleventh graders may be best able to take advantage of rhetorical specification. This result underscores the importance of composing experiences for students at this age.

According to the NAEP results, the top twelfth-grade writers are more limited when writing persuasively than for either of the other rhetorical categories used in the study:

Their persuasive writing similarly revealed a clear understanding of the basic rhetorical features of persuasion, but
continuing difficulty in the use of evidence in support of
effective arguments. (p. 98)

Along with the NAEP findings, this study argues for
continued practice with sound writing tasks.

Finally and happily, we see that college freshmen are
affected less by rhetorical specification than are other groups
(Table 6 & Figure 6); they can usually "make something out of
nothing." The writers in this study had experience and
instruction composing, having just completed one semester of
entry-level composition (in addition to other past writing experiences). At this level, students have not only matured as writers,
but also, and perhaps more importantly, have benefitted from
their experiences composing.

*I asked Eileen Oliver how she felt about her findings. Again, she
referred to knowledge gained through her experience as a teacher but
illustrated an important teacher-researcher connection in this quantitative study. She also shared an interesting anecdote as an "aside." Though
this portion of the interview does not directly relate to any particular cell
in the matrix, Oliver expressed her excitement here, a voice she chose to
keep out of her report.*

Oliver: I was pretty excited [about the results] because it's always nice
to know you're on the right track. What I found was that writing
prompts *do* make a difference and they make "different differences"
depending upon the age group. I sensed that as a teacher, and was
encouraged to see this validated as a researcher. I was puzzled by the
data that said "audience" (whether there was one stated or not) did not
make a significant difference. During my dissertation defense it was
none other than James Kinneavy who explained this phenomenon, saying that he, too, had had such an outcome. His explanation was that
students don't really "buy it" when the prompt says, "Pretend you're
writing to . . ." They know they're still just writing to a teacher. That
made sense to me.

This kind of analysis is very informative. No, it doesn't tell the whole story. But, coming from someone in the humanities (readin' and writin' and talking about books), it was very exciting to see that something one has a tacit awareness of as a teacher can really be proved through systematic analysis.

PEDAGOGICAL IMPLICATIONS

The purpose of this study was to examine what kinds of effects (if any) varying degrees of topic, purpose, and audience specifications have on the writing quality of seventh-, ninth-, and eleventh-grade students and college freshmen. The results of this study may have several implications for pedagogy:

Assessment

- Although this study does not specifically look at reading skills, the earlier discussion regarding confusing and poorly written writing prompts necessitates considering this issue. When creating a writing prompt, assessors must distinguish between reading ability and writing skills. If the reading task is confusing or difficult, the writer's poor performance may be due to poor reading rather than poor writing skills.
- The purpose of the assessment should determine the nature of the prompt. That is, the goal of providing the best writing prompt from which all students can write is different from a goal of "separating the good writers from the poor writers" through prompts designed for that purpose.
- If audience information is provided, it should be realistic; an inauthentic or conflicting audience may create problems for writers.

Instruction

- Experience generating prose is crucial for all writers. As Shaughnessy (1977) still reminds us, basic writers are writers with no experience. Further, young writers need the freedom, practice, and guidance to develop into good writers. Looking at the writing samples from this study the developmental factor is clear.

- Seventh graders differ from college freshmen in the most obvious ways. They do not write as extensively or as clearly as their older counterparts. They are young adolescents, and their interests and concerns are also egocentric and adolescent. They need short, relevant topics which engage them and make them want to write. For them, not getting to eat lunch on "the bench" like the eighth graders is a great problem. They write passionately about such things. On the other hand, eleventh graders are beginning to make decisions that will affect their future lives. Their writing reflects this change. They write intense essays about "Who Am I?" and "Where Will I Be Next?" They are engaged in writing that requires them to be introspective. The subject matter chosen by these various age levels reflects the developmental interests of adolescents in making choices about what they want to read, and their tastes change as they mature.

- The elaborated topics the ninth graders responded to in this study indicate that at this age we can begin to manipulate topics and provide writers with more information and suggestions.

- As writers enter their later teens, they are better able to write for different, more difficult rhetorical purposes. By this time, they should be comfortable (and have had practice) using many modes of discourse.

- Audience adaptation should increase in level of difficulty as the writer develops. Teachers should encourage students to observe the ways in which their writing changes according to audience specification. Attention to difference in language register, syntax, and vocabulary all figure in the response to changing rhetorical demands. Conversation about audience helps students to watch for and create more realistic writing situations. junior and senior high school students should be accomplished in revising essays to accommodate audience.

Effective and rigorous composition instruction pays off. As writers mature, they build on their prior experience to produce better quality prose. The findings here indicate that rhetorical specification in writing prompts does make a difference. Good topics and clear purposes assist students in developing higher quality work than when these elements are either not clear or are lacking. We see that complementarity in topic and audience also facilitates good writing. Further, the value of various aspects of writing prompts is different across age levels. However, the issue of audience is still unresolved. Though complementarity of topic and audience was significant, the lack of significance for audience as a main effect calls for more work in this specific area.

The findings in the present study are suggestive only; they provide some evidence that various rhetorical elements could be explicitly introduced to students at certain ages. However, the design and statistical results of this research are far from conclusive. Additional research is needed to learn more about the interaction of topic, purpose, and audience, together with an analysis of samples of successful student writing to find out how these students have used the elements in the assignment prompts.

I asked Oliver how this research had changed her teaching. In her answer, she articulated responses to two cells in the matrix (Audience x Question and Audience x Purpose). She also hints at an interesting look at voice (the Researcher x Publication cell). While Oliver produced a traditional report here, she shares her research in other ways: she applies it herself to her work with her own students and she uses it to train future teachers. Such "publication" in these other forms suggests that the traditional researcher's voice (often criticized for being impersonal and disinterested) can lead to other kinds of voices when research findings are applied to other contexts.

Oliver: I certainly have used this research (why else do we do it?). And I think it's very important for people to conduct research that matters.

The best part of all this is that I am an "English teacher educator" and thus have had many classes of students who are going out into the junior and senior high schools, community colleges, and colleges and will teach writing. This information has been really useful to share with them as well. It's one thing to have anecdotal evidence. It's much better to support that with "hard data."

APPENDIX A

Combinations of More and Less Information About Topic, Purpose, Audience

More Information About Topic (T+): Everyone has a complaint about his or her school. The problem may be, for example, too much homework, not enough dances or sports activities, or too few clubs. In any case, most of us feel that some educational need is being ignored by teachers, administrators and parents.

Less Information About Topic (T-) Everyone has a complaint about his or her school. Most of us feel that some need is being ignored.

More Information About Purpose (P+) What is your complaint? Write an essay telling how this problem affects your everyday life and how you would suggest correcting it.

Less Information About Purpose (P-) What is your complaint? Discuss.

More Information About Audience (A+) Your essay will be forwarded to a parents' group interested in the welfare of its students.

Less Information About Audience (A-)

Assignment #1 T+P+A+: Everyone has a complaint about his or her school. The problem may be, for example, too much homework, not enough dances or sports activities, or too few clubs. In any case, most of us feel that some educational need is being ignored by teachers, administrators and parents.

What is your complaint? Write an essay telling how this problem affects your everyday life and how you would suggest correcting it. Your essay will be forwarded to a parents' group interested in the welfare of its students.

Assignment #2 T+P+A-: Everyone has a complaint about his or her school. The problem may be, for example, too much homework, not enough dances or sports activities, or too few clubs. In any case, most of us feel that some educational need is being ignored by teachers, administrators and parents.

What is your complaint? Write an essay telling how this problem affects your everyday life and how you would suggest correcting it.

Assignment #3 T+P-A-: Everyone has a complaint about his or her school. The problem may be, for example, too much homework, not enough dances or sports activities, or too few clubs. In any case, most of us feel that some educational need is being ignored by teachers, administrators and parents.

What is your complaint? Discuss.

Assignment #4 T+P-A+: Everyone has a complaint about his or her school. The problem may be, for example, too much homework, not enough dances or sports activities, or too few clubs. In any case, most of us feel that some educational need is being ignored by teachers, administrators and parents.

What is your complaint? Discuss. Your essay will be forwarded to a parents' group interested in the welfare of its students.

Assignment #5 T-P+A+: Everyone has a complaint about his or her school. Most of us feel that some need is being ignored.

What is your complaint? Write an essay telling how this problem affects your everyday life and how you would suggest correcting it. Your essay will be forwarded to a parents' group interested in the welfare of its students.

Assignment #6 T-P+A-: Everyone has a complaint about his or her school. Most of us feel that some need is being ignored.

What is your complaint? Write an essay telling how this problem affects your everyday life and how you would suggest correcting it.

Assignment #7 T-P-A+: Everyone has a complaint about his or her school. Most of us feel that some need is being ignored.

What is your complaint? Discuss. Your essay will be forwarded to a parents' group interested in the welfare of its students.

Assignment #8 T-P-A-: Everyone has a complaint about his or her school. Most of us feel that some need is being ignored.

What is your complaint? Discuss.

APPENDIX B

Holistic Scoring Guide

Holistic scoring is defined as any procedure which stops short of enumerating linguistic, rhetorical, or informational features. The ranking procedure used in this study was adapted from that used by the Educational Testing Service (see References). For information regarding that adaptation please contact the author.

APPENDIX C

Examples of Students' Compositions

Essay #1-Assignment #4 (T+P-A+) *Ninth-Grade Writer*

Everyone going to school, especially high school, has at least one or two complaints about their school. My main complaint is the present policy of a closed campus at lunch for the freshmen and sophomores.

At the moment, juniors and seniors are permitted to leave campus for lunch; freshmen and sophomores are not. The punishment for breaking this policy is two hours D-hall for the underclassman who left the campus, and four hours D-hall for the upperclassman who took him or her out to lunch.

Presently, this policy is not one hundred percent enforceable. I, myself, and I know many others too, go out to lunch on a regular basis. Some freshmen and sophomores look like a junior or senior, and pass right by the teacher on duty. For both first and second lunch, there is a teacher, standing by the doors, watching for freshmen and sophomores leaving campus. They can't possibly stop them all, and many walk by casually with no problem at all. This problem came up before the school board, but was presently turned down. They said that there were not enough strong reasons to completely open up the campus. This was a disappointment for students and many teachers. Here at _____ High School, this is a very popular issue. Many students are hoping for an all-open campus but many feel it's a lost cause.

Essay #2-Assignment #1 (T+P +A+) Eleventh grade writer

In our era of fitness and well-being for everyone, it surprises and disappoints me to find that_____High School has very few true exercise classes for those who need the conditioning but don't have the time or inclination to join a sports team. Never before has America been so concerned with the physical condition of the business person as well as the athlete, but _____ High School is slow to reflect these healthy attitudes. We need to glance away from our star athletes long enough to give our less-active students some better P.E. classes.

This is the age in which jogging, swimming, and sit-ups are at the peak of popularity but there are many students who don't get a chance to exercise simply because they don't have the time. _____High School offers many sports activities which provide a good workout-but only if the participants stay after school or come early each day, sacrifice weekends and evenings, and miss school-sometimes quite often. This schedule becomes a strain when one also has home-work to do and other activities, such as music, art, and of course, a social life. There are those who thrive on it, but for others, the peaceful, easy life is a hundred times better. Or perhaps sports takes a back seat to those other activities. There is also the chance that those who would like to participate don't have the skills needed and don't make the team. Without school sports, the only alternative is to join a health spa or work out alone-the first too expensive, the second not much fun, and both hard to keep up on one's own. Besides, neither are much help if you don't have enough time in the first place.

The answer to this problem is simple. There are many slow-moving P.E. classes taken by those who need their 1 fi years of credit. Nothing would be easier, or more fun, than to add or change those classes and provide fun, physically demanding classes ones which require that hour of hard exercise but don't demand after-school work. There is already one physical conditioning class with running and weight lifting more of these could be added, as well as swimming, aerobic dancing, and others-perhaps even bicycling or walking! The variety would attract more people, and more of our generation could join the healthy crowd live longer, feel better, lose weight, tone muscles-before long we could all look like Jane Fonda or Arnold Schwartzeneger! The exercise craze is a good one; so why not expand it to today's young people? Everyone needs the chance to lead the healthiest life possible from the football team captain to the valedictorian, and <u>everyone</u> in between.

Essay #3-Assignment #3 (T+P-A -) Eleventh-grade Writer

School is an institution that will never die. This institution should be made easier to handle for the student though. It should be made so the student will be able to endure it. There are not many problems in our school though. Our school is one of the best schools that I have attended. Our school's problems are minor problems compared to most schools. It is nice looking and well kept as well. School should be a fun time of life used in preparation for the entrance into the real world where you have to make your own living and support yourself. School will live on as long as there are students to attend them.

This school's major problem is the price of yearbooks. I could not see myself laying out twenty-five dollars for something that I might not receive. The books are not worth the price that they are charging for it. The yearbook staff is raking in the money and the journalism teacher probably pockets the profit for his own. I bet they make over five dollars a book which is not that much until you consider them selling about a thousand books. Then they make about five-thousand dollars. What does a journalism class do with five-thousand dollars? They could buy anything they needed and still have money left. Yearbook at this school are a major rip-off.

Another problem at this school that needs to be solved is the problem of having too many clubs. There should be fewer clubs and more membership in the clubs. This would bring about more pride in the clubs that there are. To solve this problem, the requirements to get a grant to have a club need to be stricter. To many clubs come about that have no real purpose but to meet, eat, and drink. What do not just call this a party instead o a club? The requirements to get into the club should be stricter also. Clubs here are too easy to get into. You need to have a C average for one qualification that most clubs have here. Clubs are problems but could be solved using the outlines above. Our problems are not as bad and numerous as the problems in the other schools. Our problems can be solved easily also.

_____ High School already has a good tradition in the two year's that it has existed. Problem-solving brings about school pride. Here at _____ High School everyone has pride in their school.

SUMMARY

Oliver's answers to all of these questions articulate the processes and decisions made in the context of both rhetorical and research issues. Further, Dr. Oliver pointed to the usefulness of numerical data in our teaching and how naturally such data grows from questions related to our experience, instinct, and curiosity.

While such researchers are often criticized for "confirming the obvious," Oliver argued, throughout her interview, for what she instead called "balance" and "validation." The interplay between the subjective and objective, between rhetoric and dialectic, between narratives and numbers, and between a teacher and a researcher are well-illustrated here—all within the rich context of the desire to know, to confirm, to test one's beliefs for the purpose of practical application later while enriching the scholarship of our field at the same time.

Upon reviewing Oliver's interview, I noticed that I asked questions related to all cells in the Contextualist Research Paradigm Matrix but one: the "Researcher x Publication" cell, which asks, "How do I want to be perceived as a researcher in the final presentation? What voice would best enhance what I'm trying to say?" Oliver's interview, however, gave her an opportunity to construct a second voice—one that did not appear in her actual report. Surely, the amount of complicated data she had, the importance of her literature review, and the length of the study limited the space available for an additional personal voice in the report. The voice that Oliver chose for her study, then, is a most sensible one in the context of her work. In her interview, Oliver demonstrated a clear sense for the role and value of traditional research reports in our field, especially related to her own teaching.

In the context of other studies, however, such a report can be constructed with a personal voice as well. Chapter six will present my own pilot study on the differences in students' responses to red and blue ink in basic writing classrooms. For my report, I chose several voices, but the context in which I conducted this pilot differs greatly from Oliver's. My purposes for conducting the study were to examine our lore about red ink in the classroom and to test (or in Oliver's words, to validate, to provide balance for) that belief in our scholarship. Another purpose for sharing this pilot study along with Oliver's study is to demonstrate another form for research that relies on numerical data—one that does not refute or reject the form chosen by Oliver, but one that provides an alternative well-suited to some research contexts in which we find ourselves asking and exploring questions.

NOTES

1. When I began to look for a traditional study for this chapter, I decided to review the last two years of *RTE*: First, *RTE* has become a symbol of quantitative research in our field and has, at times, been criticized for it. Second, I focused on the last two years in order to find recent works. Therefore, I reviewed nine issues of *RTE*: May 1995 through May 1997. In those nine issues were forty-four articles (excluding notes from editors and announcements). I first eliminated twenty-two unrelated articles (four studies in teaching literature, five annotated bibliographies, two letters from readers, a memorial to Alan C. Purves, eight essays, and two "Viewpoints"). I then eliminated nine studies that used no numerical data and eight studies that gathered numerical data but did not share full analyses of data *or* converted the data to a qualitative report. Of the five articles remaining that presented full analyses of data, one was Eileen Oliver's. Since Eileen Oliver had been one of my undergraduate professors when we were both at St. Cloud State University (and since I had no further criteria for choosing one of the five over the others), I asked her first, simply because I knew her.

   When I first contacted Dr. Oliver, I did not reveal to her *why* I was interviewing her, except to say that I wanted to ask her questions about her study and that my use of her article and interview would be positive. Her answers, then, were not unfairly constructed for the purpose of helping me make my point.

2. "The Writing Quality of Seventh, Ninth, and Eleventh Graders, and College Freshmen" is copyright 1995, National Council of Teachers of English. Reprinted here by permission of the publisher.

3. Email discussions with Oliver occurred from October 26, 1997 to June 17, 1998. She has approved final printing of this chapter, my use and interpretation of her comments here, and the reprinting of her text. I'd again like to thank Eileen for her generous and patient assistance with this chapter.

6 A CONTEXTUALIST RESEARCH PARADIGM
A Demonstration

In the most traditional form, research reports often exclude personal experience or even the use of first person, resulting in texts that sometimes sound awkward ("the authors conclude . . .") or impersonal and a-contextual ("the literature has failed to show . . ."). Our own sensitivity to context in composition studies has guided the perception that such traditional reports are, therefore, insensitive to context. As shown in chapter five, this is not the case, as Oliver articulated answers to most of the questions in the Contextualist Research Paradigm Matrix. However, the appearance of the traditional report is a part of the perceived problem. While I contend that numerical evidence is never stripped of the context of personal observations, intuition, and experience, the concise manner in which numerical evidence is often presented in traditional reports often creates, for readers unfamiliar with or lacking training in traditional reports, the illusion that it is.

Choosing such a traditional form (and the voice that accompanies it) is understandable and appropriate in several contexts. In the context of Oliver's study, for example, she needed to share a lengthy literature review, articulate complicated data and data analyses, and discuss practical applications of the study—elements necessary for a persuasive and informative piece given the nature of her study. To add more personal anecdotes or to construct a personal voice would have taken too much space and would have distracted readers' attention from other, more important issues at *that* moment, in *that* context. Regardless of the reasons for Oliver's rhetorical decisions, however, she made each decision appropriately in the context of her work.

In other contexts, however, a blend of styles would be appropriate, too. In this chapter, I will present another study, but this pilot study will blend a "narrative" with the traditional-looking text, creating an alternative form for reporting research that composition scholars might find more attractive and readable if they decide the context warrants such a blended form. This blended form makes the context for the project more visible and more readily perceived by its very appearance and its use of personal voice, experience, and anecdotes— a context more visible to the untrained eye, in contrast to the need for training to understand the full context of a more traditional report. The numerical data presented in this pilot study, then, is more obviously "contextualized" within the narration of the process and anecdotes that express the curiosity that guided the study. At the same time, I do not intend to recommend this form as the *best* alternative for all studies, for to do so would, once again, ignore context.

While this blend of styles is one of the purposes of the following study, it meets a second purpose as well: the following study tests one small piece of our commonly accepted lore by asking, "Is red ink all that bad?" What would happen if we experimented by using red ink with some students and another color with other students? What would students then say about that ink color when we ask them how it makes them feel? How true is our lore? Driven by my own memory of red ink on my own papers as a student (and the encouragement I felt from my teachers), I conducted an experiment that tried to assess students' feelings about red ink. For me, there was a discrepancy between my own memories, experiences, and intuition and the oral and written lore that criticizes the use of red ink in our field. Thus, in Annis's terms, my own "believer's level of understanding" conflicted with the beliefs about an "issue" held by the "appropriate objector group."

The Contextualist Research Paradigm presented in chapter four is at work here. For example, readers will notice that the dominant voice is, first, a personal one, as I recall experiences that have framed my view of red ink. Then, the voice becomes a critical one, questioning and commenting on some available literature. As I reveal my methods and data, my voice continues to narrate and describe events, but it treats the data accurately in traditional ways when needed. Finally, my tone turns argumentative in the discussion section but returns to the

Figure 6.1

A Contextualist Pardigm for Rhetoric and Composition:
Responses in Context of Red Ink / Blue Ink Study

Rhetorical Issues

	The Social (Audience)	The Personal (Researcher)	The Factual (Evidence)
Question / Issue	I imagine readers who either believe red ink lore or have questioned it themselves; teachers, tutors, myself, the field	I'm curious because avoidance of red ink doesn't address larger issues. As a student, I didn't perceive red as negative. My studies in cognition suggest that red might be effective for attracting students' attention.	Question should be worded for hypothesis testing to guide the experiment. Ethical issues? I'm confident students will not be pained by the red pen.
Purpose	My research will benefit mostly teachers, by examining lore. It will help students if we think about our commenting styles differently.	This study might be the first of its kind. Other literature refers to red ink casually—assumptions, not "tests" or full examination.	I need evidence that is both numerical and anecdotal—to measure the anecdotal against the numerical.
Method(s)	Most others, in print and in conversation seem to accept the lore of red ink as a punishing element in a teacher's comments or discuss red ink as something from our past.	I can use my own classes and find another teacher willing to participate. I can design my own instrument and analyze my own data. Weaknesses: what if the other teacher is too different? I won't have a large group of subjects.	Data readily available: my experience and observations. Data to be gathered: Students' response to survey. Available literature will help outline the lore.
Publication	To question lore, the final report should include lore, but go beyond that. Start with lore, then numerical data.	I want to be perceived as serious but playful—a calm easy voice. Intro: questioning/calm; Methods: accurate / friendly; Discussion: argumentative and questioning; Conclusion: return to questioning calm.	My data is interesting: few significant differences, but red received higher average for all but one item. In this context, it's enough evidence to rethink lore but not enough to claim that students prefer red.

Research Issues

personal inquisitive voice with which I started. Therefore, I decided to adopt not just one voice, but several, as needed for the larger context of this study and in the smaller and different sections of the report. Figure 6.1 shows the Contextualist Research Paradigm matrix with my answers to each set of questions proposed in the original matrix (see chapter four).

Certainly, I made more decisions than I can possibly show in this space, but I hope that readers will see the intersection of the rhetorical and research issues that formed the context in which I conducted and shared the study and how these decisions appear in the final product of the study below. Further, I did not keep track of the order in which I encountered these decisions. The process of making these decisions was much messier than the matrix might suggest, and readers should be aware that the matrix simply shows *which* decisions I made, not at what time or in what order.

Undoubtedly, critics of traditional research models have argued that such research serves the trivial or obvious; here, a study about red ink might seem, at first, trivial. Yet this study is designed as a demonstration beginners might find instructive, and it attempts to answer a question that pervades our lore and sometimes our literature. Why do we subscribe to the notion that red ink is always negative? Could data gathered from classroom research help us rethink that lore?

RED INK / BLUE INK: DOES IT REALLY MATTER WHAT WRITING TEACHERS USE?[1]

When I think of red, I think of many things: the red oversized sweater that draws compliments from friends and students every time I wear it; that very special Valentine I hope to get one day; the funny family story about my police-officer grandfather not allowing my mother to own red shoes because "every prostitute on Washington Street" did, too; a man I once dated who looked especially handsome in red and less so in other colors; the single red rose I carried in my youngest sister's wedding; the comments and encouragement (in red ink) from several wonderful teachers who made me, too, want to be a teacher someday.

Red comments on my papers and tests did, in fact,
"scream" as we think they do. They yelled, "this is *important!*"
and "here's an error to correct in the future"—screaming and
yelling that drew my attention, that motivated me, that focused
my energy on working harder, becoming stronger. But teachers
also had positive things to say, and I don't recall any of them
switching ink color to do so. Still in red, their positive comments
would shout: "You're terrific!" and "I like your writing!" and, on
occasion, a "Hallelujah!" or two.

Later, when my training in composition began in a writing
center, I learned more narrow meanings for red ink. Typical of
lore, my indoctrination into the dangers of red ink was mostly
oral—listening to professors, attending conferences, and
reinforcing the notion in hallway chatter. Soon, I, too,
associated red ink with "old-fashioned" pedagogies, the kind
that writing centers and new-paradigm teachers would stay far
away from. Teachers who bled all over student papers were a
part of the problem that writing tutors were there to correct, to
provide salvation for the victims—the students. Numerous
Tutors' Columns in the *Writing Lab Newsletter* reinforced the
horrors of red ink.

In one *Tutors' Column*, "Leggo My Ego," Babcock (1995)
related the euphoric rush of power he felt when he was first
hired as a tutor, including lofty images/fantasies of power and
glory: "I, cackling my rapture, pinned endless stacks of bad
term papers to dart boards with flying red pencils" (10). In the
end, Babcock relinquished such notions of power in favor of
"tutor speak."

In the Spring of 1997, one day I had a short break from my
duties as a faculty tutor in a writing center, so I took the opportunity to grade a couple of last-minute papers for a class I would
teach that afternoon. Much to the horror of two tutors on duty at
the time, I used the only pen I had in my purse: red. Their questions, in short, were filled with dismay and centered on the
notion that someone like me (i.e., someone in a doctoral
program in composition at the time, someone in writing centers,

someone who should be well-versed in composition theory) would use, of all things, a red pen. They asked me everything but "Where have you *been?!?*"

We cannot deny that red ink is still a part of our educational framework, our image. Even in a search for the phrase "red pen(s)" on the World Wide Web via AltaVista, dozens of websites (too many to count, really) provide lists of school supplies for elementary and middle school children—including the red pens necessary for peer review of written texts. Indeed, red is still frequently used by editors, even though our negative image of red evolved to the point that writing teachers now avoid it.

Red ink with all its ills has become such a standard part of our lore, that when it is mentioned in our scholarship, these references are often casual references in nature, as if readers will automatically know what we mean. Harkin (1991), in fact, used red ink as a descriptive element of what lore is in the first place:

> Lore comprises the rituals of our profession, like teaching the modes, sitting in a circle, assigning double-entry notebooks, using a red pen, forming peer-group workshops. (125)

In Furnish's (1995) plea for writing teachers to examine their hatred of grading writing, one of Furnish's assumptions is that writing teachers' frustrations are related to their writing too much—"they use more red ink than they should if both teacher and student are to keep things in perspective" (493) (see also Sommers, 1982)—but the red pen results also in the scarlet-letter shame that students must wear:

> Most teachers mark the writing they grade by using the proverbial red ink to show students that writing is fraught with the peril of costly or shameful error. (493)

The association we have with error (and, therefore, with shame) is commonly seen. Hawisher and Selfe (1991), in a review of technology in the composition classroom, warned us against using technology to move us forward only in the same old, bad ways of the old paradigm:

> We need to talk about the dangers of instructors who use computers to deliver drill-and-practice exercises to students or of instructors who promote the use of style analyzers to underscore student errors more effectively than they did five years ago with red pens. (61)

For Gage (1986), red ink was also associated with error, especially in creating students' superstitions that good writing means good grammar:

> For such students, grammar is a gigantic, invisible mine field through which they must navigate or be destroyed— when they least expect it—by red ink. They have often suffered this sort of injury . . . (16)

Gage was not alone in constructing a violent image for red ink in the composition classroom. For others, the red pen is not only associated with grammar or error, but is also an eerie symptom of teachers' undemocratic power and authority in the classroom—an authority that is, academically speaking, violent. For Briggs and Pailliotet (1997), such violence comes from the authority asserted by "those uninformed and dangerous teachers who churned out bloodied texts, who scorned their students, who abused the power vested in them by the institution" (57).

This is war, it seems. Mine fields, blood, destruction, and casualties—all brought on by the only pen that is truly mightier than the sword: that red one. For Briggs and Pailliotet, however, teachers generally seem to be losing the war, and since we are already dubbed "dangerous," it seems natural to become "armed" as well:

> In a system that doesn't allow high school teachers the same opportunities to use the bathroom as students, who can fault teachers for asserting their power with the red pen? (57)

Power, glory, shame, and violence: Can one ink color really do all that? As our understanding of assessment improves, do our students feel more shame with one color than with another? The oral and written lore of red ink—pervasive in our field—is clear. Given my own experiences, however, I have to question: Is it accurate?

THE STUDY

The following pilot study sought to determine the effects of red ink on students' perceptions of teacher comments. In short, I was curious: do students respond negatively to red ink if teachers use red ink? The following study compares blue and red ink in basic writing courses in hopes of confirming or contesting the lore of red ink in our profession.

If our lore "holds true," the students subjected to the pain of red ink in this study should have felt that teachers who used red ink were unfair, harsh, negative, authoritative. I would expect students to perhaps become fearful of those comments and, by extension, of the teacher. But at the same time, I intuitively hypothesized that red ink *wouldn't* matter. If the lore indeed remained true, students should prefer blue ink over red, but I instead predicted no difference between students' responses to red vs. blue ink.

What I learned, however, surprised me.

METHOD

Subjects

In the Fall of 1997, I asked my friend and colleague, Greg Siering, to participate in this study with me. First, I knew that Greg was teaching two sections of basic writing at the same times my two sections of basic writing were held. Second, I wanted the other teacher to be male, to counterbalance for gender effects. Further, Greg and I are approximately the same age, were ABD in Ball State's doctoral program in composition, and were teaching the 50-minute courses not only at the same time (1:00 and 3:00, MWF) but in the same building. As a general rule, neither of us used red ink in our comments on student papers, and throughout our friendship, we have often agreed on composition theory, politics, and pedagogies.[2]

Our four sections of basic writing had a total of 57 students completing a survey at the end of the course. The fall semester course (ENG 101) is the first half of a year-long sequence for basic writers (ENG 101/102) at Ball State University. At Ball State, students are placed in basic writing based on high school rank and Verbal SAT scores. Exceptions can be made for small high schools and for students successfully testing into another course.

Procedure

For this study, I chose to compare red ink with only blue ink in order to gain a simple comparison at this time. First, blue is a common ink color that should draw no response from students based on merely color. Second, blue should stand out (as red does) from students' texts, which are often printed in black ink. I chose not to involve pencil, which would introduce the variable of a different writing utensil rather than a different ink color. Future studies could compare red ink to more unusual ink colors that might be similar to red, such as pink or purple—for a discussion of fuchsia, see Bartosenski (1992)—or involve more neutral colors such as pencil or green ink.

To counterbalance for the effects of class meeting times on the outcome of this study, I used red ink in my 1:00 section and blue in my 3:00, and Greg used red ink in his 3:00 section and blue in his 1:00. The table below shows the design of the study and the number of students participating:

TABLE 6.1

Design of the Study and Number of Participants

	Red Ink	Blue Ink
Cindy	1:00 (N=15)	3:00 (N=14)
Greg	3:00 (N=12)	1:00 (N=16)
Total (N=57)	27 Students	30 Students

Greg and I used red ink for one class and blue ink for the other on all student writing: journals, rough drafts, exercises, and final drafts. As Greg and I discussed *how* we comment on students' papers, we learned how similar we are: we both concentrate on global concerns, such as organization, development, and focus; we both avoid thorough editing of texts and instead find error patterns, marking the first few to show the student the pattern, and then encouraging the student to find the rest on his/her own (or with help in a conference); we both give summary comments at the end with a mix of positive comments and suggestions for improvement; we both ask questions about content if we're confused, offer praise for good ideas, or offer comments about how we might personally relate to what a student is saying. Given the idiosyncratic nature of teacher comments, I was glad to find another teacher so similar to my own commenting style in the context of teaching basic writing courses.

Instrument

On the last day of class, students evaluated Greg and me for the English Department, a standard procedure every term. In addition to the standard evaluation that the Department gives Writing Program students, we asked our students in this study to complete a survey (see Appendix). I made four packets of the survey and coded them for the four groups (cr, cb, gr, gb), using the teacher's first initial to separate packets by teacher (c or g), then using the first initials of red and blue to separate packets by color (r or b).

Limitations

Because my primary concern here was to assess the effect of red vs. blue ink, I did not gather demographic data at this time, although such inquiry could be done in the future, assessing, for instance, differences in gender or age in response to ink color. One of my classes that participated in this study was nearly all-male; therefore, a split balance between men and women in this study could be found only if I sought other courses. For now, because the subject group was already small, and because I saw this study as a pilot, I decided not to "make the group smaller" by dividing it further into subgroups (by gender, for example).

RESULTS

First, Question 7 on the survey was designed to test students' memories of their teachers' choice of ink colors. Students were asked, "What ink color did your teacher use when making comments on your papers?" and were given choices of a) blue, b) red, c) green, d) pencil, and e) I don't remember. Most students (46 out of 57, or 80%) correctly remembered the ink color used on their papers. Interestingly, however, more students whose papers were marked in red remembered the color accurately: only 2 out of 27 students (or 7%) in the red group remembered incorrectly, while 9 out of 30 in the blue group (or 30%) remembered the ink color incorrectly. I performed a 2 X 2 chi square analysis and found a significant difference between the two groups for correctly remembering ink color ($\chi^2_{(1)} = 4.657$, $p < .05$), suggesting that students whose papers were marked in red remembered the ink color better. Although a chi square revealed a significance difference, a phi coefficient revealed that the relationship (.286) between ink color and memory may be somewhat weak, possibly due to the small number of students in this pilot. Therefore, although students in this study tended to remember red better than blue, there are likely to be too many exceptions to a firm conclusion on this point.

But overall, and surprisingly, red ink seemed to be slightly favored on average by students in this study. As Table 6.2 shows, students whose papers were marked with red ink thought their teachers' comments were more fair (Question 1), encouraging (Question 2), and constructive (Question 3), based on the mean scores given to the first three questions. Table 6.2 shows the mean scores and standard deviations for student responses on the first three questions. Those who saw only red ink judged their teachers' comments more favorably on average, though no differences were statistically significant.[3]

Notice that of these three items, the blue group had higher standard deviations in two of the items—teachers' fairness and encouragement—indicating that students in the red group agreed more consistently in their responses to these items.

TABLE 6.2

Student Judgments of Teacher Comments

(5 = strongly agree; 3 = Neutral; 1 = strongly disagree)
Red N = 30; Blue N = 27

		Red	Blue
1. I feel my teacher made very fair comments on my papers. ($F_{1,53} = 2.95$, p>.05)	M	4.67	4.33
	SD	0.595	0.796
2. My teacher gave me adequate encouragement in his/her comments. ($F_{1,53} = 1.00$, p>.05)	M	4.57	4.37
	SD	0.575	0.755
3. My teacher used constructive criticism rather than negative. ($F_{1,53} = 2.95$, p>.05)	M	4.48	4.37
	SD	0.775	0.727

TABLE 6.3

Emotion toward Teacher Comments

(5 = strongly agree; 3 = Neutral; 1 = strongly disagree)
Red N = 30; Blue N = 27

		Red	Blue
4. I looked forward to reading my teacher's comments.	M	4.59	4.40
	SD	0.596	0.68
5. I like that my teacher writes on my papers. ($F_{1,53} = 1.00$, p>.05)	M	4.74	4.80
	SD	0.453	0.41

Because the issue here centers on students' emotional responses to red ink, I was sure to ask about their feelings, such as looking forward to reading teacher comments and simply "liking" the fact that the teacher commented at all. Table 6.3 shows the average score given to Questions 4 and 5 on the survey, items that I hoped would illustrate students' emotional responses to teacher comments. As Table 6.3 shows, students whose papers were marked in red ink responded more favorably to one item, but less favorably to another.

Though there was no significant difference between red and blue ink on Question 4 ($F_{1,53}$=.87, p>.05), it's surprising that students in the red ink group rated this item more favorably at all. Differences in responses to Question 5, however, showed that students whose papers were marked in blue "liked" that their teachers wrote on their papers, an item I had hoped would determine if red vs. blue ink had an effect on students' sensitivity to their papers being marked in the first place. This difference, too, was not significant ($F_{1,53}$=.38, p>.05), though this item was the only one in which blue had a higher mean than red.

Table 6.4 shows students' responses to Question 6, which tried to determine how students reacted to the amount of comments teachers provided. The question asked if teachers, in the students' opinions, wrote "an adequate amount" on their papers, but it did not seek to determine if students felt teachers wrote too little or too much. For the purposes of this study, "too little or too much" is another issue: students' negative or positive response to the item, regardless of the reason, is all I sought here. One student, in a written comment on the survey, however, indicated that the teacher did not write enough; otherwise, no data to that effect was gathered.

Note that the standard deviation for the blue group is more than four times higher than the red group's variability, suggesting a much higher consistency with which the students in the red group responded to this item. There was also a significance difference ($F_{1,53}$=8.48, $p < .01$) in students' responses to the amount of comments Greg and I made on

TABLE 6.4

Amount of Teacher Comments

(5 = strongly agree; 3 = Neutral; 1 = strongly disagree)
Red N = 30; Blue N = 27

		Red	Blue
I feel my teacher wrote an	M	4.59	4.40
adequate amount: not too much,	SD	0.596	0.68
not too little.			

their papers. Students in the blue ink group were significantly
more dissatisfied than the red ink group, but there were no significant differences between Greg's group and mine, as Table
6.5 shows.

TABLE 6.5

Analysis of Variance for Question 6:
Students' Satisfaction with Amount of Comment

Source	df	Mean Sq	F	Sig
Teacher	1	0.37201	0.65	0.4242
Ink Color	1	4.86258	8.48	.0053*
Teacher X Ink	1	0.63616	4.11	0.2971
Residual	53	0.57358		

*p<.01

In spite of all of the questions on this survey, I was most
interested in students' responses to Question 9, which asked
them to comment on the nature of red ink. While I expected no
significant difference among students' responses to this
question, I was surprised that of 27 students whose papers
were marked in red ink, *none* of them described red as having
a "harsh, negative" tone. In contrast, 40% of the students
whose papers were marked in blue ink suggested that a
"harsh, negative tone" is associated with red ink. More
surprisingly, 19% of the students in the red ink group indicated

that red is "bright and cheerful," while only 4% of the blue ink group suggested the same.

In other words, the only students in this study who responded negatively to red ink were students whose papers were *not marked in red*. Table 6.6 shows the percentage of responses to each choice given in Question 9:

TABLE 6.6

Students' Descriptions of Red Ink
(percentages will not add to 100%. Two students did not answer this question.)

Descriptions of Red Ink	Red	Blue
Red ink has a harsh, negative tone.	0%	40%
Red ink is easy to see.	78%	50%
Red ink is bright and cheerful.	19%	3%

A 2 x 3 chi square analysis showed a significant difference in how students perceived red ink ($X^2_{(2)}= 15.71$, $p < .001$), and a phi coefficient of .53 indicates a fairly strong relationship between the ink color actually used with students and their perceptions of that ink color. Further, the fact that the majority of students (78%) in the red ink group thought that red ink is easy to see fits well with the higher accuracy with which students in the red ink group recalled the color used on their papers (Question 7, discussed earlier).

Question 8 asked students to recommend an ink color for their teachers to use in the future. They were given options of a) blue, b) red, c) green, d) pencil, e) it really doesn't matter to me, and f) other (with a note for them to specify). I wasn't surprised to see that the majority of students (52.5%) noted that it didn't matter to them. However, the second-highest recommendation (overall) was for red ink, with 37% of the red ink group recommending red and even 17% of the blue ink group recommending that red be used in the future. Table 6.7

shows the percentages of students' future recommendations, divided by which ink color their teacher had used. Only one student marked "other," recommending purple.

To conduct a chi square analysis, I deleted the categories not under consideration here—green, pencil, and other—and kept only red, blue, and "it doesn't matter." In a 2 x 3 chi square, then, I found a significant difference among students'

TABLE 6.7

Student Recommendations for Future Ink Color
(Percentages are rounded.)

Recommendation	Red	Blue	Total
Blue	4%	27%	16.0%
Red	37%	17%	26.0%
Groon	0%	0%	0.0%
Pencil	4%	3%	3.5%
Doesn't Matter	55%	50%	52.5%
Other	0%	3%	3.0%

recommendations for future ink color ($X^2_{(2)} = 6.77$, $p < .05$) (phi coefficient = .35), suggesting that most students in this study really don't care what ink color we use. The second most popular recommendation, however, was for the ink color with which students were already familiar: for students in the red group, red was the second-highest recommendation; for students in the blue group, blue was the second-highest recommendation. We could explore this issue in future research: if students had not been given "it really doesn't matter" as an option, would we see the "familiar" color chosen most frequently?

I ended the study at the end of Fall 1997 when these students completed ENG 101, the first half of the basic writing sequence (ENG 101/102). When the same students came back for ENG 102 in Spring 1998, I did not ask Greg to continue the red/blue study, and I decided to end my part of the study in the second semester by switching to a third ink color— black, which I felt was more "neutral."

One day during ENG 102, however, some students began
to discuss their talents as creative writers. Without any prompt-
ing from me, though we were about to do a creative writing
assignment, my students began to wonder: were they better
creative writers or academic writers? As the discussion
continued, I commented on what I felt were my own
strengths—academic writing—and noted that I'm probably a
better critic than a creative writer. One student laughed, "Yeah!
I can tell! All those red marks on my papers!" Other students
laughed good-naturedly, but one student turned to face the
first: "You still get RED? I only get BLACK!" Looking at me, he
moaned and accused, "That's just so unfair!" Interestingly, the
first student remembered red comments, even though I had
switched to black ink. Another noticed the switch in color but
felt he was somehow getting "less."

DISCUSSION

These surprising results, which showed either no difference
in students' reactions to red vs. blue ink or showed that red ink
was slightly preferred to blue should cause our field to rethink
the lore of red ink that it has created. Most results here were
not statistically significant, so I cannot make a claim as strong
as "students prefer red ink." At the same time, I was surprised
to see *any* preference for red ink at all, especially in the context
of our commonly-held belief that red ink is negative. If the lore
remained "true," we should have seen a much greater
preference for blue ink. I believe that these results were due to
two factors in particular.

First, the context in which the red ink lore began has
changed. Surprisingly, the lore has not. In early research on
teachers' comments, much discussion focused on "negative"
vs. "positive" commentary (Schaub, 1997). Other research
showed the ineffectiveness of some kinds of comments, such
as thorough editing of the text, cryptic remarks in the margin
(such as "awk"), or simple grades with no explanation.
Applebee (1981) and Anson (1989) reported that the amount of

teacher comments on merely surface errors was as high as 71% and 75%, respectively.

In that context, the lore of red ink began: the accepted practice of more negative comments than positive ones, and the frequent attention to error. Since then, teachers are more informed about the effects of their comments, and several texts have been devoted solely to the art of teacher commentary.[4] Given changes in the way our field treats assessment, this pilot study suggests the need to rethink the lore that accompanies assessment as well.

In spite of changes in our profession, the lore that has defined that profession remains unchanged, and North's (1987) prophetic statement—that once something has been added to lore, it cannot be removed from it—has proven not only to be true, but unfortunate as well, especially in the evolving contexts in which we work.

Second, our own construction of the red ink lore has been based, in part, on our own literary training. "Red," after all, is never "missed" by the literary critic or the English teacher as a significant choice of color by a writer. For us, red means death, blood, war, lust, or danger—because we have been trained to see it as such. How else has a simple ink color so easily conjured so many violent images in our scholarship?

Blue, too, is quite symbolic—of sadness, water, air, tranquility—yet, we do not give much attention to that. Nor do we give attention to the white paper and black ink our students use, though such colors are as equally traditional for students as red pens are for teachers.

If we were to supplement our literary interpretations with cognitive interpretations, we would come to understand that red ink does not *deserve* this attention. It simply *grabs* our attention: a color as bright and as bold as red, meaningful in literary circles, is simply, in cognitive terms, salient, especially on student papers produced on traditional white paper with black ink. Perhaps our students have not been victimized by the red pen so much as we have been victimized by our lack of understanding of such cognitive principles as "perception" and "human memory."

And what about our students? For most of our freshmen, such literary training has not been so deeply ingrained. How can we assume that their reaction to red ink will be as literary as ours and, therefore, as negative? Students in this study suggested the most practical reason for using red: it's easy to see. And don't we want them to do just that? See—not "see as we see," but, simply, "see."

CONCLUSION

In our quest to embrace democratic pedagogies, red ink has become a symbol of all that we hope to avoid. From political, literary, and emotional standpoints, then, we have constructed the belief that red ink in our communication with students via our comments on their papers is negative, violent, and hurtful. Research that validates or refutes such beliefs must, in contrast, examine as objectively as possible such "truths." While this pilot study (or others like it) cannot examine deeply an individual's response to ink color, it does suggest the power of such research to examine broadly the equally broad belief we hold regarding ink color.

Do we really want to maintain such a deeply held belief about something as silly as ink color? Do we really believe that students are more affected by the color of our comments than by the content or tone? And in our quest to examine authority and power in the classroom (and our own paradoxical willingness to embrace authority and power in order to "give" some to our students), shouldn't we admit that removing red ink from the situation is merely a bandage and not a cure?

Such passionate attention to ink color diverts our attention from other, more important, issues—as unpleasant as some of those issues might be (even more unpleasant than the odious red pen). For instance, when an undergraduate peer tutor from our writing center began her first high school teaching job after graduation, she called me one night, appalled to learn her school's policy that all teachers *must* use red ink on students' work. Although, as writing center director at the time, I didn't recall talking about red ink in particular, our tutor training program did include numerous readings in which red ink was portrayed as the enemy, and this was one tutor in particular who attended as many professional conferences as she could, where she was undoubtedly exposed to the lore. Now an English teacher herself, this former tutor, because of her training, couldn't escape the lore of red ink and, more importantly, couldn't escape the passion surrounding such lore.

Because I felt partly responsible for her distress, I spent several minutes encouraging her to calmly ask her principal for the origin of the policy, and I pointed out a possible and unfortunate cause: if her school had trouble with students falsifying records, changing grades, or forging teachers' signatures, a standardized ink color might be a part of their solution to preventing such problems. I told her a story of a high school classmate of my own, who once erased and then changed some of his grades written in pencil in our senior English teacher's gradebook when she left her gradebook unattended one day.

Although I became a teacher one day myself, my own adolescent past included a talent for forging teachers' signatures on hall passes—a harmless prank, or so I thought, until I grew up and learned more about schools and their legal responsibilities. Fortunately, no one for whom I had written a hall pass had been injured or had caused harm to someone else.

This former tutor had been so fortunate to have worked mostly with highly motivated, sincere, honest college students in our writing center. Unfortunately, we teachers also know that not all students are the same, and especially in the context of working with teenagers, we know their desire to test the limits sometimes—an unfortunate impetus for much classroom policy/policing.

But on the brighter side, colors—even red—are useful in many ways. For instance, my own students recently reminded me of the importance of color-coding their papers—or what

Bartosenski (1992) called "painting a paper"—something I often encourage my students to do. Two of my most motivated students in a basic writing course in the Spring of 1998 (the red ink group in this very study) were often models of collaboration—Ryan and Chad shared their papers with each other in and out of class, energetically discussed the points they were trying to make, made helpful suggestions that they accepted or rejected, asked critical questions, called me in to settle several disputes, but refused to "do the work" for each other.

One day, during a peer review session, Ryan brought my purse from the front desk to where I was sitting with another group of students in the back of the room. "Do you have a red pen?" Ryan asked, handing me my purse. "Chad needs to color-code his paper. It's all messed up." From across the room, Chad laughed at himself, yelling, "Yeah! It's a mess! But we just figured it out!"

Could such excellent collaboration among students even occur in a classroom in which the teacher used the threatening red ink? Could such rapport develop in this classroom (with authoritative red ink) to the point that a student feels comfortable bringing me my purse from across the room? Could such excellent skills at self-assessment and peer review emerge in a classroom bloodied by a red pen? Of course. Because there's so much more to my teaching and yours than the color of an ink.

Studies such as this one provide a deeper look into our beliefs—what they are, where they come from, and whom or what are they for. As teachers frequently grapple with how to comment on student papers, the avoidance of red ink should not provide a superficial kind of relief. Just as we ask ourselves hard questions about how to word those comments or how much to comment (and where), we should examine more fully the effects of what those comments look like—not assuming, uncritically, that one color is "off limits" and the others are all somehow (equally) acceptable. Further, research such as this will not only test those beliefs, but could also place our beliefs in the larger context of student-teacher rapport, assignment making, cognition, and individual conferences. As our field rapidly changes, so must our lore—especially when that lore doesn't make sense to the people who matter the most—our students.

What's next for my classroom, my students, and the pens in my purse? To be honest, I'm not sure. Should I continue using red ink? I discovered during this study a strange outcome of limiting ourselves to only one color. One night I discovered that I had no red pens at home, but I had to grade papers from the "red ink group." I ran to a nearby 24-hour supermarket to purchase more. It would have ruined my study if I had used another color, but my office was farther away than the supermarket. I laughed all the way there, "Oh, I see. *This* is why we shouldn't use red ink!"

In the semester following this study, I first started using black ink consistently, but later I randomly used whatever writing utensil I first grabbed out of my well-used purse whenever I graded papers: pencils, blue pens, red pens. It didn't matter, I thought, but in the back of my mind the question remained, "doesn't it?" These students remembered red, responded somewhat more favorably to red, and, on one day, even asked for red.

Next, then, will be more experimentation because I can't quite decide what to do. I started this study thinking that ink color didn't matter at all. Now I suspect that it does, but not in the way our lore has taught us. I would first like to continue gathering data in the same manner from more students, perhaps adding interviews that will give fuller descriptions of students' reactions to our red ink lore. A different study could compare (instead of ink color) consistency of ink color: some classes would get a systematic rotation of varied colors, and others would get a steady use of one color. If we keep switching colors, will students' attention be drawn instead to the content of our comments? Will it matter at all? Only future experimentation will reveal that.

SUMMARY

Similar to the interview with Eileen Oliver, this study demonstrates the potential collapse of the qualitative/quantitative dichotomy. The red ink/blue ink pilot study presented here shares, on the one hand, features of both anecdotal and numerical evidence; on the other hand and more accurately, it presents, on the whole, *neither*. It is instead a study that explores a question in the context of the researcher's curiosity, experience, and available resources—a study that demonstrates a Contextualist Research Paradigm that encourages us to explore our research not simply as "qualitative" or "quantitative," but—simply, and more broadly defined—as research: research conducted in contexts that may produce varied processes/decisions and products/forms.

If we paid attention to only form here, a traditional report would not have the personal voice, narrative threads, anecdotes, or "asides" that I shared for the purpose of illustrating my point of view and examining all kinds of evidence available to me in the context of this study. Similarly, a purely "qualitative" study would not have focused on numerical data and conducted such descriptive and inferential statistical analyses. Attending instead to context, I presented this study in the form most appropriate for what I wanted to know—a decision I made in the process of research that resulted in a product that shares a blend of voices, styles, and forms—all dictated by context.

Applying a Contextualist Research Paradigm has great potential for reconstructing our field—our teachers, researchers, and scholarship. Especially as we conduct and read research, attending to contextualist principles will allow us to examine and accept our research for what it is in its moment—understanding strengths and limitations, knowing that one study never pretends to answer everything about the nature of our work. All research methods have limits—and all research methods have potential—depending on the contexts in which we ask and explore our research questions.

Chapter five, through an illustration, examined the potential of a Contextualist Research Paradigm and its accompanying matrix—to see the breadth of this concept called "research." Chapter six, through a demonstration, explored its potential further. Chapter seven will outline other specific needs our field must meet in order to fully embrace a new contextualist paradigm and chapter eight will speculate on the future of composition research.

NOTES

1. Ball State University approval for this study is filed under IRB protocol ID #98-48.

2. I'd like to thank my friend and colleague Greg Siering for participating in this study, even though he normally does not use red ink (though not out of concern for students' reactions, but his own distaste for how the color looks on the page—in his own words, "it's an aesthetic thing").

3. Statistical significance in this study was determined through stepwise regression analysis through which all variables (teachers, class times, and ink color) were factored in separately to ensure that no differences existed because of differences in teacher, differences in class times, or differences in group sizes per ink color (Greg, for example, had more students in the blue ink group, and I had more students in the red ink group). Computer analysis determined that these differences in group sizes and some other variables produced no significant differences. While the F-values reported here look much like a standard ANOVA, conducting a stepwise regression analysis is a more "sophisticated" way of conducted an ANOVA in some contexts.

4. See, for example, White, Lutz, & Kamusikiri (1996) *Assessment of Writing: Politics, Policies, Practices*; White (1994) *Teaching and Assessing Writing*; Anson (1989) *Writing and Response*; Straub & Lunsford (1995) *Twelve Readers Reading: Responding to College Student Writing*; and Zak & Weaver (1998) *The Theory and Practice of Grading Writing: Problems and Possibilities*.

APPENDIX

Response to Teacher Comments
* please do not put your name on this form *

Please rank the following (5 = strongly agree; 3 = neutral;
1 = strongly disagree)

1. I feel my teacher made very fair   5 4 3 2 1
   comments on my papers
2. My teacher gave me adequate   5 4 3 2 1
   encouragement in his/her comments
3. My teacher used constructive   5 4 3 2 1
   criticism rather than negative
4. I looked forward to reading my   5 4 3 2 1
   teacher's comments
5. I like that my teacher writes on   5 4 3 2 1
   my papers
6. I feel my teacher wrote an   5 4 3 2 1
   adequate amount: not too much, not too little

Please circle the answers that apply to you:

7. What ink color did your teacher use when making
   comments on your papers?
      a. blue
      b. red
      c. green
      d. pencil
      e. I don't remember
8. I'd like to recommend the following ink color to my
   teacher in the future:
      a. blue
      b. red
      c. green
      d. pencil

    e. it really doesn't matter to me

    f. Other: _____

9. Please circle the statement that is most fitting to you
   (please circle only ONE):

    a. Red ink has a harsh, negative tone

    b. Red ink is easy to see

    c. Red ink is bright and cheerful

7 PREDICTOR VARIABLES
The Future of Composition Research

> Rhetoric has as its domain all aspects of the argumentative
> mode of discourse including logic, dialectic, and the
> methodology of science.
>
> Walter Weimer, 1979

To fully embrace the Contextualist Research Paradigm, we must take other steps that will enable us to do so. This chapter will focus on specific recommendations for changing the direction of our research trends: reconsidering MLA as a style manual, understanding the exclusionary voices of our storytellers, incorporating our research in our teaching, training our researchers more completely in a wider range of research methods and statistics, and embracing numbers as natural phenomena. All of these specific recommendations are made with an eye toward the overall context of our field's quest to define itself and construct its boundaries in an accurate, respectable, and flexible manner.

MLA VOICE, MY VOICE

When I began this project, I was writing in MLA style. I later changed to APA, but I couldn't explain why—something about MLA style bothered me in this work. I thought perhaps APA would make more sense if only because of my interest in science and psychology and in numerical evidence. And, personally, I've always preferred APA to MLA anyway. But, still, I couldn't figure out why.

MLA treats text as a "living" object of study, always in front of us, always available to us. Therefore, if I were to write about Milton's *Paradise Lost* or Morrison's *Paradise*, I would use present tense for both, regardless of how old or how new those texts are, or how many centuries separate the two. That is the convention of literature and of literary criticism—and justifiably so. The novel, the poem, the short story—works of literature—can always be interpreted, reinterpreted, criticized, but the work itself will not change. Once it is published, it's published. It's "there." Forever. Thus, present tense treats the text adequately—the work "is."

In composition, however, in spite of numerous publications that will also be there "forever," our texts serve a different purpose: constructing theory, presenting research, and discussing pedagogy are acts that focus not on the *product* of the text that resulted from such inquiry, but on the *process* of thinking that was used to arrive at that text in the first place and the later application of those ideas to our work. Yet, because of our ties to literature, we continue to use MLA style in our own publications[1]—as if the scholarship we are reviewing is "present" in text form rather than "past" in thought form. And because our texts are based on theory, research, and pedagogy (rather than fiction), our use of MLA ties the theories, research, and pedagogies to their authors in the present tense as if those authors still believe—still currently "live" in—that theory, research, or pedagogy. In other words, the present tense that MLA requires for treatment of *text*, is transferred instead, in composition, to treatment of *authors*. As a result, our criticism, citations, and use of composition scholarship locks the author—rather than the text—in present tense.

Consider, for example, Bushman's (1998) use of Flower's (1979) cognitive description of writer-based and reader-based prose:

> Linda Flower *explains* this phenomenon in cognitive terms and, like Vygotsky, *believes* that a writer must "transform" one's "writer-based prose" into "reader-based prose." (10, emphasis mine)

Citing a theory that is almost 20 years old in a manner that makes Flower (and, worse, Vygotsky) "still believe"—always—something she published in 1979 de-contextualizes our work. To write about composition publications in the present tense creates the illusion that our authors, regardless of the amount of time that has passed, still believe their theories of twenty years before.

Because the constraints of MLA documentation demand present tense, composition publications that require MLA style limit our authors and decontextualize our work in four ways: 1) the authors currently writing and publishing must use present tense advocated by the MLA regardless of what is best in the context of their work, 2) present tense for both our discussion/analysis/commentary and our source citations makes it more difficult for readers to distinguish between the author's own voice and the voices of other texts to which the author refers, 3) present tense does not allow authors who are being cited to have their own works viewed in the context in which they were originally published, and 4) authors cited in present tense are locked into what they *believed* (in 1979, in Flower's case) as if those works will always represent what those authors are thinking *now* (i.e., Flower can't learn anything more after 1979 that would change her mind).

Present tense, as required by MLA when reviewing scholarship, has a certain "indefinite" tone to it, suggesting "always, forever," while at the same time a certain "definitiveness" to it, suggesting a "rigid, locked" status of our scholarship and our scholars. In reality, our past publications are so often revisited, revised, and extended beyond themselves, and, certainly, the authors themselves continue to grow, change, and refine their beliefs. Frequent interchanges of ideas through our scholarship create new theories, new research, new pedagogies, even from the authors who once proposed the "old." This scholarship, in other words, is not literary and will, therefore, be "changed." While Toni Morrison, for example, might write differently in her next novel, or might write even better than she already does, no amount of criticism or questions or reviews will make Morrison change *Paradise* or change the "idea" that produced it—because no one would ever expect her to. It's literature. And that's what literature is, and that's what the MLA is historically about.

In contrast to MLA, the APA recommends past tense. Research was completed in the past, after all, and theories proposed are published in the past as well. For APA, the context of time is important, which is why the year is placed near the authors' names in APA citations.[2] To show the difference that using APA can make in composition scholarship, consider the following paragraph, a combination of reference and commentary, printed earlier in this work. The passage is in APA style, with the verb phrases highlighted:

But such a study *takes* time and, worse, *requires* quantifying and analyzing data (numbers, in other words), and Elbow *warned* us in the same book that any reduction of anything to a single number is "untrustworthy" (251). Never mind that Elbow *warned* us also in the beginning of the same book that his reflections *were* biased and that he, like Gulliver, *was* a less-than-reliable narrator (vi). The current climate of our field (one of new favoritism toward qualitative forms of research) *has produced* a battle for trustworthiness between a number and a narrative. And the narrative clearly *wins*—not because it necessarily *offers* more (or more accurate) information than the other, but because the narrative *offers* one kind of information that we clearly value more.

The past tense in reference to Elbow helps separate his voice (established by past tense) from my own voice and commentary (established by present tense). Past tense here also ties what Elbow *said* only to the specific work being cited, not to "Elbow's thoughts generally and for all time," keeping his words tied closely to the specific context in which they were written—the most honest and fair look at any author in the first place.

Further, in my own classrooms, I am reminded of my students' needs to learn APA documentation for their own fields. On the first day of class in Composition II (which has a focus on research), I give students a survey, asking about their familiarity with MLA documentation, their comfort with computers and the library, and other questions, including "What is your major?" Most students are majoring in fields that require APA: education, social work, psychology, and so on. Other students are undecided. As a writing teacher, it is my duty to discuss not only MLA, but APA also, and, more importantly, to allow students to choose one or the other for their research projects, as they decide which is more appropriate in the context of their research and their futures. Several students opt for MLA because they've been taught MLA in Composition I and ultimately choose the familiar (and, of course, some decide that MLA is more appropriate for their tasks). Most students, however, are grateful for the chance to learn APA, and, similar to my own experience as a psychology major (in which only one professor figured out that no one else was teaching APA documentation and format), they feared no one was ever going to help them learn it.

I propose that composition scholars abandon MLA as a style manual. Using other styles such as APA will help us establish our voices more clearly, will help us understand our scholarship and our scholars in their contexts more strongly, and will more accurately reflect the notion that our authors frequently refine their ideas and beliefs.

VOICES, STORYTELLERS, POWER, AND TENURE

Researchers have many voices. Even the so-called impersonal voice of traditional research—the voice that is seen as voiceless because it is drowned by a system of other researchers, other theories, data, and a traditional format for a report—is, in itself, a voice nonetheless: a voice chosen by the researcher at that moment, in that context of his/her research shared in the most appropriate forum, a voice that chooses at the moment to focus readers' attention on issues other than itself. A researcher's voice in the most traditional-looking research report isn't as "drowned" as we might think: adhering to styles such as APA helps distinguish researchers' voices (using present tense for discussions, conclusions, experience, commentary, analyses) from the voices of others (using past tense for literature reviews and for descriptions of methods). Such clarification, in fact, helps reveal the full context in which a researcher is operating by clearly outlining the sources—such as "formal" publication *and* "informal" interaction with others—of a researcher's thoughts (Gilbert & Mulkay, 1984).

Adopting any voice—as varied as those voices might be—is a rhetorical act, a rhetorical decision, made by a writer in a particular context. Unfortunately, several composition scholars now advocate a "personal voice" through storytelling as the only necessary voice in our scholarship, regardless of other necessities, regardless of the writer's own personal decision to do otherwise, and regardless of the context in which the researcher is writing.

And who are the storytellers in composition today? For the most part, we have two groups of scholars in composition from whom we readily accept the story. First, the "big names." Peter Elbow, Louise Phelps, Teresa Enos, Joe Trimmer, Donald Graves, the presidents of our organizations—these names have earned the right to tell stories because they paid their dues earlier with traditional scholarship. (How else does someone become a keynote speaker? We all *have* stories, of course, but not everyone is allowed to *tell* one at a convention in front of everybody.) Spack (1997) commented on the unwillingness of mainstream journals to publish "the personal," citing Gebhardt's (1992) admission that during his tenure as editor of *CCC* (1987-1993), "personal perspective essays" were reserved for "leaders" of our field (20). In other words, once a scholar has established a reputation via other, more traditional forms of scholarship—including a doctoral dissertation—the rules that govern their scholarship lighten up. Storytellers emerge when our field has granted them the privilege to do so.

In Trimmer's *Narration as Knowledge* (1997), for example, who were the storytellers? Lad Tobin, Toby Fulwiler, Wendy Bishop, James Clifford, Chris Anson, Sondra Perl, Lillian Bridwell-Bowles . . . There were only a few "names" I didn't recognize at first—names I felt I probably *should* know but didn't (in the neverending remnants of graduate-student guilt that comes from not studying absolutely *everything*). But most of the names I *had* studied. I had to study them in order to earn my degree, write my exams, and earn the privilege of writing a dissertation. What's next for me? That depends. If I earn a "name," can I, too, tell stories? For now, my stories had better be embedded in the larger context of scholarship, research, and dissertation-like citations to everybody else's name but my own.

For those who argue that stories are somehow automatically "inclusive"—that they allow everyone to have a voice and do not systematically marginalize anyone—consider Gunner and McNenny's (1997) description of how they invited speakers to the Conference on Basic Writing, held at CCCC 1997 in Phoenix:

> In inviting the workshop speakers, we were quite aware of the political truism that the voices heard are the voices that validate. To have our issues "spoken into existence," in a sense, we looked in some cases to have speakers who themselves wield some professional and institutional power. Victor Villanueva, Gary Tate, Jacqueline Jones Royster, Ira Shor: were they themselves not so committed to inclusiveness, our invitations to them would really have been a kind of exploitation, of their names, status, and labor. (3-4)

Invited to ride the coat-tails of this inclusiveness, paradoxically validated by the institutional and professional power granted to the few, were newcomers, new storytellers: with Gary Tate, John McMillan and Elizabeth Woodworth; with Jacqueline Jones Royster, Rebecca Greenberg Taylor. Indeed, storytellers at this conference were ones with names and power, who invited and mentored a few fortunate graduate students and junior faculty to become storytellers and temporarily attach their otherwise powerless names to ones with power—the leaders of our field whose personal perspectives we value.

Undergraduates form the second group of composition scholars we readily allow to tell stories: the peer tutor. Especially in venues like the "Tutors' Column" of the *Writing Lab Newsletter*, undergraduate peer tutors are encouraged to share their experiences and tell their stories. That's OK. Because they're still undergraduates, we don't expect extensive knowledge of the scholarship in our field. And because the work of the peer tutor is commonly described as beginning primarily in "practice" rather than in "theory," we value their experiences and stories before they become tainted, while they're still honest, and while they present and publish—not for tenure, but for *knowledge*, for learning, for the challenge of it all, and sometimes just for fun or, especially, for that good feeling we all get afterwards.

In other words, the two groups in composition most likely to be storytellers (and be readily accepted as such) are those who have achieved status ("big names") and those who couldn't care less about status yet (undergraduate peer tutors). In the meantime, those who are somewhere in the gray middle of the spectrum (graduate students, new Ph.D's, non-tenured professors, adjunct faculty) have not yet earned the privilege of just telling stories (as if everyone would listen) but have moved beyond the undergraduate years when that's almost all we had to share.[3]

While systems for achieving tenure are being questioned currently, we are still tenure-seeking professionals who understand the value of institutional power and are, therefore, still bound by older rules governing the granting of tenure at most universities. Can telling stories alone earn us tenure? Probably not. But *theorizing* the role of storytelling in our scholarship, *epistemizing* storytelling, surely can. Spurred on, perhaps, by contentions such as Boyer's (1990) that "a new vision of scholarship is required . . . to clarify campus missions and relate the work of the academy more directly to the realities of contemporary life" (13)—to reward faculty time spent teaching and mentoring students, not just time spent as researchers—we have inferred license for the personal, anecdotal research that we now prefer.

But Boyer also reminded us that when current tenure systems were formulated, "research *per se* was not the problem. The problem was that the research mission, which was appropriate for *some* institutions, created a shadow over the entire higher learning enterprise" (12). To help rewrite those missions in a way that would help us value both research and teaching, Boyer identified four kinds of scholarship in a model that does not suggest we stop doing traditional research, but that places our research in the larger cycle, the larger context, of our scholarly work (17-25):

1. The Scholarship of Discovery
   - knowledge for its own sake
   - traditional definition of "research"
   - asks, "what is there to know?"
2. The Scholarship of Integration
   - dependent on and related to the scholarship of discovery
   - connects knowledge to larger contexts, ideas, other disciplines
   - asks, "what does this knowledge mean?"
3. The Scholarship of Application
   - dependent on and related to the scholarship of discovery and integration
   - applies knowledge to useful contexts
   - asks, "who or what can this knowledge help?"
4. The Scholarship of Teaching
   - transmitting, transforming, and extending the discovery, integration, and application of knowledge
   - makes others aware of the application of integrated discoveries
   - asks, "what more do we need to know?" (return to discovery)

In casual conversations with others in my field, I've often heard Boyer's name mentioned in support of the "scholarship of teaching," as if he separated teaching from this model, elevating it above the larger context of discovery, integration, and application of knowledge. Instead, Boyer argued, "What we urgently need today is a more inclusive view of what it means to be a scholar—a recognition that knowledge is acquired through research, through synthesis, through practice, and through teaching" (24). For Boyer, "inspired teaching keeps the flame of scholarship alive" (24)—all scholarship. And though it appears in varied forms, such scholarship must not be so separate from our teaching.

TEACHING OUR RESEARCH

One argument frequently put forth in defense of experience-based narratives is that such narratives create closer ties between our research and our teaching. We *are* quite good at sharing stories and research about our teaching, but we so seldom do the reverse: teach our research. Some scholars have asked this question before: "Why don't we teach our research or our theory to our students?" Troyka (1984), for instance, proposed that basic writers read texts from the classical rhetoric that first shaped our field. Schilb (1991) argued that composition students should be "coinquirers into the ramifications of cultural studies and postmodernism" as students "may hunger for genuine intellectual substance" (187). Harkin (1991) contrasted our field to chemistry, where research will ultimately be taught in chemistry courses. Research in chemistry is an integral, necessary part of *learning* chemistry. We would be hard-pressed to assert that we, too, pass on our research to our students in a manner that will help them engage fully in the study of writing. Frequent use of texts like readers and handbooks indicates that we still prefer, in spite of a so-called new paradigm, to rely on examples/models, study questions, and rules.

Unless we share our research with our students, we won't like the answer to a most difficult question: "Whose knowledge do we advance when we conduct research and publish our inquiry?" For now, the answer is "ours," not our students'. And whose knowledge *should* we serve in the end? A text such as Elbow and Belanoff's *Community of Writers*, for instance, offers clear case studies of writers in action, including the authors. What would happen if we provided students with excellent case studies such as those with other research: Brand's (1989) research on affective responses to writing, Jensen and DiTiberio's (1989) research on the MBTI, Straub's (1997) research on teachers' comments, Oliver's (1995) research on writing prompts, Johnson's (1991) review of the history of writing in the last century?

Incorporating more of our research into our composition textbooks, of course, places greater demands on our field. First, it requires that we stop arguing about research so much and start doing some (see Charney, 1996; Barton, 1997). Second, it requires that our research be useful not only to teachers, editors, and tenure committees, but also, and more importantly, to the students who need it. Teaching our research will make us more accountable for that research, will open a different and necessary dialogue about research with students (and, by extension, ourselves), will present our discipline to our students in the full, rich context of its long history and varied inquiry, and will invite students to conduct their own inquiry into the nature of composing—outcomes that will bridge more solidly the gap we have created between our teaching and our scholarship and research.

But are we prepared to do so?

TRAINING OUR RESEARCHERS

Numerous scholars have pointed to the lack of training in research and statistics by composition graduate programs designed to produce "humanists." Lauer and Asher (1988), Hayes and Young, et al. (1992), North (1985), and Ede (1992), to name only a few, have all commented in some way on our limited training. We can still find composition programs that require more literature than composition or that require at least some literature training instead of training in research design and statistics.

In an online survey of eight doctoral programs in composition (March 1998, consortium-l@mtu.edu), none of the eight respondents indicated that their programs require a course in statistics, and only one-half, or four, of those programs provided training in "quantitative" research methods, though three of those four blended these methods in the same course as "qualitative." All eight respondents indicated that research and research designs relying on numerical evidence are not highly valued in their programs. Further, four of the eight respondents indicated that scores on the Quantitative section of the GRE are less important than Verbal and Analytical scores, and two indicated that Quantitative *and* Analytical scores are less important than Verbal scores when admitting doctoral students to their programs. Only one respondent indicated that all three sections are treated equally, and one chose not to answer the question. Thus, in addition to not consistently providing training for our doctoral students, we do not highly value potential and important indicators of their math training, ability, or anxiety. While these eight programs might not be representative of the broader field and of all doctoral programs, the eight programs in this survey represent the training currently provided to 182 doctoral students.

Add to this inadequate textbooks designed to train the composition researcher (as reviewed in chapter two), and the result is that our training (if we receive any at all) is, at best, potentially misguided. Our strongest and most comprehensive text yet is Hayes and Young, et al. (1992), *Reading Empirical Research Studies: The Rhetoric of Research.* As the title suggests, the editors focused on the rhetoric of research: "the scientist is to be seen as a practicing rhetorician" (8). The collection of eighteen studies, with comments on strengths and weaknesses by the editors and reflections by the original authors, is an excellent text for any course on research. A special chapter is devoted to how to read traditional research reports, all couched in an argument similar to the one I am making here: "By and large, those responsible for maintaining and improving writing instruction in this country cannot, without further training, access the work that could help them carry out their responsibilities better" (6). Still, editors of this text, as others have done, refer readers elsewhere for the most difficult part of the research process—statistical analysis.

At the same time, graduate students are under more pressure than ever to publish their work while still in graduate school. The job market is such that the standard "publish or perish" pressure often reserved for the tenure line has trickled down to the graduate student—not in the same way, of course (one wouldn't be kicked out of graduate school for not publishing), but in a way that may block our full entrance to the field in the first place—perishing before they even start. In the October 1997 *MLA Job Listing*, for instance, numerous composition positions required "substantial" publication experiences, and one posting even noted "preferably a book."

In other words, graduate students are pushed to publish before they are fully trained researchers. And, certainly, they are capable of publishing the kinds of work they are trained to do: textual analysis/criticism, theoretical explorations, political debates, stories. Therefore, the trend of criticizing research, arguing about research, defending preferred methods more often than actually exploring all kinds of research will likely continue unless our training programs change.

Anderson (1998) speculated on the ethics of our research, a component of research we also omit if our programs neglect full training. Anderson questioned the ethics of sharing unpublished student essays or quoting their spoken words (64) in much of our research—most quoting and sharing we see in our qualitative research—and hoped to make readers aware of the NCTE and CCCC guidelines for securing students' permission to do so. For Anderson, our field, in contrast to the social sciences, lacks training in research ethics.

> the social sciences' extensive discourse on research ethics is so deeply embedded in those fields that it constitutes a form of tacit knowledge. . . . For example, knowledge of the *APA Ethics Code* is so pervasive in psychology that most books on psychology research methods don't even mention it. Composition's pioneering introductions to social science research methods (Kirsch and Sullivan; Lauer and Asher) resemble similar books written by social scientists because they discuss techniques only—but differ because they are not set in a context that includes a rich, disciplinary discussion of the techniques' ethical dimensions. (65)

Anderson included sample permission forms as appendices to his article and questioned our use of them in most research thus far. Indeed, our training in research methods is so limited that we should be concerned about the ethics of the research we publish. No graduate course on research in composition should omit discussion of ethics and practice writing IRB proposals, for example, and no course that requires graduate students to conduct an educational study should omit the IRB proposal and approval as a required assignment. Writing such proposals demands that the writer be clear, convincing, and knowledgeable of the methods employed—all in the context of why the research question is important and how the research findings will be used.

Composition scholars need training in a wide range of research methods—and in statistics—but one course alone won't do the job. Ideally, courses would be offered concurrently with other content-driven courses and in a manner that fits well with the overall context of the program, allowing students the opportunity to design studies on issues of interest to them. A small, manageable study such as the red ink/blue ink study presented in chapter six offers a model of the kinds of designs and statistical analyses students could learn in the context of their own questions, becoming more sophisticated in design as they move on. Graduate students should never be pressured to produce publishable manuscripts of those fledgling studies—they must first learn, make those false starts, discover those mistakes, and, by the end of their programs, be stronger for it. Does "just practicing" research methods in a classroom make them less "real"? No. Like practicing medicine or writing student papers, we recognize that such practice always feeds long-term goals.

To help train researchers, our field needs a text that explains statistics in contexts that composition researchers will understand. The bowling alley study throughout chapters two, three, and four in this work provided, I hope, a beginning. Though a bowling alley study might seem silly, humor is a useful step toward dissolving the tension that surrounds quantitative research in our field. In plain language, in simple contexts (at first), research design and statistics can be explained as a means of making decisions, as a process for finding out something interesting, and as procedures that can actually be enjoyable and playful.

NUMBERS IN CONTEXT

Finally, let's return to that primary "culprit" in the qualitative-quantitative rift: the number. That untrustworthy, reductive, impersonal number. And let's admit that, sometimes, in some contexts, numbers might *not* be important, or they might *not* be the only way to look at something. But then let's try to understand when they *are* important and when they do, in fact, mean something, depending on context. Numbers naturally appear frequently and, certainly, in varied contexts: in our personal lives and our teaching lives.

For instance, the next time you're at the supermarket, notice how often you compare prices, compare labels for fat grams, compare packages for quantity. Remember when you started thinking about retirement? Understanding interest rates, investment options—dollars—suddenly became important, just as balancing a checkbook once did. When you get your blood pressure checked, you don't accept a vague "it's fine" or "it's a tad high" from a medical professional, do you? No, give me the numbers, doc. And if a loved one, diagnosed with diabetes, tells you that her blood sugars are better or worse or the same, you take the time to learn what those numbers mean, right? If you've ever found pleasure in winning a card game, in your favorite team winning an important playoff game, in your teenager passing the written test to get a driver's license, you've learned that numbers can be fun—and fun to think about. If you've ever argued with a loved one, unable to explain why you're angry except that the other person did such-and-such a number of times or said such-and-such once too often, then you know the power of quantifying behavior in a personal argument.

If numbers can teach us something about our very livelihood in these personal situations, what else could they possibly help us learn? In our daily lives, depending on contexts, numbers inform our health, share our love, express our anger, plan for our futures, and give us pleasure. And, sure, come tax time, they might give us ulcers, but that's not *because* they're numbers—it's the *context* in which we're using them that we loathe.

In the context of our teaching, numbers affect us every day. For those who teach freshman composition, yearly increases or decreases in enrollment might affect our jobs. Retention efforts across the nation focus on increasing the numbers of students who persist to graduation, efforts that affect the students in our classrooms. Those who serve on committees that attend to issues such as starting salaries, merit pay, graduate admissions, stipends, and hiring decisions need to be sensitive to the numbers involved in those particular contexts. When we talk to students in conferences about how many times they missed a Friday, or how often a certain kind of error appears, or how many journal entries they have yet to do, we use numerical patterns to help us communicate with students, help us understand what to focus on next, and help us determine whose problems are purely academic and whose might be more personal. In peer review sessions, when students notice that a classmate used a certain word six times in one short paragraph, they point it out and quantify it in order to help that student reduce wordiness or redundancy, an important insight in the context of reader response.

If numbers, frequencies, and patterns that can be quantified give us insight on our students' problems, or their written work, or on our professional concerns, what else could they help us learn? Certainly, not all student behaviors can or should be quantified, but we naturally quantify the ones we can as a necessary step toward teaching, toward helping.

We know that those numbers reveal something to us—possibly revealing a story somewhere.

8 CONCLUSIONS (AND BEGINNINGS)

What will composition look like in the future if we abandon numerical evidence entirely and tell stories instead? How would we tie all of those stories together, and how, exactly, would we find them useful to our teaching? We might learn one day that our postmodern critique of scientism has resulted not in a new understanding of the role science plays in our culture, but in a chaotic individualism through which we amass a body of scholarship we are ultimately unable to contain, describe, or, in the end, use. How will our field be portrayed to others if constructed of a mass of stories one must be an insider to understand or appreciate—stories we are unable to debate, falsify, or evaluate?[1] And if it takes only one liar to destroy the credibility of us all, how will we continue to *believe* the stories we hear? And to what will we turn when we lose trust—again?

As with most trends in composition, a new one will most likely be just around the corner. Then we will realize that the story can exclude and marginalize some voices, that there are other voices just as valid as the personal, that we need new research to examine broader issues and to put our stories to the test, and that in order to do all of this, we need to be better trained as researchers, armed with a wide range of methods available to us—methods able to answer the wide range of questions we will so naturally raise within so many varied contexts. Storytelling can enhance any kind of inquiry, certainly, but diverse inquiry can aid the power of those stories at the same time, if we do not limit the forms of evidence we seek, the political ideologies we seek to uphold, and the written forms we favor and find pleasing.

As reviewed in chapter one, the new storytelling trend has gained a strong hold on our scholarship, our beliefs, and, most importantly, our means of justifying those beliefs. However, the current value of storytelling in our field has been enhanced, in part, by arguments that simply devalue the research that relies on numerical evidence. Further, our own history (and desire to escape the remnants of 19th century thought in particular) has added to our quest for something new, something different, as shown in chapter two. Math avoidance and anxiety, the fight against male-dominated science, and a preference for works that are more literary than traditional reports, as illustrated in chapter three, have added fuel to the qualitative/quantitative dichotomy (and dichotomous language) we currently face in our field.

While a theory such as a Contextualist Theory of Epistemic Justification, presented in chapter four, may provide us a lens through which to see our research and our research contexts differently—and to recontextualize a most harmful division among competing theories of epistemology—we must take other active steps in order for our field to fully realize, in practical terms, the value of such a changed vision. After all, our field is currently divided in such a way that an inclusive theory such as a Contextualist Theory of Epistemic Justification cannot be embraced at all unless we first understand how best to open the doors necessary for it to work. Otherwise, such a theory will remain only that—a theory, one that makes sense in our scholarship only.

To apply a Contextualist Theory of Epistemic Justification in a useful, practical manner, the Contextualist Research Paradigm Matrix in chapter four focuses on questions that researchers must ask in the contexts formed by simultaneous and intersecting research issues and rhetorical issues. Such questions, asked honestly from the desire to learn and to share, will help us focus on available means for learning in that context, rather than relying on trends that are merely popular or writing styles that we prefer. The questions in the matrix point to larger issues, such as conducting research that is useful not only to us, but also to our students, and maintaining ethical standards while exploring a research question. Further, the questions in the matrix are deliberately general—to start the process of later, more specific questions that will vary due to context.

The reprint in chapter five of Oliver's (1995) study on rhetorical specification in writing prompts, together with an interview in which she articulated several decisions she made during the process, provides an example of a researcher (and a study) at work within the matrix. Oliver made decisions based on a combination of factors: usefulness to her readers (other teachers), benefits to students in our classrooms, fairness in relation to her data, validation of her own experience. Similarly, chapter six presents the red ink/blue ink study to demonstrate the matrix—the research process—at work as well, though my own decisions in that study, because of a different context, resulted in a product that differs from Oliver's but is no less accurate. Both chapters five and six reveal the complicated processes that guide researchers in the construction of their final products—complicated, varied processes that may result in varied products. Indeed, the final product of any researcher's endeavors, regardless of kind, can ultimately share, in the limited space of a final product, only parts of those processes—processes that a Contextualist Research Paradigm helps reveal.

A contextualist paradigm enables us to systemize that inquiry while still maintaining the flexibility of our multidisciplinary field. In a Contextualist Research Paradigm, one *kind* of research is not automatically more valuable than another, and one *kind* of evidence does not guide our quests. Instead, full attention to the rhetorical tradition that has guided our field from the start *and* full understanding of the processes of research that guide our inquiry converge to provide a new foundation upon which our scholars can see our own research and research questions differently—a vision that can provide stability *and* growth at the same time.

For Phelps (1988), our field had been engaged in the quest for a new genre that would adequately express what we believe about "the personal nature of knowledge," but in the "meantime, we are seeing hybrid, tortured, mixed, and often unsuccessful discourse forms" (vii). While Phelps did not specify what she meant here, or to what kinds of texts she referred, I recognize my own text as deliberately hybrid and mixed. In my own quest to search not for *a* new genre, but for a new lens through which to see the eclectic forms of knowledge that inform our work in varied contexts, I could not—as Phelps did—narrow such a quest to a path of theory only. To do so would demand that genre dictate inquiry, not the reverse.

In the context of this inquiry, then—a quest for an inclusive Contextualist Research Paradigm for Rhetoric and Composition—this work produced not one genre of text, but six: 1) I told several stories, of course, as my own personal experiences and conviction guided this quest; 2) I referred to and analyzed theory and research in a traditional, academic manner because theory and research, too, informed the quest; 3) I constructed a mock study for the purposes of demonstrating decision-making and research procedures in a research context; 4) I reprinted Oliver's (1995) study for readers' scrutiny and 5) conducted an interview with Dr. Oliver that also illustrated decision-making in context; and 6) conducted a new pilot study to illustrate the value of research for testing our lore.

Such a hybrid text is not tortured, but is necessary for exploring *and* conveying a new understanding of the eclectic epistemic foundations of our work—as teachers and as researchers. The mix of texts presented here aids our understanding of the context in which our current, too narrow preference for research methods has grown and furthers our understanding by examining reasons for that trend.

Composition's quest to define itself as a discipline has recently resulted in our gravitation toward the narrow path of storytelling in a misguided and unsuccessful attempt to define the field via genre, personal anecdotes, and politics rather than the contexts in which we find ourselves teaching, researching, and asking questions. Our attempt to become a respected academic discipline by simultaneously countering academic tradition has focused our attention on the political, rather than the epistemic, goals of our publications. At the same time, our quest to shed our own history of constructing a mechanical, drill-oriented paradigm that ignored students' voices has led us to an equally limited paradigm focused on our own voices rather than on research that will benefit our students.

Should we stop telling our stories? Absolutely not. We must, in fact, keep telling them in order to create the fullest interplay among various kinds of evidence, but then we must seek that variety, too.

Numbers alone won't reveal everything we need to know. Stories alone can't do it, either. But when researchers stop defining their work by method only—and focus more on the research question in a research context, applying a new contextualist paradigm, understanding that all research methods are, indeed, epistemic—then the full power of any data, be it story or number, will truly blossom into the knowledge our field seeks and the discipline we hope to become.

NOTES

1. For a recent review of the potential for theory to silence debate (and, therefore, silence voices), see Porter (1998), "Methods, Truth, Reasons," *College English*, April 1998.

REFERENCES
for Eileen Oliver's
"Writing Quality, etc."

Applebee, A., Langer, J., Mullis, I., Latham, A., & Gentile, C. (1994). *NAEP 1992 writing report card.* Princeton, NJ: Educational Testing Service.

Bamberg, B. (1982). Multiple-choice and holistic essay scores: What are they measuring? *College Composition and Communication, 33,* 404–406.

Black, K. (1989). Audience analysis and persuasive writing at the college level. *Research in the Teaching of English, 23,* 231–253.

Bortz, D. (1962). The written language patterns of intermediate grade children when writing compositions in three forms: Descriptive, expository, and narrative. *Dissertation Abstracts International, 30,* 5332. (University Microfilms No. AAC 7010386)

Braddock, R., Lloyd-Jones, R., & Schoer, L. (1963). *Research in written composition.* Urbana, IL: National Council of Teachers of English.

Breland, H. M., & Griswold, P. A. (1981). *The assessment of writing ability: A review of research.* (Research Rep. No. 84–12). Princeton, NJ: Educational Testing Service.

Brossell, G. (1983). Rhetorical specifications in essay examination topics. *College English, 45,* 165–173.

Cherry, R. (1989). Fictional scenarios and rhetorical specification in writing tasks: A cautionary note. *Journal of Advanced Composition, 9,* 151–161.

Cooper, P. L. (1983). *The assessment of writing ability: A review of research.* (Research Rep. No. 84–12). Princeton, NJ: Educational Testing Service.

Craig, S. G. (1988). *The effect of intended audience on language functions in written argument at two grade levels.* Unpublished doctoral dissertation, The University of British Columbia, Vancouver.

Cronbach, L. (1970). *Essentials of psychological testing (3rd ed).* New York: Harper & Row.

Crowhurst, M., & Piche, G. (1979). Audiences and mode of discourse effects on syntactic complexity in writing at two grade levels. *Research in the Teaching of English, 13,* 101–109.

Educational Testing Service. (1987). *Scoring guide.* Princeton, N.J.: Author.

Elbow, P. (1987). Closing my eyes as I speak: An argument for ignoring audience. *College English, 49,* 50–69.

Engelhard, Jr., G., Gordon, B., & Gabrielson, S. (1992). The influences of mode of discourse, experiential demand, and gender on the quality of student writing. *Research in the Teaching of English, 26,* 315–336.

Farrell, E. (1976). The beginning begets: Making composition assignments. In R. L. Graves (Ed.), *Rhetoric and composition: A sourcebook for teachers* (pp. 220–224). Rochelle Park, NJ: Hayden Book Company.

Flower, L., & Hayes, J. (1981). The cognition of discovery: Defining a rhetorical problem. *College Composition and Communication, 31,* 21–32.

Frank, L. (1992). Writing to be read: Young writers' ability to demonstrate audience awareness when evaluated by their readers. *Research in the Teaching of English, 26,* 277–299.

Freedman, S., & Robinson, W. (1982). Testing proficiency in writing at San Francisco State University. *College Composition and Communication, 33,* 393–398.

Greenberg, K. (1982). Competency testing: What role should teachers of composition play? *College Composition and Communication, 33,* 366–376.

Herrington, A. (1979). Judgment: Designing a proficiency exam. In A. Allen & R. A. Donovan (Eds.), *Critical issues in writing* (pp. 24; 26–29). New York: Bronx Community College of the City of New York.

Hoetker, J. (1982). Essay examination topics and students writing. *College Composition and Communication*, 33, 377–393.

Hoetker, J., & Brossell, G. (1986). A procedure for writing content-fair essay examination topics for large-scale writing assessments. *College Composition and Communication*, 37, 328–336.

Hoetker, J., & Brossell, G. (1989). The effects of systematic variations in essay topics on the writing performance of college freshmen. *College Composition and Communication*, 40, 414–421.

Huot, B. (1990). The literature of direct writing assessment: Major concerns and prevailing trends. *Review of Educational Research*, 60, 237–263.

Keech, C. (1982, April). *Unexpected direction of change in student performance*. Paper presented at the Annual Meeting of the American Educational Research Association, New York.

Kincaid, G. (1970). Some factors affecting variations in the quality of students writing. *Dissertation Abstracts International*, 13, 733 (University Microfilms No. 5922)

Kroll, B. (1985). Rewriting a complex story for a young reader: The development of audience-adapted writing skills. *Research in the Teaching of English*, 19, 120–139.

Leu, D., Keech, C., Murphy, S., & Kinzer, C. (1988). Effects of variation in a writing test prompt upon holistic score and other factors. In J. Gray (Ed.), *Properties of writing tasks: A study of alternate procedures for holistic writing assessment* (pp. 15–23). Berkeley, CA: Bay Area Writing Project.

Maimon, E., & Nodine, B. (1978). Measuring syntactic growth: Errors and expectations in sentence-combining practice with college freshmen. *Research in the Teaching of English*, 12, 233–244.

Matsen, P., Rollinson, P., & Sousa, M. (Eds.). (1990). *Readings from classical rhetoric*. Carbondale, IL: Southern Illinois University Press.

Mellon, J. (1976). Round two of the National Writing Assessment-interpreting the apparent decline of writing ability: A review. *Research in the Teaching of English*, 10, 66–74.

Moffett, J. (1968). *Teaching the universe of discourse*. Boston: Houghton Mifflin.

Murphy, J. (Ed.). (1990). *A short history of writing instruction: from ancient Greece to twentieth-century America.* Davis, CA: Hermagoras Press.

Murphy, S., & Ruth, L. (1993). The field-testing of writing prompts reconsidered. In M. Williamson & B. Huot (Eds.), *Validating holistic scoring for writing assessment: Theoretical and empirical foundations* (pp. 266–302). Cresskill, NJ: Hampton Press.

Odell, L. (1981). Defining and assessing competence in writing. In C. E. Cooper (Ed.), *The nature and measurement of competency in English* (pp. 95–138). Urbana, IL: National Council of Teachers of English.

Perron, J. (1977, April). *Written syntactic complexity and the modes of discourse.* Paper presented at the Annual Meeting of the American Educational Research Association, New York.

Piche, D., Michlin, M., Johnson, F., & Rubin, D. (1975). Relationships between fourth graders performances on selected role-taking tasks and referential communication accuracy tasks. *Child Development*, 46, 965–969.

Prater, D., & Padia, W. (1983). Effects of modes of discourse on writing performance in grades four and six. *Research in the Teaching of English*, 17, 127–134.

Rafoth, B. (1989). Audience and information. *Research in the Teaching of English*, 23, 273–291.

Redd-Boyd, T., & Slater, W. (1989). The effects of audience specification on undergraduates' attitudes, strategies, and writing. *Research in the Teaching of English*, 23, 77–108.

Roen, D., & Willey, R. J. (1988). The effects of audience awareness on drafting and revising. *Research in the Teaching of English*, 22, 75–88.

Rosen, H. (1969). *An investigation of the effects of differentiated writing assignments on the performance in English composition of selected fifteen- and sixteen-year-old pupils.* Unpublished doctoral dissertation, University of London, U.K.

Rubin, D., & Piche, G. (1979). Development in syntactic and strategic aspects of audience adaptive skills in written persuasive communication. *Research in the Teaching of English*, 13, 293–316.

Ruth, L., & Murphy, S. (1984). Designing topics for writing assessment: Problems of writing. *College Composition and Communication*, 85, 410–422.

San Jose, C. (1972). Grammatical structures in four modes of writing at fourth grade level. *Dissertation Abstracts International*, 33, 5411. (University Microfilms, No. 73–95, #063).

Scardamalia, M., & Bereiter, C. (1986). Research on written composition. In M.C. Wittrock (Ed.), *Handbook of Research on Teaching* (3rd ed.) (pp. 778–803). New York: Macmillan.

Shaughnessy, M. (1977). *Errors and expectations*. New York: Oxford University Press.

White, E. (1985). *Teaching and assessing writing*. San Francisco: Jossey-Bass.

White, E. (1994). *Teaching and assessing writing* (2nd ed.). San Francisco: Jossey-Bass.

Witte, S. (1992). Context, text, intertext: Toward a constructivist semiotic of writing. *Written Communication*, 9, 237–308.

Witte, S., & Faigley, L- (1981). Coherence, cohesion and writing quality. *College Composition and Communication*, 32, 189–204.

WORKS CITED

Alston, W. P. 1989. *Epistemic justification: Essays in the theory of knowledge.*
Ithaca: Cornell University Press.

Anderson, P. V. 1998. Simple gifts: Ethical issues in the conduct of person-based composition research. *College Composition and Communication,* 49: 63–89.

Angeles, P. A. 1992. *Dictionary of philosophy* (2nd ed.). New York: Harper Collins.

Annis, D. 1978/1993. A contextualist theory of epistemic justification. In L. P. Pojman, ed., *The theory of knowledge: Classic and contemporary readings,* 280–287. Belmont, CA: Wadsworth Publishing Company. (Reprinted from *American Philosophical Quarterly,* 15: 213–19).

Anson, C. 1989. Response styles and ways of knowing. In C. Anson, ed., *Writing and response,* 332–66. Urbana: National Council of Teachers of English.

Applebee, A. 1981. *Writing in the secondary schools: English and the content areas.* Urbana: National Council of Teachers of English.

Aristotle. Trans. 1991. *On rhetoric: A theory of civic discourse.* Translated by G. A. Kennedy. New York: Oxford University Press.

Babcock, M. 1995. Leggo my ego. *The Writing Lab Newsletter,* 19.5: 10–12.

Barton, E. 1997. Review: Empirical studies in composition. *College English,* 59: 815–27.

Bartosenski, M. 1992. Color, revision, and painting a paper. *The Writing Center Journal,* 12: 159–73.

Battersby, J. L. 1996. The inescapability of humanism. *College English,* 58: 555–67.

Beach, R. 1992. Experimental and descriptive research methods in composition. In G. Kirsch & P. A. Sullivan, eds., *Methods and methodology in composition research,* 217–46. Carbondale: Southern Illinois University Press.

Beach, R., Green, J. L., Kamil, M. L., & Shanahan, T. 1992. *Multi-disciplinary perspectives on literacy research.* Urbana, IL: National Council of Teachers of English & National Conference on Research in English.

Berkenkotter, C. 1989. The legacy of positivism in empirical composition research. *Journal of Advanced Composition,* 9: 69–82.

Berkenkotter, C. 1991. Paradigm debates, turf wars, and the conduct of sociocognitive inquiry in composition. *College Composition and Communication,* 42: 151–69.

Berlin, J. A. 1984. *Writing instruction in nineteenth-century American colleges.* Carbondale: Southern Illinois University Press.

———. 1987. *Rhetoric and reality: Writing instruction in American colleges, 1900–1985.* Carbondale: Southern Illinois University Press.

Berthoff, A. 1990. *The sense of learning.* Portsmouth, NH: Heinemann, Boynton/Cook.

Bonjour, L. 1985. *The structure of empirical knowledge.* Cambridge: Harvard University Press.

Booth, W. C. 1963. The rhetorical stance. *College Composition and Communication,* 14: 139–45.

Boyer, E. L. 1990. *Scholarship reconsidered: Priorities of the professoriate.* Princeton: The Carnegie Foundation for the Advancement of Teaching.

Braddock, R., Lloyd-Jones, R., & Schoer, L. 1963. *Research in written composition.* Champaign, IL: National Council of Teachers of English.

Brand, A. G. 1989. *The psychology of writing: The affective experience.* New York: Greenwood.

Briggs, L. 1998. Narrative as response to writers: Making connections. *The Writing Lab Newsletter,* 22.7: 1–4.

Briggs, L., & Pailliotet, A. W. 1997. A story about grammar and power. *Journal of Basic Writing,* 16: 46–61.

Brodkey, L. 1987. Writing ethnographic narratives. *Written Communication,* 4: 25–50.

Bushman, D. 1991. Past accomplishments and current trends in writing center research: A bibliographic essay. In J. Simpson & R. Wallace, eds., *The writing center: New directions,* 27– 38. New York: Garland Publishing.

Bushman, D. 1998. Theorizing a "social-expressivist" writing center. *The Writing Lab Newsletter,* 22.7: 6–11.

Campbell, G. 1776/1990. Excerpts from *Philosophy of rhetoric.* In J. L. Golden & E. P. J. Corbett, eds., *The rhetoric of Blair, Campbell, and Whately,* 145–271. Carbondale: Southern Illinois University Press.

Carroll, L. A. 1997. Pomo blues: Stories from first-year composition. *College English, 59:* 916–33.

Carter, K. & Spitzack, C. 1989. *Doing research on women's communication: Perspectives on theory and method.* Norwood, NJ: Ablex Publishing Corporation.

Charney, D. 1996. Empiricism is not a four-letter word. *College Composition and Communication,* 47: 567–93.

Chiste, K. B., & O'Shea, J. 1988. Patterns of question selection and writing performance of ESL students. *TESOL Quarterly,* 22: 681–84.

Clifford, J. 1986. Introduction: Partial truths. In J. Clifford & G. E. Marcus, eds., *Writing culture: The poetics and politics of ethnography,* 1–26. Berkeley: University of California Press.

Connors, R. J. 1981. The rise and fall of the modes of discourse. *College Composition and Communication,* 32: 444–55.

———. 1983. Composition studies and science. *College English,* 45: 1–20.

———. 1995. Women's reclamation of rhetoric in the nineteenth century. In L. W. Phelps & J. Emig, eds., *Feminine principles and women's experience in American composition and rhetoric,* 67–90. Pittsburgh: University of Pittsburgh Press.

———. 1996. Teaching and learning as a man. *College English, 58,* 137–57.

DiPardo, A. 1992. 'Whispers of coming and going': Lessons from Fannie. *The Writing Center Journal,* 12: 125–44.

Dyson, A. H., & Genishi, C. 1994. *The need for story: Cultural diversity in classroom and community.* Urbana, IL: National Council of Teachers of English.

Ede, L. 1992. Methods, methodologies, and politics of knowledge: Reflections and speculations. In G. Kirsch & P. A. Sullivan, eds., *Methods and methodology in composition research,* 314–32. Carbondale: Southern Illinois University Press.

Elbow, P. 1990. *What is English?* New York: The Modern Language Association.

Emig, J. 1982. Inquiry paradigms and writing. *College Composition and Communication,* 33: 64–75.

Enos, T. 1996. *Gender roles and faculty lives in rhetoric and composition.* Carbondale: Southern Illinois University Press.

Ferris, D. R. 1994. Rhetorical strategies in student persuasive writing: Differences between native and non-native English speakers. *Research in the Teaching of English,* 28: 45–65.

Fitzgerald, S., Mulvihill, P., & Dobson, R. 1991. Meeting the needs of graduate students: Writing support groups in the center. In J. Simpson & R. Wallace, eds., *The writing center: New directions,* 133–44. New York: Garland.

Flower, L. 1989. Cognition, context, and theory building. *College Composition and Communication,* 40: 282–311.

Foucault, M. 1972. *The archaeology of knowledge.* New York: Pantheon Books.

———. 1977. What is an author? In *Language, counter-memory, practice: Selected interviews,* 113–38). Ithaca, NY: Cornell University Press.

———. 1980. *Power/Knowledge: Selected interviews and other writings, 1972–1977.* New York: Pantheon.

Furnish, S. 1995. Loving grading writing. *CLA Journal,* 38: 490–504.

Gage, J. T. 1986. Why write? In A. Petrosky & D. Bartholomae, eds., *The teaching of writing,* 8–29. Chicago: University of Chicago Press.

Gannett, C. 1995. The stories of our lives become our lives: Journals, diaries, and academic discourse. In L. W. Phelps & J. Emig, eds., *Feminine principles and women's experience in American composition and rhetoric,* 109–36. Pittsburgh: University of Pittsburgh Press.

Gates, B. T. & Shteir, A. B. 1997. *Natural eloquence: Women reinscribe science.* Madison: University of Wisconsin Press.

Gates, H. L. 1987. *The classic slave narratives.* New York: Penguin.

Geertz, C. 1973. *The interpretation of cultures.* New York: Basic.

Gere, A. R. 1985. Empirical research in composition. In B. McClelland & T. Donovan, eds., *Perspectives on research and scholarship in composition,* 110–24. New York: Modern Language Association.

Gilbert, G. N., & Mulkay, M. 1984. Contexts of scientific discourse. In *Opening Pandora's box: A sociological analysis of scientists' discourse.* Cambridge: University of Cambridge Press.

Gill, G. E. 1992. The African-American student: At risk. *College Composition* and Communication, 43: 225–30.

Gradin, S. L. 1995. *Romancing rhetorics: Social expressivist perspectives on the teaching of writing.* Portsmouth, NH: Boynton/Cook, Heinemann.

Green, L. D. 1990. Aristotelian rhetoric, dialectic and the traditions of *Antistrophos. Rhetorica,* 8: 5–27.

Gunner, J., & McNenny, G. 1997. Retrospection as prologue: Afterthoughts on motive. *Journal of Basic Writing,* 16: 3–6.

Hagaman, J. 1981. On Campbell's *Philosophy of rhetoric* and its relevance to contemporary invention. *Rhetoric Society Quarterly,* 11: 145–54.

Hairston, M. 1982. The winds of change: Thomas Kuhn and the revolution in the teaching of writing. *College Composition and Communication,* 33: 76–88.

Harding, S. 1986. *The science question in feminism.* Ithaca: Cornell University Press.

Harding, S. 1987. Introduction: Is there a feminist method? In S. Harding, ed., *Feminism and methodology,* 1–14. Bloomington: Indiana University Press.

Harding, S. 1991. *Whose science? Whose knowledge? Thinking from women's lives.* Ithaca, NY: Cornell University Press.

Harding, S., & O'Barr, J. F. 1987. *Sex and scientific inquiry.* Chicago: University of Chicago Press.

Harkin, P. 1991. The postdisciplinary politics of lore. In P. Harkin & J. Schilb, eds., *Contending with words: Composition and rhetoric in a postmodern age,* 124–38. New York: The Modern Language Association.

Harkin, P., & Schilb, J. 1991. *Contending with words: Composition and rhetoric in a postmodern age.* New York: The Modern Language Association.

Harste, J. C. 1992. Foreword. In R. Beach, J. L. Green, M. L. Kamil, & T. Shanahan, eds., *Multidisciplinary perspectives on literacy research,* ix–xiii. Urbana, IL: National Council of Teachers of English and National Conference on Research in English.

Hawisher, G. E., & Selfe, C. L. 1991. The rhetoric of technology and the electronic writing class. *College Composition and Communication,* 42: 55–65.

Hawkins, K. 1989. Exposing masculine science: An alternative feminist approach to the study of women's communication. In K. Carter & C. Spitzack, eds., *Doing research on women's communication: Perspectives on theory and method,* 40–64. Norwood, NJ: Ablex Publishing Corporation.

Hayes, J. R. 1992. A psychological perspective applied to literacy studies. In R. Beach, J. Green, M. Kamil, & T. Shanahan, eds., *Multidisciplinary perspectives on literacy research,* 125–40. Urbana, IL: National Conference on Research in English/National Council of Teachers of English.

Hayes, J. R., Young, R. E., Matchett, M. L., McCaffrey, M., Cochran, C., & Hajduk, T. 1992. *Reading empirical research studies: The rhetoric of research.* Hillsdale, NJ: Lawrence Erlbaum Associates.

Healy, D. 1995. Writing center directors: An emerging portrait of the profession. *Writing Program Administration,* 18: 26–43.

Herrington, A. 1989. The first twenty years of *Research in the Teaching of English* and the growth of a research community in composition studies. *Research in the Teaching of English,* 16: 117–38.

Hillocks, G., Jr. 1986. *Research on written composition.* Urbana, IL: National Council of Teachers of English.

———. 1992. Reconciling the qualitative and quantitative. In R. Beach, J. Green, M. Kamil, & T. Shanahan, eds., *Multidisciplinary perspectives on literacy research,* 57–68. Urbana, IL: National Conference on Research in English/National Council of Teachers of English.

Hobson, E. H. 1992. Maintaining our balance: Walking the tightrope of competing epistemologies. *The Writing Center Journal,* 13: 65–75.

hooks, b. 1989. *talking back: thinking feminist, thinking black.* Boston: South End Press.

Hunzer, K. M. 1997. Misperceptions of gender in the writing center: Stereotyping and the facilitative tutor. *The Writing Lab Newsletter,* 22.2: 6–10.

Irmscher, W. F. 1987. Finding a comfortable identity. *College Composition and Communication,* 38: 81–7.

Jacobs, S. 1997. Review: Reflections on pedagogical study. *College English,* 59: 461–69.

Jensen, G. H., & DiTiberio, J. K. 1989. *Personality and the teaching of composition.* Norwood, NJ: Ablex.

Johnson, N. 1991. *Nineteenth-century rhetoric in North America.* Carbondale: Southern Illinois University Press.

Kail, H., & Allen, K. 1982. Conducting research in the writing lab. In M. Harris, ed., *Tutoring writing: A sourcebook for writing labs,* 233–45. Glenview, IL: Scott, Foresman and Company.

Kamil, M., Langer, J., & Shanahan, T. 1985. *Understanding research in reading and writing.* Boston: Allyn & Bacon.

Keller, E. F. 1985. *Reflections on gender and science.* New Haven: Yale University Press.

Kerlinger, F. N. 1986. *Foundations of behavioral research* (3rd ed.). New York: Holt, Rinehart and Winston.

Kinneavy, J. L. 1971. *A theory of discourse.* Englewood Cliffs, NJ: Prentice-Hall, Inc.

Kirsch, G. 1992. Methodological pluralism: Epistemological issues. In G. Kirsch & P. A. Sullivan, eds., *Methods and methodology in composition research,* 247–69. Carbondale: Southern Illinois University Press.

————. 1993. *Women writing the academy: Authority, audience, and transformation.* Carbodale: Southern Illinois University Press.

Kirsch, G., & Sullivan, P. A. 1992. *Methods and methodology in composition research.* Carbondale: Southern Illinois University Press.

Kuhn, T. S. 1970. *The structure of scientific revolutions* (2nd ed.). Chicago: University of Chicago Press.

Langellier, K. M., & Hall, D. L. 1989. Interviewing women: A phenomenological approach to feminist communication research. In K. Carter & C. Spitzack, eds., *Doing research on women's communication: Perspectives on theory and method,* 193–220. Norwood, NJ: Ablex Publishing Corporation.

Langer, J. 1987. "Musings . . . red herrings in language research: Qualitative versus quantitative methods. *Research in the Teaching of English,* 21: 117–19.

Lauer, J., & Asher, J. W. 1988. *Composition research: Empirical designs.* New York: Oxford University Press.

Lauer, J. 1995. The feminization of rhetoric and composition studies? *Rhetoric Review,* 13: 276–86.

Lerner, N. 1997. Counting beans and making beans count. *The Writing Lab Newsletter,* 22.1: 1–4.

Lunsford, A. A. 1981. Essay writing and teachers' responses in nineteenth-century Scottish universities. *College Composition and Communication,* 32: 434–43.

Lunsford, A. A. 1991. Collaboration, control, and the idea of a writing center. *The Writing Center Journal,* 12: 3–10.

Meier, D. 1997. *Learning in small moments: Life in an urban classroom.* New York: Teachers College Press.

Meyer, R. J. 1996 *Stories from the heart: Teachers and students researching their literacy lives*. Hillsdale, NJ: Lawrence Erlbaum Associates.

Miller, S. 1992. Writing theory :: Theory writing. In G. Kirsch & P. A. Sullivan, eds., *Methods and methodology in composition research*, 62–83. Carbondale: Southern Illinois University Press.

Moss, B. J. 1992. Ethnography and composition: Studying language at home. In G. Kirsch & P. A. Sullivan, eds., *Methods and methodology in composition research*, 153–71. Carbondale: Southern Illinois University Press.

Murphy, C, & Sherwood, S. 1995. *The St. Martin's sourcbook for writing tutors*. New York: St. Martin's Press.

Nike Corporation. 6 June 1998. A woman is often measured (advertisement). [Online]. Available: www.cam.org/~jfc/Nike/Nike4.text.

Neuleib, J. W., & Scharton, M. A. 1994. Writing others, writing ourselves: Ethnography and the writing center. In J. A. Mullin & R. Wallace, eds., *Intersections: Theory-practice in the writing center*, 54–67. Urbana, IL: National Council of Teachers of English.

Newkirk, T. 1992. The narrative roots of the case study. In G. Kirsch & P. A. Sullivan, eds., *Methods and methodology in composition research*, 130–52. Carbondale: Southern Illinois University Press.

Noble, D. 1992. *A world without women: The Christian clerical culture of western science*. New York: Alfred A. Knopf.

North, S. M. 1984. Writing center research: Testing our assumptions. In G. A. Olson, ed., *Writing centers: Theory and administration*, 24–35. Urbana, IL: National Council of Teachers of English.

———. 1985. Designing a case study method for tutorials: A prelude to research. *Rhetoric Review*, 4: 88–99.

———. 1987. *The making of knowledge in composition: Portrait of an emerging field*. Upper Montclair, NJ: Boynton/Cook.

O'Donnell, T. 1996. Politics and ordinary language: A defense of expressivist rhetorics. *College English*, 58: 423–39.

Oliver, E. I. 1995. The writing quality of seventh, ninth, and eleventh graders, and college freshmen: Does rhetorical specification in writing prompts make a difference? *Research in the Teaching of English*, 29: 422–50.

Paulos, J. A. 1995. *A mathematician reads the newspaper*. New York: BasicBooks.

Phelps, L. W. 1988. *Composition as a human science: Contributions to the self- understanding of a discipline.* New York: Oxford University Press.

———. 1989. Images of student writing: The deep structure of teacher response. In C. M. Anson, ed., *Writing and response: Theory, practice, and research,* 37–67. Urbana, IL: National Council of Teachers of English.

———. 1991. Practical wisdom and the geography of knowledge in composition. *College English,* 53: 863–85.

Phelps, L. W., & Emig, J. 1995. *Feminine principles and women's experience in American composition and rhetoric.* Pittsburgh: University of Pittsburgh Press.

Polanyi, M. 1964. *Personal knowledge: Towards a post-critical philosophy.* New York: Harper and Row.

Porter, K. J. 1998. Methods, truths, reasons. *College English,* 60: 426–40.

Pratt, M. L. 1991. Arts of the contact zone. In *Profession 91,* 33–40). New York: The Modern Language Association of America.

Radencich, M. C., Eckhardt, K., Rasch, R., Uhr, S. L., & Pisaneschi, D. M. 1998. University course-based practitioner research: Four studies on journal writing contextualize the process. *Research in the Teaching of English,* 32: 79–112.

Ray, R. 1992. Composition from the teacher-research point of view. In G. Kirsch & P. A. Sullivan, eds., *Methods and methodology in composition research,* 172–89. Carbondale: Southern Illinois University Press.

Rose, M. 1988. Narrowing the mind and page: Remedial writers and cognitive reductionism. *College Composition and Communication,* 39: 267–302.

Rose, M. 1989. *Lives on the boundary.* New York: Penguin.

Royster, J. J., & Taylor, R. G. 1997. Constructing teacher identity in the basic writing classroom. *Journal of Basic Writing,* 16: 27–50.

Schiebinger, L. 1993. *Nature's body: Gender in the making of modern science.* Boston: Beacon Press.

Schilb, J. 1991. Cultural studies, postmodernism, and composition. In P. Harkin & J. Schilb, eds., *Contending with words: Composition and rhetoric in a postmodern age,* 173–88. New York: The Modern Language Association.

Schmidt, P. A. 1996. *Beginning in retrospect: Writing and reading a teacher's life.* New York: Teachers College Press.

Schriver, K. 1989. What are we doing as a research community? Theory building in rhetoric and composition: The role of empirical scholarship. *Rhetoric Review,* 7: 272–88.

Schriver, K. 1992. Connecting cognition and context in composition. In G. Kirsch & P. A. Sullivan, eds., *Methods and methodology in composition research,* 190–216. Carbondale: Southern Illinois University Press.

Selzer, J. 1998. Review: Scrutinizing science. *College English,* 60: 444–50.

Shapin, S. 1996. *The scientific revolution.* Chicago: University of Chicago Press.

Shea, C. 1996, April 16. Psychologists debate accuracy of 'significance test.' *The Chronicle of Higher Education,* 42: A12, A17.

Shepherd, L. J. 1993. *Lifting the veil: The feminine face of science.* Boston: Shambhala.

Smagorinsky, P., & Smith, M. W. 1997. Editors' introduction. *Research in the Teaching of English,* 31: 157–60.

Smagorinsky, P., & Smith, M. W. 1998. Editors' introduction. *Research in the Teaching of English,* 32: 121–25.

Snow, C. P. 1965. *Two cultures and the scientific revolution.* Cambridge: Cambridge University Press.

Snyder, B. R. 1990. Literacy and numeracy. *Daedalus,* 119: 233–57.

Sommers, N. 1979. The need for theory in composition research. *College Composition and Communication,* 30: 46–9.

———. 1982. Responding to student writing. *College Composition and Communication,* 33: 148–56.

Spack, R. 1997. The (in)visibility of the person(al) in academe. *College English,* 59: 9–31.

Steen, L. A. 1990. Numeracy. *Daedalus,* 119: 211–32.

Stewart, D. C. 1983. The nineteenth century. In W. B. Horner, ed., *The present state of scholarship in historical and contemporary rhetoric,* 134–66. Columbia: University of Missouri Press.

Stotsky, S. 1997. From the editor. *Research in the Teaching of English,* 31: 5–6.

Straub, R. 1997. Students' reactions to teacher comments: An exploratory study. *Research in the Teaching of English,* 31: 91–119.

Straub, R., & Lunsford, R. F. 1995. *Twelve readers reading: Responding to college student writing.* Creskill, NJ: Hampton Press.

Sullivan, P. A. 1992. Feminism and methodology in composition studies. In G. Kirsch & P. A. Sullivan, eds., *Methods and methodology in composition research*, 37–61. Carbondale: Southern Illinois University Press.

Sullivan, P. A., & Qualley, D. J. 1994. Pedagogy in the age of politics. Urbana, IL: National Council of Teachers of English.

Taylor, C. A. 1996. *Defining science: A rhetoric of demarcation.* Madison: University of Wisconsin Press.

Tobias, S. 1978. *Overcoming math anxiety.* New York: Norton.

———. 1987. *Succeed with math: Every student's guide to conquering math anxiety.* New York: College Entrance Examination Board.

Trimbur, J. 1993. Foreword. In G. Kirsch, *Women writing the academy: Audience, authority, and transformation*, ix–xi. Carbondale: Southern Illinois University Press.

Trimmer, J. F. 1997. *Narration as knowledge: Tales of the teaching life.* Portsmouth, NH: Heinemann, Boynton/Cook.

Troyka, L. Q. 1984. Classical rhetoric and the basic writer. In R. J. Connors, L. S. Ede, & A. A. Lunsford, eds., *Essays on Classical Rhetoric and Modern Discourse*, 193–202. Carbondale: Southern Illinois University Press.

Ward, S. 1995. The revenge of the humanities: Reality, rhetoric, and the politics of postmodernism. *Sociological Perspectives* [Online] 38: 109–28. Available: Expanded Academic ASAP: http://sbweb3.med.iac-net.com/infotrac/session/5/892/ 9881937/21!xrn_1&bkm_21.

Weimer, W. 1979. *Notes on the methodology of scientific research.* Hillsdale, NJ: Lawrence Erlbaum Associates.

Welch, N. 1997. Review: Telling tales about teaching writing. *College English*, 59: 939–45.

Wells, S. 1996. Women write science: The case of Hannah Longshore. *College English*, 58: 176–91.

Yeo, R. R. 1986. Method and the rhetoric of science. In J. A. Schuster & R. R. Yeo, eds., *The politics and rhetoric of scientific method*, 259–97. Boston: D. Reidel Publishing.

Zak, F., & Weaver, C. C. 1998. *The theory and practice of grading writing: Problems and possibilities.* Albany, NY: State University of New York Press.

INDEX

ABOUT THE AUTHOR

Cindy Johanek is assistant professor of English and directs the writing center at Denison University, where she teaches first-year composition and seminars in composition theory, pedagogy, research, and history. She earned her B.A. in English and cognitive and experimental psychology, and graduate degrees in composition and rhetoric. The study on which Composing Research is based received Ball State University's Distinguished Dissertation Award in 1999.